Social
Justice &
Church Authority

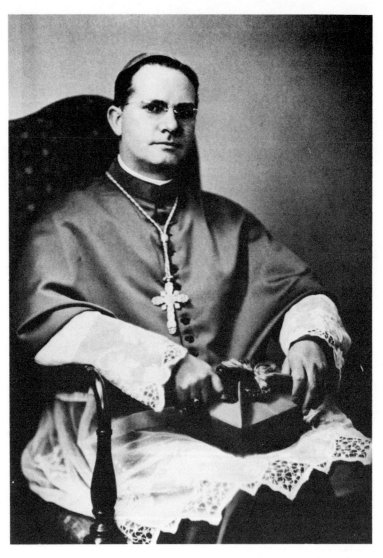

Robert E. Lucey as Bishop of Amarillo, 1934. Photograph by Edwards Studio, courtesy of the Archives of the Archdiocese of San Antonio.

Social
Justice &
Church Authority

The Public Life of
Archbishop Robert E. Lucey

Saul E. Bronder

Temple University Press • *Philadelphia*

Temple University Press, Philadelphia 19122
© 1982 by Temple University. All rights reserved
Published 1982
Printed in the United States of America

Library of Congress Cataloging in Publication Data
Bronder, Saul E.
    Social justice & church authority.
    Bibliography: p.
    Includes index.
    1. Lucey, Robert Emmet, 1891–   . 2. Catholic
Church—Bishops—Biography. 3. Bishops—Texas—San
Antonio—Biography. 4. Catholic Church—Texas—San
Antonio—History—20th century. 5. San Antonio (Tex.)—
Biography. I. Title. II. Title: Social Justice and
church authority.
BX4705.L7956B76   282′.092′4 [B]   81-18377
ISBN 0-87722-239-8   AACR2

For Ruth

Contents

Illustrations		ix
Acknowledgments		xi
Introduction		3
1	The Early Years	6
2	Social Justice and the Papal Encyclicals	21
3	Amarillo: A New Dealing Bishop	41
4	San Antonio: The Bishops' Committee and the Migrant Farm Worker	65
5	The Confraternity of Christian Doctrine and Operation Latin America	87
6	New Life and a Renewed Church	100
7	Coming Apart	130
	Epilogue	163
	Notes	165
	Bibliography	195
	Index	209

Illustrations

Robert E. Lucey as Bishop of
Amarillo, 1934   *frontispiece*

Lucey and Family, ca. 1912   51

Lucey and Cast of St. Patrick's Seminary Play,
undated   51

Lucey as a Seminarian in Italy, 1913   52

President Truman and Lucey with Members of
the Commission on Migratory Labor, 1951   115

Lucey in Medellin, Colombia, during
International Catechetical Week,
August 11–17, 1968   115

President Johnson and Lucey at the signing of
the Medicare Extension Bill, 1966   116

Acknowledgments

The Archbishop's story spanned nearly ninety years. Telling his story has taken nearly five, plus the help of many friends and colleagues. Nathan I. Huggins of Harvard University consistently managed to ask the right question at the right time and saw a dissertation to completion. To him, my first and special thanks. Walter Rundell, Jr., David O'Brien and Monsignor John Tracy Ellis gave the manuscript a careful reading. To Right Reverend Egbert Donovan and Fathers Joseph Bronder, John Murtha and Douglas Nowicki of Saint Vincent Archabbey I owe much for their untiring support.

During my two years in San Antonio I acquired many debts, for which I can offer only token repayment: to Monsignor Charles Grahmann for turning a cold storage bin into a cold work room; to Father Alois Goertz for his warm friendship; to John and Anna Verstegen, Len and Kitty Bronec, Roselis and Jim Wilson, and Bob and Carol Taylor for their unlimited hospitality; and last, to Archbishop Robert E. Lucey for receiving me so openly.

Among the many archivists who put up with questions and waged a few arguments I want to thank Sister Gertrude Cook and Mrs. Opelia Tennant of San Antonio, Father Francis Weber of Los Angeles, and Sister Nellie Rooney of Amarillo.

For my parents and my wife, Ann, I have the gratitude of a son and a husband, and to my sister, Ruth, for her sustaining love, I dedicate this book.

Social
Justice &
Church Authority

Introduction

Robert Emmet Lucey, the former Roman Catholic Archbishop of San Antonio, Texas, was born in Los Angeles on March 16, 1891. He was ordained to the priesthood in Rome in 1916 and spent the next eighteen years working in the archdiocese of Los Angeles. In 1934 he was consecrated bishop and appointed to the diocese of Amarillo, Texas, where he labored until elevated to the archdiocese of San Antonio in March, 1941. For nearly thirty years Archbishop Lucey presided over the Catholic Church in San Antonio, until age and controversy forced his retirement in June, 1969.

The key tension of Lucey's life was between his social liberalism and his ecclesiastical conservativism. His support of organized labor in the 1920s and 1930s, his pioneering work on behalf of Mexican Americans and migrant farm workers in the 1940s and 1950s, and his commitment to racial integration and social justice for the poor in the 1960s identify him with the liberal cause. At the same time, Lucey was a rigid ecclesiastical conservative, honoring Church authority and respecting its hierarchical nature. He fused his personality with his episcopal office, tolerated no criticism from within the Church, and dealt harshly with those who challenged his word.

The story of Robert E. Lucey is, therefore, that of a pioneer in the area of social justice whose liberalism depended upon the certainty of order as provided by traditional

3

Church authority. It was his appropriation of the authority of the Church that enabled him to espouse vigorously the Church's liberal social teachings and train a group of priests in his image as a social reformer.

Although the Church's teachings and Lucey's commitment to them did not change during his life, the Archbishop lost his effectiveness as a social champion because he could not accept the more liberal understanding of ecclesiastical authority occasioned by the Second Vatican Council of 1962–1965. Ironically, Lucey's downfall as a social liberal came about because of the liberalization of authority in the Church and at the hands of the very priests he had trained so thoroughly in social action.

The Archbishop was eager to have his story told. Confident of his accomplishments, he was generous with his papers and in granting interviews and rarely hesitated to express opinions about the controversies of his public life. He shared very little about his personal life, however. He was a public man, and it was his work, his example, that counted and that he wanted publicized. His private life, such as it was, he judged unimportant for public consideration.

Lucey's public life allowed no room for personal relationships. He explained that he had "sacrificed the warmth that comes from friendships due to my commitment to social justice." Perhaps his public life also conveniently screened a natural shyness, while his use of the episcopal office contributed to the absence of confidants.

A final point. The Archbishop saw the world mostly in blacks and whites. He appears two-dimensional because he was that way. His mind did not tolerate doubt. Issues were clear to him; answers followed just as clearly. In later years, particularly after the Second Vatican Council, this absoluteness of mind was the source of his undoing.

Lucey will be remembered for placing the Church squarely on the side of the poor and exploited. He will also be remembered for personifying the limitations of ecclesiastical authoritarianism. In the end, Lucey was a churchman dedicated to the cause of social justice, but he was also a hierocrat who understood only paternalistic relationship. It is this conflict that lies at the heart of his story.

1. The Early Years

Perhaps Mary Lucey had been too busy with the children that summer day to have missed hearing the train whistle telling her that John, her husband, would be home for dinner soon. An experienced freight conductor for the Southern Pacific Railroad, John Lucey spent three days out of five on the Los Angeles–Indio run and was in the habit of signaling his wife with the train's whistle as he pulled into Shorb Station, a few miles outside Los Angeles. Two long toots meant that supper should be ready in thirty minutes.[1]

A neighbor brought Mrs. Lucey the news. There had been an accident; John had been killed. When she got to the railroad station, what was left of her husband's body was covered with a blood-soaked sheet. "They wouldn't even let her see him, the train had cut him so badly," the Archbishop said.[2]

Years later, Robert E. Lucey, the retired Archbishop of San Antonio, recalled the experience. The time was 1900. He was nine years old, the fourth child of John and Mary Lucey:

> My father had to register the train as it passed through the station. The train didn't stop, either, just slowed down. He would run along the tops of the cars to the engine, swing down to the ground and register the train, then catch the caboose as it went by. He had to do that rain or shine; it didn't matter what the weather was, he had to do it.[3]

The Los Angeles County Coroner's report certified that John Lucey was killed on June 25, 1900, when he fell between two box cars attached to a moving Southern Pacific freight train, "the fall being caused by the lurching of the train."[4] The death was ruled accidental, and the railroad company was exonerated from all liability. The Archbishop remembered that his mother received a small sum of money from the Southern Pacific as compensation for her husband's death, but, he said forcefully, "That didn't go far in keeping our heads above water. It was barbaric how companies treated their workers in those days, just barbaric."[5] Time had not softened the trauma that sowed the seeds of a social conscience.

The 1900s were years when reformers marched for the rights of the common man. The first two decades of the twentieth century witnessed great compaigns to fight corruption and inefficiency in government, to regulate and control big business, and to improve the lot of the urban poor, especially through social welfare legislation.[6] Robert Lucey was too young to understand the reform philosophy of Progressivism, but he had questions reflecting his sense of the injustice of his father's death. Why didn't the trains have to stop when they came into the station to register their freight? Why did his father have to work at such a dangerous job? Now that he was dead, who would take care of the family? Why didn't someone force the railroad company to help? Similar questions were being asked by reformers calling for the enforcement of work safety rules and some kind of insurance or compensation for workers injured or killed on the job. As he grew up, the seeds of his social conscience took root in his Catholicism. Social justice would become his cause, and he would make many a march for it.

The Lucey family had made something of a march of their own. John Joseph Lucey was born in Boston in July, 1847, and worked on the railroad as a young man. His father had come from County Cork in Ireland years earlier and settled briefly in Canada before migrating to Boston. John Lucey was a short man, about five feet six inches tall, but powerfully built, weighing nearly two hundred pounds. An old photograph shows a broad-shouldered, handsome man with strong features and a full handlebar moustache.[7]

Family tradition has it that it was on one of his railroad runs from Boston to upper New York State that he met and fell in love with Mary Nettle, a petite and beautiful woman twelve years his junior. John and Mary were married on November 11, 1879, at Saint Patrick Church in Brasher Falls, New York. Two children came in three and a half years, Mary Ellen in 1880 and Mark John in 1883. Brasher Falls was not their home for long. The railroad was headed west in the 1880s, and the Lucey family went with it, first to Tucson, Arizona, where a third child, Dennis, was born in 1888, and finally to Los Angeles in 1889. The family had completed its cross-country march.[8]

The Luceys were only one of many families making their way to Southern California, particularly Los Angeles, in the 1880s, attracted by the productivity of the land, the mild climate, and the transcontinental railroad. Census figures show that the population of Los Angeles, terminus for the Southern Pacific and Santa Fe railroads, increased from 11,000 in 1880 to 50,395 in 1890. Moreover, by 1900, when the city's population exceeded one hundred thousand, Los Angeles retained an air of middle-class Christian respectability that its sister city to the north, "the Paris of the West," had long since lost, or, some say, never had. Hollywood, oil, real estate, and tourists had not yet overwhelmed Los Angeles with destructive wealth, and its citizens were not so far removed from their Puritan heritage as to forget the divine call to industry and virtue. In fact, the city was beginning to bustle with business, and the city fathers kept its virtue intact by shutting down the gambling houses in 1896 and forcing saloons to close on Sundays a few years later. By 1906, as one historian noted, Los Angeles boasted that it had more churches than any other comparable city in the country.[9]

John Lucey found employment as a freight conductor with the Southern Pacific Railroad, a company that virtually controlled Los Angeles in the early 1900s.[10] He chose freight over passenger service because of the few extra dollars involved; the Luceys needed the extra money. In June, 1889, not long after they moved into their first home on South Chestnut Street in the Boyle Heights section of Los Angeles, they were greeted with the birth of another son, Edmund.[11]

The joy of a newborn was short-lived, however. Diphtheria claimed the life of two-year-old Dennis in 1890. Four years later the same disease took the life of another Lucey, Leroy, born in 1892.[12] In between came Robert Emmet, born on March 16, 1891, one day ahead of schedule: "I did everything fast. My mother expected me on Saint Patrick's Day and intended to name me Patrick, but I couldn't wait. I guess I've been that way all my life." Robert was born at home but not without incident. His mother told him he had been born blue, and perhaps the lack of oxygen had something to do with the deafness in his right ear, an embarrassing inconvenience he was to experience all his life.[13]

The Lucey family continued to grow, with the births of Catherine in 1895 and Margaret Mary in 1897 completing the household. John and Mary talked for many hours about the prospect of more children straining their already tight budget before deciding to start payments on a newer home in the Lincoln Heights section of Los Angeles. After Margaret's birth, the family moved into a two-story frame house on Avenue 24, located in Sacred Heart Parish, a middle-class Irish and German neighborhood, staunchly Catholic.[14]

Robert learned his ABCs from the Dominican sisters who taught at Sacred Heart Grade School and was soon serving as an altar boy for Father Michael McAuliffe, the pastor of the parish church. Robert found a friend in the priest and would return to him for advice in the coming years.[15]

Early in life Robert began what was to become a habit of taking things into his own hands. One day he picked up his baby sister, Margaret, and carried her around the living room to stop her crying. A misplaced pillow brought the two to the floor, Robert fracturing his hip in the fall. When spinal paralysis developed from the injury, the worried parents called for help. As the Archbishop told the story, the doctors prescribed chloroform and neck exercises: "They would give me this chloroform and then come up behind the bed, grab hold of my head and twist it," he related. "You could hear me shriek two blocks away!"[16]

When the doctors gave up twisting, Mrs Lucey turned to the Dominican sisters for the only other kind of help she knew. The sisters prayed and her son recovered. The Archbishop discounted any miraculous explanation for his remarkable recovery but did claim some exemption from routine illness. "You see, an ordinary sickness doesn't hit me at all. I have to have some special disease. Somehow the paralysis went away, and in a few weeks I was back running in the streets with the other kids."[17]

Mrs. Lucey was active in Sacred Heart Parish, but her involvement took second place to bringing up her children. There was no doubt about who raised the Lucey youngsters to know, love, and serve God. "My father was a kindly sort of man," the Archbishop reminisced, "but his job kept him away from home much of the time. He was smart enough, however, to leave a good deal of the discipline of the family to my mother. He let her see to it that we obeyed, and we did."[18]

After her husband's death in 1900, Mrs. Lucey did not remarry but chose instead to raise the children herself. She was a woman of strong character and the spiritual center of the family, "a very regular Irish mother," as one of her neighbors described her.[19] Her photograph in the family album shows eyes that knew how to laugh and a mouth set firm against hard times. And hard times there were.

Without a husband's paycheck she had to take in boarders to make ends meet, and the children, too, felt the pinch. Mary Ellen was employed in a local department store and contributed her salary to the upkeep of the family. Edmund, nicknamed "Dee," signed on as an office boy with the Santa Fe

Railroad and likewise added his earning to the family income. Robert himself worked after school at LaSage's Shoe Store, wrapping packages and doing odd jobs.[20]

The thought of becoming a priest grew gradually in Robert. He may have first considered a religious vocation as early as his grade school years when his older brother Jack left for the seminary. Robert did not pattern himself after his brother, but he saw something compelling in Jack's commitment to the priesthood. A similar influence came from his childhood friend, Father McAuliffe. As the old Archbishop once remarked, "I had been an altar boy for several years, and you can't come that close to fire without being warmed." Then, too, there was Robert's mother, who undoubtedly felt great happiness in yielding another son to the service of God.[21]

To chart the faith of any person is risky, for it sometimes involves making assumptions about the working of the hand of God in the human heart, assumptions not shared by everyone. There was an element in Lucey's choice of vocation that cannot be explained solely on the basis of reason. That element was his desire to do God's will.[22] There was a danger, of course, to which the future Archbishop was not immune, that one could confuse this divine will with one's own.

Lucey took his first step toward the priesthood in 1905 when he began high school as a day student at Saint Vincent College, a Catholic preparatory school operated by the Vincentian Fathers. Located on Grand Avenue about a thirty-minute trolley ride from the Lucey home, Saint Vincent had been founded after the Civil War by a small group of priests under the encouragement of Thaddeus Amat, Bishop of Monterey–Los Angeles. By the time Robert enrolled, Saint Vincent had both a coeducational secondary level and a college division, and judging from articles appearing in the student magazine, the school seemed to cultivate a rather liberal point of view, at least on labor relations.[23]

"The Church and the Labor Question," for example,

appeared in the *Saint Vincent College Student* in 1904 and gave unstinted praise to Pope Leo XIII's encyclical *Rerum Novarum*, which proclaimed the right of workers to form unions. Another surviving issue of the magazine carried a valedictory address entitled "The Dignity of Labor," in which the Pope's letter was lauded for its recognition of the dignity of the worker's way of life, and called for more papal leadership in this area.[24]

In his two years at Saint Vincent, Robert achieved some distinction. As a freshman he took third place in the English department's annual public-speaking contest, and the following year he won that prestigious competition with a recitation of "The Ride of Jennie McNeal." The gold medal awarded for elocution was donated by the LaSage brothers, Robert's current employers, but no collusion was ever suggested.[25]

In September, 1907, Lucey enrolled at Saint Patrick's Seminary in Menlo Park, California. After the first of many train rides between Los Angeles and San Francisco, the high school junior arrived at the seminary and was impressed by its spacious campus and the Romanesque design of its buildings. A cornerstone inscription read: "Saint Patrick Seminary, dedicated to the patron saint of a great Catholic race to which the vast majority of our own people belong."[26] Robert, however, a native son of Los Angeles, did not think of himself then as Irish, and never did.

Saint Patrick's Seminary was located on an eighty-six-acre tract of land in the Santa Clara Valley and formally opened in September, 1898, with twenty-eight students enrolled in the "classical" department. By 1907 the student enrollment had climbed to eighty. The Sulpician Fathers, noted for their "excellent discipline," were in charge.[27] The seminary itself was divided into two wings. Robert's brother Jack was on the senior side with the other philosophy and theology students, while the younger Lucey began on the junior wing, remaining there until he finished his last two years of high school and first two years of college. In accordance with standard seminary policy, Robert could not associate with Jack or any "senior" except at specially designated free times, but on those occasions the brothers would walk around the flower garden and talk. Robert made friends with several other seminarians from Los Angeles, although "particular friendships" were forbidden by the rules.[28]

At Saint Patrick's, rules governed eating and sleeping, study and recreation, keeping silence in hallways, the dormitory, and the washrooms; other rules specified when one could write home and required that unsealed letters be placed on the prefect's desk in case the rector wanted to screen them. It was a strict, regimented schedule the students followed, almost as rigid as the one their notorious neighbors lived by, and comparisons were frequently drawn. "We used to call the seminary the penitentiary," a former student recalled. "There was only one difference between Saint Patrick's Seminary, where we were, and San Quentin, which was thirty miles away. . . . They got beans on Tuesday and we did not get them and wanted them."[29]

Like most high school students, Lucey was not beyond bending a few rules. One night he and a friend raided the seminary dining room for French bread and apples. When the rector inquired about the missing provisions the next morning, the undetected culprits professed ignorance of the break-in. A classmate's diary entry summed up the adventure: "It was great."[30]

Life at Saint Patrick's also had its less than light moments. "Can I see your Latin?" was heard all too often at the 8:00 A.M. study hall, as panicking students thumbed through "ponies." Chemistry Lucey could not master, but public speaking supported his academic average. "The Ride of Jennie McNeal" was trotted out again, this time with a bit more polish, and it and "The Violin's Song" were the staples in his eloquent repertoire. Acting also interested the young scholastic, as surviving lists of dramatis personae indicate. A picture of him in costume for *Antigone* suggests more of the comic than the tragic, and in fact farces like *The Hidden Gem* and *The Doctor's Assistant* were more his speed.[31] As the months went by, an admirer assessed his steady accomplishment: "Emmet surely is a pride to the South [Los Angeles]. He is very good in every kind of athletics and leads nearly every study he is taking up."[32] When high school graduation came in 1909, Robert Lucey could look back at his performance with a certain measure of satisfaction.

But looking back was the farthest thing from his mind. Time seemed to be on wheels. Jack was ordained in 1909 and assigned to a parish in Los Angeles. Robert completed his first two years of college and in 1911 moved into the senior wing of the seminary, skipping the first year of philosophy studies in the transfer. He was now called "Mr." Lucey and had a private room. The spiritual regimen was also tighter, with hours assigned for confession, spiritual conferences, monthly retreats, and days of recollection. There were regular faculty evaluations of his progress. Perhaps this more serious tone had something to do with Robert's decision not to see anymore a friend he had met in Oakland. A priest must have no doubts about his vocation.[33] At twenty Lucey was becoming more set in his ways. "He was very stubborn, you know," a classmate once said of him. "He would stubbornly stick to the last on anything he felt was right and wanted done, and he would have it done his way."[34] The accuracy of this observation would be demonstrated time and again as the years passed by.

The social battles of the day were beginning to draw Lucey's attention. While at Saint Patrick's he had heard Father Peter C. Yorke, the pioneer labor priest, speak in San Francisco in support of the city's unions in their battle against open shop employers. Yorke cited *Rerum Novarum* in defense of the worker's right to join a union. The priest's firebrand style was attractive, and his concern for the ordinary workingman struck a sympathetic chord in Lucey.[35] *A Living Wage*, the widely acclaimed book by Father John A. Ryan, professor of moral theology at Saint Paul Seminary in Saint Paul, Minnesota, echoed Yorke's ideas and provided a theoretical basis for workers' rights.[36] In later years Lucey, too, would seek to revise the institutional arrangements of American economic life. Although he had neither Yorke's fire nor Ryan's brilliance, he came to share their devotion to the cause of social justice. But for now the names of Yorke and Ryan and others floated unattached in his mind. It would be years before he would make firm connections between what they stood for and the message he was to preach.

Thoughts about social justice were pushed to the back of his mind when Lucey learned through the seminary grapevine that his Bishop, Thomas Conaty, intended to send a student to Rome in the fall of 1912. He was delighted when Conaty chose him to go to Rome to complete his theological education. By late September he was in Boston, waiting to sail for Italy.[37]

The S.S. *Canopic* listed Robert Emmet Lucey on its register along with another seminarian bound for Italy named Raymond McGowan. The two could hardly have been more different in appearance and habit. Lucey was meticulous, given to pressed trousers, combed hair, and shiny shoes; McGowan had a style that charitably could be called rumpled. Lucey was punctual; McGowan barely managed to run across the gangplank before the ship steamed out of port. But Lucey and McGowan struck up a friendship on board that was to last a lifetime. They were kindred spirits and became allies in the fight for social justice.[38]

The travelers were met at the dock in Naples by two North American College students, attended the opera there that night (an interest Lucey was never to lose), and the following morning took the train to Rome.[39] For the next four years, Lucey lived at Via dell'Umilta, 30, the North American College residence, and attended classes at the Urban College on the Piazza de Spagna.

What was it like to be an ecclesiastical student in Rome in

1912? What understanding of the nature, purpose, and operation of the Church would a student acquire? What intellectual
atmosphere prevailed in Catholic seminaries at that time?
One historian has stated that the issue that overshadowed the
Catholic Church's intellectual centers from 1907 until well
after World War I was modernism.[40] This heresy provided the
background for Lucey's theological training in Rome.

Condemned by Pope Pius X in his 1907 encyclical, *Pascendi Dominici gregis*, modernism can be defined as a group
of propositions that included "most attempts then being
made by European Catholics, priests and laity, to incorporate
the most recent non-scholastic research and scholarship into
the development of theology and scripture studies." Tools of
research and directions of thought condemned in the encyclical included historical criticism, literary exegesis separate
from dogma, Bergsonian intuitionism, Neo-Hegelianism and
Neo-Kantianism. The Pope also issued a general warning
against "all systems of thought by whatever name which
expounded an evolutionary theory of religion, or suggested
that the Church had reshaped external truths in every period
of history according to its understanding, or otherwise
threatened the validity and the stability of dogma."[41]

In a perceptive essay on the impact of modernism on the
American priest, Michael Gannon produced a profile of a
"typical" modernist: "he was a philosopher, a believer, a
theologian, an historian, a critic, an apologist and a reformer." The source of his heresy was not his wide learning but
his alleged use of it "to subvert the very kingdom of Christ,"
most especially by suggesting that "the essence of Christianity
lay not in intellectual propositions nor in creeds, but in the
very processes of life."[42] Pius X had such people in mind when
he wrote in *Pascendi*: "None is more skilled, none more
astute than they, in the employment of a thousand noxious
devices; for they play the double part of rationalist and
Catholic, and this so craftily that they easily lead the unwary
into error. . . ."[43] He did not mince words about how mod-

ernists were to be dealt with. If a professor in a seminary or Catholic university was found to be stained with modernism in any way, he was to be excluded "without compunction." If an administrative officer in the Church fell victim to modernism, he was to be employed only in "the lowest and most obscure offices." To further guard against this evil, the Pope ordered that vigilance committees be set up in every diocese to detect and stamp it out.[44]

A veritable witchhunt ensued. Books, journals, and newspapers dealing with theology were scrutinized for error and sometimes censored. Priests were forbidden to gather at congresses except on rare occasions because it was at such meetings that modernists propagated their views. Nor were they permitted to follow courses of study at secular universities if such courses were available at Catholic institutions. In a series of statements extending through 1913, Pius X decreed that all doctrinal decisions of the Pontifical Biblical Commission were binding, that all candidates for ordination were to take an oath against modernism, and that Catholic institutions were to establish Thomism as the sole system of thought and the scholastic method as mandatory. Finally, the Pope discouraged "all disinterested activity among clerics preparing for ordination."[45]

The historian E. E. Y. Hales has written of the lives destroyed by the excesses of the anti-modernist witchhunt: "We shall never know how many valuable shoots, which might have brought forth good fruit, were killed alongside the dangerous errors when the bomb was dropped, nor how many men were prevented thereafter from ever thinking at all because some had fallen into error." Hales notes that "a kind of intellectual sterilization" was the cost of using high explosives against critical thinking.[46]

The repression had two long-range effects on the intellectual life of Catholic priests. It spread fear and suspicion among Catholic intellectuals and virtually extinguished enthusiasm for creative scholarship. In the United States this result was exemplified in the termination of the *New York Review*, the first scientific Catholic theological journal in the country. Founded in June, 1905, by Sulpician priests on the faculty of Saint Joseph Seminary in Dunwoodie, New York, the *Review* was an advanced publication promoting the study of theology and scripture in conjunction with the natural, historical, and social sciences. Although never officially condemned by Rome, the journal ceased publication in June, 1908, citing financial problems stemming from a diminished circulation. As Michael Gannon points out, however, the *Review* had fallen into official Roman disfavor, which, given the atmosphere of the times, was fatal.[47]

The anti-modernist repression also gave rise to a new philistinism among Catholic clerics. Catholic philosophy and theology alone had the whole truth, and this made further intellectual inquiry unattractive, unnecessary, and dangerous. Later, when canon law was codified in 1918, Catholic answers, already indisputable, were cemented into unchangeable and unchallengeable precepts. *Roma locuta, causa finita.*[48]

One final consideration is appropriate. Before the Second Vatican Council, seminaries were seen largely as dispensaries of knowledge where packaged answers to vital questions were passed on to future priests. Seminaries were understood to be not so much for intellectual as for character development. Authority, discipline, and order were given the highest priority. In fact, seminary training paralleled military training. These ecclesiastical bootcamps turned out "soldiers of Christ," armored with an unshakable confidence in the Catholic Church as the sole repository of truth.[49] This is no less true of the North American College in Rome in Lucey's time.

With the modernism controversy providing the background for his theological training, Robert Lucey began life at "dell Nord." The college had been the brainchild of Archbishops John Hughes of New York and Francis Patrick

Kendrick of Baltimore. Having come to Rome for the proclamation of the dogma of the Immaculate Conception in 1854, the two American prelates persuaded Pope Pius IX that the United States should have a collegiate residence in Rome as other nations had. The Pope agreed, and after acquiring and renovating an old convent on Via dell'Umilta, opened the North American College on December 8, 1859.[50] In his Spartan cell, Lucey found a bed, desk, and chair, plus a small kerosene lamp for light. The room was unheated, and there were no windows for sunlight.

A typical day at the North began and ended with bells, the first at 5:30 in the morning, the last at 10:00 at night. In between came daily mass, meals and recreation, and classes. In general Lucey, while not oustanding, did well academically.[51]

Thinking back on his four-year theologate, Archbishop Lucey recalled one lasting impression: "To study in Rome involves more than just theology and philosophy. What impresses you is the impact of the whole tremendous organization known as the Catholic Church."[52] For Lucey, Rome was the heart of the Church. Here lay the authority. Here was the power and ceremony and sanctity. It was an experience he never forgot.

On May 14, 1916, Robert Emmet Lucey was ordained a priest in the Church of Saint Apollinarius in Rome.[53] No one from his family could be present for the celebration, but in a sense the young priest now had a new family, the institutional Roman Catholic Church, to which he gave unwavering loyalty. In years to come Lucey would be shocked to learn that some priests considered it lacking in humanity.

The day after ordination Father Lucey said three masses at the Tomb of Saint Peter and took time to bask in the glow of his triumph. Then it was back to business. He devoted the next few weeks to preparing for his doctoral examinations, which he passed, and was awarded the degree in June. Lucey's years in Rome were over; it was time to go home. He traveled through northern Italy to France and sailed from Bordeaux on July 15, 1916, on the French ship *La Touraine*. Ignoring the captain's warning to spend the first night aboard ship fully dressed and bundled in a life preserver for fear of German U-boats, Robert pulled on his pajamas and awoke the next morning to a peaceful Atlantic scene.[54] He arrived in New York about ten days later and was back in California by mid-August, ready to begin the work of a parish priest.

2. Social Justice and the Papal Encyclicals

Robert Lucey eagerly took up his first assignment as assistant pastor at Saint Vibiana Cathedral in downtown Los Angeles. His duties as a newly ordained curate were typical: saying mass and hearing confessions, visiting the sick, taking the parish census, and something he had always enjoyed, preaching. The times, however, were not typical. Not long after Lucey returned from Rome, the United States joined the war in Europe, and he volunteered for military chaplaincy in the army. The young priest had his papers processed and all arrangements made when an unexpected tragedy struck. On December 27, 1917, his older brother Jack suffered a ruptured appendix and died. Lucey's superior, Bishop John J. Cantwell, told him that his trenches were now in Los Angeles and gave him a temporary assignment as administrator of Jack's former parish.[1]

Other parish assignments followed. In 1920 Lucey was sent to Immaculate Heart of Mary Parish as assistant pastor, with the additional task of serving as chaplain of the Newman Center at the University of California at Los Angeles. After a year at the Center, he approached Bishop Cantwell for money to renovate and expand its facilities, but the Bishop had something else in mind. He told Lucey to forget about the Newman Center and offered him the post of director of the Bureau of Catholic Charities for the Monterey–Los Angeles diocese. Lucey refused the assignment and stalked out of the Bishop's office.[2]

By Cantwell's own admission, heading the Catholic Charities Bureau was "one of the lousiest jobs in the diocese," an evaluation stemming in part from the general disesteem for professional social work at the time. Lucey himself knew the reputation of Los Angeles social workers: "Statistical Christs" they were called, more concerned with numbers than with people.[3] Furthermore, Lucey had had no training in social work. He did not relish taking up an assignment that he might bungle, losing the respect of people and the Church. Nevertheless, his Bishop had asked him, and how could he refuse? The next morning he acceded to Cantwell's wishes. "Accepting that job changed my whole life," Archbishop Lucey was later to recall. "It set me on a completely different course."[4] The decision marked the beginning of a five-year tenure in the bureau that, in turn, spurred Lucey to develop a philosophy of social justice that was to guide him throughout his life.

The principal sources of the philosophy Lucey fashioned in the years between 1921 and the coming of the New Deal were the social encyclicals of Leo XIII and Pius XI.[5] These official Church teachings provided the underlying principles and the authority for Lucey's social activism and gave shape and definition to his work in California and beyond.

Written in 1891, Pope Leo XIII's encyclical *Rerum Novarum* appeared at a time when nineteenth-century economic liberalism and the increasing concentration of wealth and industrial power were making workers' lives more narrow and precarious. The solution to this evil, Leo stated, lay neither in the abolition of private property nor in class warfare as the socialists proclaimed but in the recognition of the rights and dignity of workers. To hold private possessions was clearly in accord with nature and an inviolable right. Moreover, it was a great mistake to believe that "class is naturally hostile to class; that rich and poor are intended to live at war with one another." On the contrary, just as the parts of the human body fit into one another and work in harmony, "so in a State it is ordained by nature that these two classes should exist in harmony and agreement . . . so as to maintain the equilibrium of the body politic. Each requires the other; capital cannot do without labor, nor labor without capital." Thus the fundamental principles of socialism must be "utterly rejected."[6]

Leo declared that the worker had inviolable rights, too, including the right to enough of the world's goods to maintain himself and his family in "reasonable and frugal comfort." Workers owed their employers an honest day's labor, but employers in turn owed their workers a just wage, a safe and decent workplace, and reasonable working hours. The Pope charged that "by degrees it has come to pass that Working Men have been given over, isolated and defenseless, to the callousness of employers and the greed of unrestrained competition." As a result, "a small number of very rich men have been able to lay upon the masses of the poor a yoke little better than slavery itself." To remedy this situation Leo endorsed the right of workers to form unions as a means of securing just wages and reasonable hours and conditions. The Pope went one step further. He insisted that the state had the obligation to guarantee the rights of all its citizens: "Whenever the general interest of any class suffers, or is threatened with evils which can in no other way be met, the public authority must step in to meet them."[7]

For its time *Rerum Novarum* was a radical proposal, and it offered substantial support to reform. Leo's criticism of laissez-faire capitalism, his acceptance of the idea of government intervention in the economy, and the specific rights he outlined for workers were still advanced thirty years after the encyclical was written. It was a call for a reordering of social and economic life based on the moral guidelines of justice and charity.

The limitations of the Catholic reform movement must be attributed to the Church in general rather than to the encyclical itself. In the early 1900s, clerical activists like John Ryan and Peter Yorke, who recognized the existence of social and economic injustice and tried to do something about it, were exceptional. Few of their ordained brothers had come to see these evils, and fewer still were ready to admit that the American economic system could be at fault. Would not the Protestants question their patriotism? More important, these priests had simply not been equipped by their backgrounds, seminary training, or personal experience to grasp the root causes of poverty in industrial society, make informed judgments about reform proposals, and lead their people in an attack on social injustice.[8] "There is scarcely any danger, indeed, that the clergy of America will ever lose sympathy with the desire of the masses for industrial freedom and industrial opportunity," John Ryan had written in 1908, "but there is a very real danger that their sympathy will not be equalled by their knowledge. The great majority of our clergy in the United States have not yet begun to study systematically or take more than superficial interest in the important social problems of their age and country."[9] The situation had not changed substantially when Lucey took to the social justice road in the 1920s.

World War I and the ever growing demand for farm workers in the Southwest had drawn thousands of immigrants to California by the 1920s. Many of these immigrants were Mexicans, at least nominally Catholic and unmistakably poor. Their ranks would be swelled by thousands more as a result of the Calles persecution in Mexico in 1924, and as these immigrants poured into the already overcrowded and deteriorating neighborhoods of East Los Angeles, they quickly became an exploitable pool of cheap labor. It was in response to the needs of the first wave of immigrants that Bishop Cantwell established the Bureau of Catholic Charities in 1919. Covering an area from Monterey to San Diego, the bureau began with a budget of $85,000, one office, and a mostly volunteer staff. Given these limitations, it could do little more than provide stopgap assistance in the form of small handouts to some of the seemingly numberless applicants for help.[10]

When Lucey assumed the directorship of the bureau in 1921, he brought with him an attractive, energetic personality. He was a handsome man, broad-shouldered and brown-haired like his father, with sparkling eyes and a quick smile inherited from his mother. He was meticulous in his appearance, well-spoken in his words, and, as described by a fellow priest, "not timid about his ability." Lucey had a drive that soon won him the label of "ecclesiastical climber" and a curious shyness frequently mistaken for arrogance.[11]

Although he looked upon the bureau's work as essentially religious, Lucey came to define religion as concern for the whole person, body and soul. Emphasis on the one at the expense of the other was neither good social work nor a true expression of spiritual belief. He conveyed the tone of his developing religious philosophy in his report on the bureau's activities for 1921: "Any charity that serves the body without the soul, or the spiritual without the material, is of necessity limited and incomplete." If religion claimed to have value for man, it must demonstrate that value in the social arena because "today religion is judged by its social service; doctrine means little to people."[12]

His experience at the Bureau of Catholic Charities helped Lucey to link social action to traditional pastoral goals. He learned from his work with the Catholic Charities settlement houses in the barrios of East Los Angeles that if the Church was to be effective in its spiritual ministry, it had to respond as well to the material needs of its people. In a sense, it was necessary to eliminate the demoralizing effects of poverty so that the poor would be more disposed to listen to the Church's teachings.[13]

Lucey's record as an administrator demonstrated a growing social consciousness. By nearly quadrupling the bureau's annual operating budget from $85,000 in 1919 to $320,000 in 1925, he was able to expand its range of services. At the central office in Los Angeles, for instance, a full-time staff of thirty-seven salaried workers operated twenty-eight institutions, including nine boarding schools for dependent children, a maternity hospital for dependent mothers, two day nurseries, three settlement houses, and three clinics. Free medical, dental, and legal services were provided by a volunteer staff of more than one hundred doctors, nurses, lawyers, and social workers. By the time he left the bureau in 1925, Lucey had supervised the creation of branch offices in nine California cities.[14]

Lucey also brought a more professional tone to the bureau. He stressed the value of keeping records and diagnostic files on patients, the need for specially trained personnel, and thorough investigations into the backgrounds of children and foster parents before placement, as well as follow-up work on these cases.[15]

As the years went on, however, Lucey became more concerned with the causes of poverty than with its symptoms. His work in the bureau gave him a firsthand understanding of the economic injustices of industrial society. He saw how low pay, exhausting hours, and hazardous working conditions made the worker's life a misery. He learned the realities of unemployment and underemployment: "One reason why so many people were coming [to the bureau] for money," he noted, was "just to buy the necessities of life and avoid hunger." These people were forced onto the dole because "the men in the family either had no work, or they were employed part time." His bureau experience enabled him to review the social consequences of the death of a family's principal breadwinner. He learned how juvenile delinquency, crime, and illiteracy were tied together with poverty and unemployment. The upshot was that he saw the urgency of reform: "I realized more clearly that it wasn't so much giving your sack of potatoes to a poor family that solved the problem. The need was stopping the cause."[16]

Lucey's administration and his growing awareness of the

relationship between industrialism and poverty reflected the trend in Catholic welfare work after the turn of the century. Previously Catholic charitable organizations throughout the country had dealt with the problems of swelling immigration, industrialization, and the rush to the cities on what amounted to a case-by-case basis, but now the sheer volume of people and problems forced a change in direction. Increasingly the Church's resources were marshaled to deal more systematically with social problems. Fund raising and administration became more centralized, while duplication and overlapping services were gradually reduced or eliminated. This organized and scientific approach brought with it a rejection of the notion that poverty was the result of personal weakness and failure and prompted criticism of industrialism as the root cause of much suffering.[17] Lucey shared in this criticism and found support for his convictions in the official teaching of the Church.

It is difficult to determine when Lucey read Pope Leo XIII's *Rerum Novarum* and understood its implications for the first time. Perhaps it was during the first of two terms in the California State Department of Social Welfare, to which he was appointed by Governor Friend Richardson in 1925 and reappointed by Governor James Rolph, Jr., in 1931, or during his investigations of slum housing as a member of the Los Angeles Municipal Housing Commission, an appointment he accepted from Mayor George Cyer in 1925. It may have been that same year, while serving as chairman of the Committee on Industrial Problems of the American Association of Social Workers, that Lucey saw the connection between what Leo was saying and what he was seeing as he investigated working conditions in factories and shops where Mexican labor was chiefly used.[18] In any event, from the time he read the encyclical and understood it, his career was revealed to him.

The heart of Lucey's social message in pre-Depression America was the just wage. Following *Rerum Novarum* as interpreted by John A. Ryan, Lucey maintained that a just wage had to be a "living" wage, one that enabled a worker to provide himself and his family with a "decent livelihood in frugal comfort." The fundamental reason for a just wage was not to stimulate productivity and increase purchasing power; rather, the reason was found in man himself, "a creature of God, endowed with rights and obligations, personality and immeasurable dignity." Speaking before the Catholic Conference on Industrial Problems in 1928, he noted that "industry has known the muscle, brawn and sweat of man but has failed to recognize his finer human attributes." Too often modern industry "has used the laborer as a tool or a machine, and when he was worn out, he was scrapped and another took his place."[19]

The prevailing industrial ethic in the 1920s held that wages ought to be determined by the law of supply and demand, the needs of the worker playing no part in the wage contract. This view had gained official sanction in 1923 when the United States Supreme Court ruled in *Adkins* v. *Children's Hospital* that the District of Columbia's minimum wage law for women was unconstitutional on the grounds that the needs of the employee were extraneous to the wage contract, and that consequently a law fixing a minimum wage based on recognition of those needs was an unreasonable interference with liberty of contract.[20] Lucey blasted the justices' decision that an employer had no obligation to protect the health and welfare of his employees. "In other words," he wrote, "if a woman's wages were so unjust that she starves or loses her health or sacrifices her virtue, that is just too bad for the lady, but it is not the concern of the employer. . . . The employer must be free to pay starvation wages if he so chooses." Lucey called instead for the application of the principles of *Rerum Novarum.* "Until we have in this country public opinion properly informed and based on the principles outlined by Pope Leo XIII, labor must continue to fight an unequal battle for its just rights." To his dismay, however, public opinion in the country at large and in Los Angeles in particular was not "properly informed." Company unions and "yellow dog" contracts denying workers the right to unionize prevailed in industry. "Among primitive peoples," Lucey caustically remarked, "certain animals from Beetles to Bulls have been held in reverence, but in Los Angeles the Yellow Dog is sacred and industry is his priest and prophet."[21]

Five articles written in the summer of 1928 and published in the *Tidings*, the official newspaper for the Los Angeles diocese, spelled out Lucey's position on the living wage, stating as a first principle that "industrial problems are the business of the Catholic Church" because they involve moral principles. Anticipating that "some Catholics are inclined to say that the Church should preach the Gospel and let business alone," he cited Leo's teaching. "The economic problem is not poverty," Lucey stated. "It's the thing that causes poverty—the mutual relations of Capital and Labor. Therefore the Church must lay down the ethical principles of justice and charity which govern industrial relations and then get men to observe these principles."[22] He admitted that there was no easy solution to the problems of industrial relations but warned that if workers were forced to the "brink of dependency" in a land of abundance, they would turn to revolution. "If we continue to oppress the laborers of this country in the future as we have in the past," he wrote, "they may decide that our system of private property is bankrupt . . . and turn to the Communists."[23]

Referring to statistics from a cost-of-living study sponsored by the Los Angeles Community Chest in 1927, Lucey stated that mere subsistence for a Los Angeles family of five, all in normal health, required an annual wage of $1,278.60. Such an income would require a daily wage of $4.11, "if a man worked every day except Sunday and the Fourth of July." Lucey pointed out that this subsistence wage allowed nothing for personal savings, life insurance, health care, emergencies, or recreation. It provided for no births or deaths in the family, only enough "to keep life in the body for five at the lowest possible level. . . . This mere subsistence wage cannot by any stretch of the imagination be called a living wage," he wrote.[24]

To meet Leo's "reasonable and frugal comfort" criterion, a worker's yearly income must total at least $2,200, Lucey argued, basing this figure on the United States Bureau of Labor report that established the annual cost of living for a statistical family of five at between $2,200 and $2,600, depending on the section of the country. For 1926, however, Lucey found that "86% of all the employed earned less than $2,000 per year."[25] Conditions in his own state were no better. The March, 1928, report of the Bureau of Labor Statistics of the California Department of Industrial Relations revealed that of the forty-eight occupations and 140,561 workers included in the report, none reached an annual income of $2,200. Thus Lucey demonstrated that "in the richest country in the world the economic condition of many millions of citizens is pitiful and deplorable in the extreme."[26]

Going beyond what Leo had stated explicitly in *Rerum Novarum*, Lucey maintained that the worker had the natural right to such conditions of labor "as will enable him to enrich his life and achieve a complete human existence." To him this meant more than fair wages, reasonable hours, and safe working conditions. It meant that the worker must have some security against unemployment, a reasonable measure of control in doing his job, and the chance to develop his "human interests" outside the work environment, such as continuing his education and having leisure time to spend with his family. As Lucey summarized it, "A little less of machine existence and little more of liberty and life will bring [workers] the happiness which is their right."[27]

Lucey warned the wealthy that they might retain for their own use "whatever of this world's goods is necessary for their state in life," but "superfluous wealth must be used for the spiritual and temporal welfare of their fellow man." It was not the desire of the Church that the rich "retain their wealth

during life and allocate it to pious purposes only at death."
Their riches represented a stewardship for which they would
be held accountable in this life and the next.[28]

Rerum Novarum provided the underlying principles of
Lucey's social theory and gave him the authority to preach the
social gospel. Indeed, he used *Rerum Novarum* and later
Quadragesimo Anno as shields for his activities. "I hid behind
the encyclicals," the Archbishop recalled, because "social
justice doesn't sound well to people paying bad wages."
When the criticism of his "socialist" views came from within
the Church, he was quick to point out to his clerical colleagues
that he was only advancing what the Pope himself had taught.
Were they arguing against the Pope, he asked?[29]

The problem of authority was compounded by differ-
ences between Lucey's vision and that of the Los Angeles
clergy. In the 1920s the majority of Roman Catholic priests in
Los Angeles had been born, trained, and ordained in Ireland
and then shipped to the United States, where they were badly
needed for parochial work. In general these priests saw the
parish as their main responsibility: paying off debts on the
church, ministering to the spiritual needs of their parishioners, caring for the sick and dying, and the like. They worried
about their individual parishes and developed little, if any,
social awareness.

These conflicting visions of the ministry were exacerbated
by Lucey's less than humble attitude toward the foreign-born
Irish clergy. Their reaction to him was unmixed. "Lucey was a
glamour boy, a self-promoter who used people and discarded
them when they had served his purpose," one contemporary
stated. "He was respectful of those above him but tyrannical
of those below." Another priest commented: "We all felt that
he felt none of us even remotely were his intellectual equals,"
an accurate impression, according to Lucey. A third priest
contemporary, later consecrated a bishop, described Lucey in
the more diplomatic language of the episcopacy: "He wasn't a
priest's priest." Even his social message was, some of his

clerical brothers thought, motivated by self-interest. "That son of a bitch would lasso anything he could find and ride it," one of them insisted.[30]

Lucey was in fact as conscious as any priest of the possibilities of moving up the ecclesiastical ladder, but what motivated him was a truly broad vision of the Church. Even in these early years, he was concerned with the Church's "image": what role it was playing in the larger community, what contribution it could make and was making to the country. Whatever else he was, Lucey was not parochial in his vision. He was able to see beyond the problems of the parish to those of an entire society, and he felt that the Church must participate in the resolution of social and economic evils. He worked untiringly and had absolutely no capacity for clerical small talk, assiduously avoiding rectory chitchat.

Getting a hearing for his views on social justice presented something of a problem for Lucey and other social activists in the 1920s. Across the nation the economy appeared sound, and prosperity seemed an American birthright. Laissez-faire capitalism was firmly entrenched in the White House, and so long as it delivered good times, most Americans found little fault with it.[31] Moreover, the Catholic Church was experiencing a revival of the old conflicts with Protestantism, represented by Prohibition, the revival of the Ku Klux Klan, and opposition to the presidential candidacy of the Catholic Alfred E. Smith. Catholicism was associated with the immigrant and his descendants, who invariably took up life in the cities, drank beer and whiskey, and practiced a religion that, some said, came from Rome, not Jesus Christ. The cumulative effect of these conflicts was to turn the Church's energy toward self-defense and away from social reform.[32] It would require an unprecedented catastrophe for large numbers of Catholics, and non-Catholics, to take seriously a call for social change. That catastrophe struck on October 29, 1929, when the stock market collapsed and the national nightmare began.

The Great Depression called for fundamental changes in the capitalist system, and Lucey found a blueprint for those changes in the latest letter from Rome. Written in 1931 to commemorate the fortieth anniversary of *Rerum Novarum* and intended as a response to the current worldwide depression, Pope Pius XI's *Quadragesimo Anno* reviewed Leo XIII's teaching on the condition of workers and then advanced a program for the reconstruction of modern society based on the principles of justice and charity.[33]

Pius reaffirmed Leo's pronouncement on the right to private property but hedged that right with further limitations, condemning its arbitrary use and superfluous accumulation and the philosophy of rugged individualism that supposedly gave it legitimacy. He reiterated Leo's endorsement of unionism as a means of obtaining a just wage and a life of reasonable and frugal comfort, but once again went beyond Leo and insisted that the worker had the right to wages, sufficient not only to keep himself and his family in frugal comfort, but to allow for savings to meet future needs. This was the "living" wage John A. Ryan had written about in 1906 and Lucey had stressed in his speeches in the 1920s. Finally, sharpening Leo's criticism of the capitalistic system, Pius recommended that the social order be restructured along the lines of the "occupational groups system," a program that urged the cooperation of workers, employers, government, and the public in determining wages, hours, profits, and prices for the nation's industries. The Pope then concluded with a call for a moral conversion of mankind to accompany social and economic reform.[34]

In America, where nearly thirteen million people were out of work by 1932, where "Hoovervilles" and the "Bonus Army" exposed the bankruptcy of the free enterprise system, social reformers of the Catholic center took *Quadragesimo Anno* as a guide and authority for reconstructing modern society. Their principal means was to rally Catholic support for Franklin D. Roosevelt's New Deal. Moderates like Ryan and Lucey interpreted the encyclical not as an absolute condemnation of capitalism, but as a call for the use of governmental power to stabilize the economy and relieve the overwhelming suffering brought on by the Depression. Economic planning, public works programs, class legislation, and support for organized labor would help correct grave disorders in capitalism without destroying the free enterprise system itself. For Ryan and Lucey, the politics of the New Deal meshed well with the ethos of papal teaching.[35]

When *Quadragesimo Anno* was published on May 15, 1931, Lucey was pastor of Saint Anthony Church in Long Beach, California, having been promoted out of Los Angeles to this wealthy "Anglo" parish by Bishop Cantwell in the summer of 1929. After settling into the parish, and without asking Cantwell's permission, Lucey arranged for a local radio station to broadcast a weekly program in which he would speak on matters pertaining to the Catholic faith. Financed by parish funds and local community donations, "Saint Anthony's Hour" made its debut on September 7, 1930, and was aired on Sunday evenings from 5:30 to 6:00. After *Quadragesimo Anno* appeared, "Saint Anthony's Hour" quickly shifted its emphasis from the explanation of formal dogma to discussion of the Church's social teaching. With an audience that may have been statewide, the program gave Lucey a forum for his social justice message until it was terminated in early January, 1933.[36]

In a series of broadcasts running from October, 1931, to October, 1932, Lucey took up the worker's cause. What explained the present plight of the worker? Like many others, Lucey led off his explanation with a blast at the Republican party. "We were told that prosperity belonged to a certain political party in such a way that if they were returned to power, all would be well with the country," he stated. But the Depression had burst the bubble of prosperity, and with it the proud claims of the Republicans. "There is a growing respect in this country for those who demand a new deal for labor, a better distribution of wealth and income, more of justice and less of industrial slavery." The people who hold such views "are honest and intelligent," he added, "and calling them names isn't going to stop them."[37]

The basic cause of the Depression, according to Lucey, was the maldistribution of wealth and income in the United States. By claiming the lion's share of profits and allowing workers only token wage increases, greedy businessmen had undermined the worker's purchasing power. Underconsumption resulted and, in turn, forced production cutbacks and unemployment. To illustrate the problem, he cited statistics from the manufacturing industries. In 1923 the value of products in all the manufacturing industries in the country was $60 billion, and wages amounted to $11 billion. By 1929 the value of products had increased to $69 billion, but wages had gained by less than one-half billion. "In other words," Lucey explained, "we have witnessed a rapidly widening gap between production and wages, and in 1929 the gap got so wide that the whole structure collapsed."[38]

Lucey proposed to restore balance to American economic life through the adoption of the occupational group system as outlined in *Quadragesimo Anno*. He explained the program with the following example. The California oil industry, he said, ought to be organized into groups representing labor, management, and consumers with the power to regulate the industry. This occupational group would maintain standards of fairness with regard to wages, hours, prices, business practices, and profits. It would enable labor to participate in policy decisions within the industry and provide management with better control over production. Consumers would be protected by governmental action, "directing, watching, stimulating and restraining as circumstances suggest and necessity demands."[39]

As Lucey saw it, the occupational group system would bring to industry sufficient self-government to reduce or remove conflict between workers and employers and give workers a share in the ownership, management, and profits of industry. Government would be kept at a minimum, with only that amount of centralized control necessary for the common good. His interpretation of *Quadragesimo Anno* would soon find a parallel in the National Industrial Recovery Act of 1933, one of the pillars of the New Deal.

Although the Pope's plan called for the organization of both employers and workers, Lucey tended to stress labor unions and said very little about employers' associations. In broadcast after broadcast he reiterated the "innate, natural and inalienable right" of workers to organize while scoring such management tactics as the company union and yellow dog contract. Lucey denounced company unions without qualification as "a sham and a fraud," designed, like yellow dog contracts, solely to benefit employers and thus perpetuate economic injustice.[40]

The winter of 1931/32 saw an unprecedented number of people in need and private, local, and state funds unable to provide assistance. Lucey believed that direct relief was required, and only the federal government could do the job. "There is no other way," he declared. "Either the federal government will get us out of this depression, or we shall not get out of it. Make no mistake about that."[41]

Lucey supported the LaFollette-Costigan bill to appropriate $375 million to states for the direct relief of the jobless. He tore into opponents of the measure who attacked it on the grounds that federal relief would pauperize the unemployed and break their spirit. "In the name of all that is reasonable," he cried, "how can you pauperize a man who hasn't had a job in twelve months? . . . How can you break the spirit of a man whose spirit is already crushed?" In an obvious reference to President Hoover's Reconstruction Finance Corporation, Lucey asked: "If the Government of the United States can help banks and railroads and big corporations, can it not protect the humble citizen who is poor?"[42]

Lucey met all comers on the issue of relief. Responding to

the charge that federal aid would damage states and city relief agencies, he replied that his personal experience in Long Beach relief work revealed that only the federal government had sufficient resources to handle the problem. As for the fear that federal aid would damage the existing structure of the national government, he recalled for his critics American relief assistance to the Armenians and Belgians: "Our government did not perish. If we feed the children of America, how can that act of justice damage the structure of our government?" Finally, in answer to the assertion that federal relief would drain the Treasury, he pointed out that "no one cried when Congress appropriated $2 billion for the Reconstruction Finance Corporation, $500 million for the National Credit Corporation, $750 million for the Federal Reserve System."[43] Some of Lucey's listeners were bothered by his comparison of federal aid to banks and federal aid to the unemployed, noting that the former was a loan, whereas the latter was a grant. As Lucey saw it, however, the critical point was that "corporations . . . and the unemployed . . . requested federal relief, and the corporations got absolutely what they asked for, and the unemployed got absolutely nothing. The requests were not identical, to be sure, but the unemployed asked only for justice, and they didn't get it." Since federal loans to the unemployed would not help, he suggested that the federal government lend the relief funds to the states, and that the states repay the federal government by taxing larger incomes and inheritances.[44]

As the Depression deepened and the mood of the country became more desperate, Lucey linked the economic crisis with a decline in religious awareness. In a broadcast of October, 1932, he observed that except for the Roman Catholic Church, "religion as embodying revealed doctrine, definite morality and a form of worship is hastening to decay." He lamented that a great number of Americans enjoyed only "a vague relationship with God" and were "pitifully ignorant of the doctrines and ordinances of Jesus Christ." The "comparatively few" non-Catholics who still went to church were get-ting very poor instruction about religious truths. "These good people have frequently been religious, according to their light," Lucey allowed, "but unfortunately that light has been very dim." The reason was that "outside the Catholic Church definite, precise doctrine is impossible: there can be opinion and theories, but nothing certain." In words that revealed much about his training, he added: "To us who are within the fold it seems that uncertainty in religion must be maddening to those sincere people who are groping and struggling to find something solid upon which to pin their faith and hope."[45]

During the years when "Saint Anthony's Hour" was on the air, Lucey enjoyed a proper but distant relationship with Bishop Cantwell. The priest exercised enough care in what he said that he was not silenced, but Cantwell was definitely disturbed by Lucey's message. His fear of adverse public reaction to the program played a part in the Bishop's decision to end the radio broadcasts. In a letter dated December 29, 1932, Cantwell first congratulated Lucey on his radio talks, "which I follow with interest week by week," and then got to the point. Due to the strained financial conditions of the parish, he wrote, "I think it inadvisable to continue the radio talks at the expense of the parish." He added that "if the radio [program] can be financed otherwise than from the parish receipts, I am quite willing that these talks continue." Point-ing out that Saint Anthony's plant "is perhaps the finest in the diocese," he told Lucey that "the liquidation of the debt that is on the parish must be the first consideration of a parish priest."[46]

Lucey felt that factors other than financial ones were involved in the decision to end the program. "I've always been convinced that the Bishop was delighted to have an excuse to get me off the air. . . . He didn't want to stop me, but I think he felt it would be more prudent if I just shut up and did the ordinary work of a priest."[47] And with that "Saint Anthony's Hour" signed off.

Lucey nonetheless continued his attack on industrial injustice. After taking time out to rebuild his church, which was destroyed in the California earthquake of March 10, 1933, he was back on the social justice track by September, this time taking on the *Los Angeles Times* and its campaign in behalf of the open shop. In an article in the *Tidings* entitled "Catholic Social Teaching and the Open Shop," Lucey declared that the open shop ran counter to the teaching of the Church and was a criminal injustice perpetrated by employers against workers. The so-called peace it produced was "the peace of force." "When a strong man sits on the throat of a weaker man, you have a picture of Open Shop peace," he stated. "Under the Open Shop plan the worker does not fight because he cannot. That, however, is not peace but slavery."[48]

Lucey's efforts in Los Angeles and Long Beach had not gone unnoticed by the working people whose cause he made his own or by his religious superiors. Upon a recommendation from Bishop Cantwell to the Apostolic Delegate, he was appointed Bishop of Amarillo, Texas. The public announcement came on February 12, 1934.[49]

Congratulations poured in from labor unions and various social welfare organizations with which Lucey had worked. The Long Beach Building Trades Council–AFL regretted the loss of "a man who has been so close and has worked so hard for the Organized Labor movement," while the hod carriers union of that city made him an honorary member, an honor he never tired of mentioning. The Children's Protective Association of Los Angeles and the Los Angeles County Welfare Federation of Community Chests praised him for his inspiring, pioneering welfare work in California.[50]

Religious and political leaders joined in the well-wishing. Rabbi Edgar F. Magnin of the Wilshire Boulevard Temple in Los Angeles and the Reverend C. Rankin Barnes of the National Council of the Protestant Episcopal Church applauded the appointment. The Mayor of Los Angeles, Frank Shaw, and the Postmaster General of the United States,

James Farley, sent their congratulations, as did the editor of the *Long Beach Press-Telegram*, who praised Lucey for the splendid service he had rendered the city.[51]

In the customary round of honorary luncheons and dinners, Lucey was lauded for fighting for the common man and compared to John the Baptist for "voic[ing] the coming of the New Deal long before its eventuation was dreamed of by most men." The citizens of Long Beach expressed their thanks in a testimonial dinner at which, it was widely noted, only one of the evening's ten speakers was Catholic, a tribute to Lucey's broad appeal.[52]

3. Amarillo: A New Dealing Bishop

"Where the hell is Amarillo?" Robert Lucey asked himself when he learned that he was to become the new Bishop there. Giving up life in Southern California in exchange for west Texas seemed a public penance, but Lucey accepted the appointment for what it was: a testing ground for his episcopal capabilities. If he did well in Amarillo, he could expect future promotions. Looking back, the Archbishop was very direct on this point: "The long-range plan was for me to move into the San Antonio Archdiocese."[1] It took no special insight to recognize this, for Archbishop Arthur J. Drossaerts of San Antonio was advanced in years, as were the other four bishops in Texas at the time. Their careers had long since peaked, but Robert Lucey at forty-three had his future ahead of him.

The story of Lucey's years in the High Plains is one of deepening commitment to social justice, as demonstrated by his support for organized labor, the New Deal, and international peace. The years from 1934 to 1941 also tell another tale: Lucey's style of episcopal leadership and the authoritarian manner in which he implemented the social teaching of the Church in the diocese of Amarillo. These two currents ran together smoothly in the Amarillo years, although changing times and a changing Church would later force them into conflict.

The people of Amarillo welcomed Lucey with warmth and enthusiasm. "The new bishop of Amarillo, Catholic, has arrived and was met at the station by a huge crowd," a local newspaper reported. "He is a particularly handsome young man. Upstanding and well built, he is of the two-fisted type and has the manners of a courtier. If he is as progressive and alert as he looks, he should be very helpful and active in civic affairs in Amarillo...."[2] The next day, May 16, 1934, he was installed as Bishop of Amarillo at a ceremony in Sacred Heart Cathedral. Described by the *Amarillo Globe* as "a page torn from the pageantry of the Medieval Ages," the installation ceremony had all the pomp of a coronation, with twelve members of the American Catholic hierarchy of the Southwest in attendance.[3]

The Texas Panhandle was no place for the weak-kneed. First inhabited by dinosaurs and later visited by passing dignitaries like Coronado, the Panhandle by the 1870s was pockmarked with small cattle towns, stopover places on the drive to Wyoming. It was the railroad that brought the first signs of stability to the High Plains, gradually transforming cattle towns into farming communities. With the break-up of the huge ranch lands of west Texas after 1900 and the subsequent development of wheat, cotton, and sorghum as staple crops, the area grew steadily. Finally, when gas and oil were discovered in the region in the 1920s, the Panhandle population boomed. Amarillo's citizens numbered more than forty thousand by 1930.[4]

A local history of the "capital of the Plains" declared that Amarillo had "an enjoyable and healthful climate," temperatures in the summer averaging 64.9 degrees, with the mercury dipping to 39.4 on a typical winter day. Whoever recorded these temperatures must have tarried in Amarillo only as long as Coronado, for in the winter the High Plains are racked with snow and bitterly cold winds, and the summer heat soars into the 90s.[5]

In the 1930s Amarillo was a truly awful place to be. In addition to the suffering brought on by the Depression, the area was plagued with drought and dust storms. "I have never swallowed so much dirt in all my life," Lucey wrote to Bishop

Cantwell after one year in his new home. "We had dust storms almost all winter in various shades—black, gray, red and brown."[6] Of the nearly seven years he labored in Amarillo, five were drought and dust years, but through it all Lucey remained staunch. "I was hard to discourage. If I couldn't change the weather, I knew I had to learn to live with it."[7]

The condition of the Amarillo diocese in 1934 was as troubling as the weather. Lacking order and organization, the diocese resembled a frayed cloth. The new Bishop would have to pull together the loose ends, cut some away, and sew the remainder into a new arrangement.

Originally established in 1926 by Pope Pius XI, the Amarillo diocese took in an area of 72,000 square miles and a Catholic population of approximately twenty thousand. Financially, the diocese was almost totally dependent upon donations from the American Board of Catholic Missions, a committee of the National Catholic Welfare Council, and the Extension Society, a Chicago-based organization founded to support Catholic missionary activity, especially in the very poor regions of the United States. During the episcopacy of the first Bishop of Amarillo, Rudolph Gerken (1927–1934), the Extension Society alone contributed more than one hundred thousand dollars to keep the diocese afloat.[8]

Under Gerken's leadership the diocese embarked in the late 1920s on a building program that it desperately needed but could ill afford. Churches were built and remodeled; elementary schools were started; and even a college—Saint George College—was opened in 1928. To pay for all of this, Gerken relied on grants from the Extension Society and the American Board of Catholic Missions, plus private loans from relatives—an unusual arrangement, to say the least. Equally unusual was Gerken's method of keeping the diocesan financial records. "He did his bookkeeping on the back of an envelope," one priest observed.[9]

Then the Depression struck, revenues were lost, debts

mounted. Nineteen thirty-two marked the beginning of seven lean, dry years in west Texas. While the rest of the country gradually emerged from the depths of the Depression, Amarillo remained in dire poverty throughout the decade. Thousands of Catholics were numbered among the Okies who moved out of the Dust Bowl, reducing the diocesan population from thirty-two thousand in 1931 to less than twenty thousand by 1934. The Catholic exodus meant a corresponding loss of diocesan income, which, coupled with smaller grants from the Extension Society and the American Board of Catholic Missions due to the Depression, spelled hard times.[10] The result was that when Lucey arrived in May, 1934, he found the diocese deep in debt and the financial records in chaos.

His new see also lacked those special institutional features that sharpen identity and give a sense of social purpose. For example, the Amarillo diocese had no newspaper to shape and express Catholic thinking on Church and world affairs. The few diocesan organizations of the laity that existed were in disarray. The poor could not be certain of finding help from the Catholic Welfare Bureau, and the educational facilities of the diocese were staffed with poorly qualified teachers. But the clearest example of the lack of order in the diocese was the clergy.

When Bishop Gerken assumed control in 1927, he had about two dozen priests to staff the nineteen parishes and more than fifty missions scattered throughout his see.[11] The Bishop was in no position to be selective about the quality of the clergy he was able to recruit. It was no secret that Gerken was forced to accept "rejects" from other dioceses, maverick priests whose own bishops were all too willing to lend them to Amarillo or any other faraway place. These priests, frequently inferior in learning and training and not accustomed to bowing before ecclesiastical authority, worked in some harmony with Gerken, partly because of their distance from him, partly because of the high demand for their services, but most of all because of Gerken's flexibility. Mixing paternal persuasion with stronger measures on occasion, Gerken was able to maintain reasonable control by keeping a loose rein on his priests; yet such a relationship was undesirable at best. Because a number of these priests were on loan from other places and had not been incardinated into the Amarillo diocese, the parish structure of the diocese was tenuous. Were a half dozen of them suddenly to pull out and return to their original sees, the Bishop of Amarillo would be in extreme straits.[12]

The contrast between Gerken and Lucey could not have been sharper. Gerken was a warm man with an Iowa farm background, a first-namer, an outgoing person who, it was said, "never stepped on people's toes." His episcopal style was informal and loose; one did not need an appointment to see him. Gerken was close to his people and priests and was approachable as a man and a bishop. Lucey was a city boy, with a dignified air left over from his Roman training. Unlike Gerken, he needed a formal association with people before he would mix with them and was so reserved that people felt ill at ease in his presence, an atmosphere he cultivated because he felt that it gave him an advantage in dealing with others. Bishop Lucey was remembered as "well-ordered" and "very businesslike," but no one felt free to drop in on him for a chat or without an appointment. Lucey left no doubt in anyone's mind that he was the Bishop and expected to be treated as such. When he presided at liturgical functions or attended church or civic ceremonies, for example, he was very much the center of attention. Finally, Lucey did not have the common touch his predecessor had; he was a distant person, and, as one priest put it, inspired fear rather than affection.[13]

There were other contrasts as well. Gerken was more pastorally oriented, Lucey more administrative. Gerken's operations tended to be ad hoc and makeshift, while Lucey thought in broad organizational terms. Lucey was much more civic-minded than Gerken, involving himself and the Church in the affairs of the world by speaking out on social issues. The two bishops thought differently about the see city. While Gerken scattered his efforts at building up the diocese throughout the territory, Lucey concentrated his work in Amarillo itself, establishing a diocesan pecking order in terms of residence in the see city.[14] Later, in the San Antonio archdiocese, the same order would prevail, revealing which priests were currently enjoying the Archbishop's favor. Again unlike Gerken, Lucey had a maddening capacity for detail. One example will serve to illustrate the point. In the midst of the time-consuming preparations for his departure from Los Angeles, Lucey wrote to the administrator of the Amarillo diocese for the measurements of the dining room table in his new home so that a proper tablecloth could be made. He went so far as to tell the administrator how to take the measurements: "take a large piece of paper and cut it the exact size of one-half of the table. We can then fit a tablecloth to double that size for the full table."[15] One can only guess at the administrator's reaction to the letter.

One final aspect of Lucey's episcopal style deserves note—his predilection for canon law. When he came to Amarillo, the diocese did not have a trained canon lawyer, and thus he had to seek temporary assistance from outside. In a series of letters to a professor of canon law at the Catholic University of America in Washington, D.C., he inquired about the power of a bishop in cases involving diocesan appointments, incardination, and the like. In August, 1935, he wrote for an interpretation of the force of a Roman decree empowering a bishop to compel his priests to obey chancery instructions. Some priests were refusing to follow his commands—"three ne'er-do-wells who seem to take pleasure in opposing their bishop"—and he asked if he could place them under canonical precept and suspend them if necessary. "In a certain way it is a test of my authority," he wrote, "and the prudent thing to do would be probably to make them obey."[16]

Lucey was a determined man, and one toward whom few people could remain neutral. He held strong opinions and expressed them in strong language. He tolerated no dissension within the ranks, and where he led, he expected his priests and people to follow.

Lucey set about bringing order to the diocese soon after his arrival. One of the first items on his agenda was to shore up its sagging finances. He began by creating a diocesan lay board of advisors and within a year was able to record a favorable assets-to-liabilities ratio. By efficient and careful administration, he paid off the debts owed to Gerken's relatives, refinanced diocesan debts at lower interest rates, and generally brought the diocese onto a sounder financial base. At the same time he maintained good relations with the Extension Society and the American Board of Catholic Missions, tapping both agencies for more than one hundred thousand dollars over the next six years.[17] He worked hard to demonstrate the enormous needs of his diocese and win benefactors for it.

In 1934 he wrote to the executive secretary of the Extension Society that "Amarillo [diocese] lives by the grace of God and the favors of its friends" in Chicago. He told of the great drought afflicting crops and livestock, of farmers in desperation, "and poverty and desolation everywhere." Lucey portrayed the rigors of life in west Texas and the difficulties of ministering to his people. "In many instances roads, autos and people are poor. The mission collections are negligible—not enough to pay for the gasoline used in transportation, and the death of a tire from old age and hard work is a financial catastrophe. For several missions the subsidy from the Extension Society is the difference between life and death."[18] To the American Board of Catholic Missions in 1936, the Bishop announced that "old Man Drought is now spending his fifth year in our diocese" and, along with his "two pernicious children, Duststorms and Heat," had succeeded in "ruining many people's disposition and everybody's wheat crop." Again to the board, in 1938, he related how devastating the drought had been to the wheat harvest. Conditions were no better in 1939, as drought continued to plague the region. "Old Man Drought is no new phenomenon out here," Lucey stated in his annual report to the board. "He isn't even considered a visitor—he has just settled down and become one of us. . . . The only crop that did well [this year] was the one we didn't plant. The government gave us a few dollars for reducing our wheat acreage."[19]

As the financial picture started to improve, Lucey set about bringing order to diocesan institutions. He worked hard to keep Saint George College operating, a nearly impossible task in the Depression years. After its founding in the fall of 1928, the college received several donations from Mrs. Katherine E. Price, and Bishop Gerken changed the name to Price Memorial College. When the Depression struck, the school went into a financial decline, from which it recovered very slowly. In 1936 Mrs. Price endowed the college with a ten-thousand-dollar grant, and the school struggled on. Lucey catered to Mrs. Price, "our diocesan fairy godmother," and tried to better the school's academic standards. In 1938 he persuaded the Christian Brothers of the Saint Louis Province to staff it, considerably improving its academic standing.[20]

The Catholic Welfare Bureau was another means Lucey used to bring order to his diocese as well as teach the social gospel of the Church. Established in 1932 by Bishop Gerken as the Bureau for Catholic Charities, it was a small, poorly staffed, and largely inefficient operation until Lucey reorganized it into the Catholic Welfare Bureau, incorporated in March, 1935. Applying his Los Angeles experience to the Amarillo setting, he established the bureau as "a family and child welfare agency" and hired a Los Angeles social worker as its first director. Although the budget never exceeded $10,000 for any one year, the bureau was facing poverty more extreme than that Lucey had encountered in California. The agency distributed food and clothing, provided basic medical and dental care, especially for mothers and infants, made job referrals, and helped people get on their feet with emergency assistance. Lucey supervised the bureau's work closely in these years through the monthly reports he required of the director.[21]

Lucey was also pouring much of his energy into organizing the laity for "Catholic Action," a movement associated with Pope Pius XI and defined as "the participation of the laity in the apostolate of the hierarchy through prayer, study and action." Under Lucey's leadership, Catholic Action was a clerical operation directed by a priest appointed by and responsible to him. It was not a lay movement, as it was under other bishops in other dioceses.[22] The keys to Catholic Action were study clubs and lay retreats in which adult Catholics studied and discussed their faith. In Amarillo the centerpiece of Catholic Action was the Confraternity of Christian Doctrine, an organization designed to provide religious instruction to both children and adults. Lucey had been active in setting up the Confraternity in Los Angeles, and he used his experience in establishing it in Amarillo.

In a letter sent to all pastors on February 15, 1936, Lucey ordered that the Confraternity be instituted in all diocesan parishes and missions and that efforts be directed first toward adult study clubs.[23] Religious instruction was important, Lucey believed, because it led Catholics to a deeper awareness of the moral and social obligations of their religion.

The problem was that the Confraternity in Amarillo tended to be largely a paper organization. Lucey required his pastors to submit regular accounts of the progress of their parish Confraternities but was surprisingly gullible about these reports. Many of them padded attendance, but Lucey seemed not to be aware of this.[24] Much of the discussion club material was juvenile in content and hardly calculated to challenge Catholics to social action, but again the Bishop seemed oblivious.[25] He had a vision of what the Confraternity ought to have been but never grasped the practical problems of making his vision real.

Developing an effective Confraternity program was made more difficult by the indifference of many of Lucey's priests toward both the program and their Bishop. They expressed their dissatisfaction with passive resistance. The laity, too, were unaccustomed to having a fireball for a bishop, one whose grand ideas seemed as remote from them as Lucey himself.[26] His entire career as a mover and shaker in Confraternity work was flawed by an unfortunate combination of energetic drive and remoteness from pastoral realities.

Another instrument Lucey used to organize the diocese and propagate his views was the *Texas Panhandle Register*, the official diocesan newspaper, which he established in 1936. The *Register* had much the same objective as the Confraternity of Christian Doctrine—to develop an informed and enthusiastic laity. In a pastoral letter printed in the first edition of the newspaper on July 5, 1936, Lucey outlined the need for a Catholic press to help enlighten and challenge its lay readers. As he put it, "A simple trusting faith is good, but an informed faith is better." Lucey went on to say that "a diocese is like an army with officers and soldiers—clergy and people. Information, direction and inspiration must come from headquarters if there is to be unity of plan and purpose. Our vital line of communication is this weekly paper. That it may help us to present to God 'a people acceptable, a pursuer of good works,' is our hope and prayer." His weekly editorial column entitled "Observations by the Sentinel" was intended to educate Catholics in their social thinking.[27]

There was one more area to which Lucey attempted to bring order—the sensitive problem of the clergy. The installation ceremony had barely ended before the new Bishop ordered those priests who were not incardinated to incardinate immediately or leave. The letter was an ultimatum, and it eventually cost Lucey some very good and much needed priests who found their new Bishop's style offensive. On the

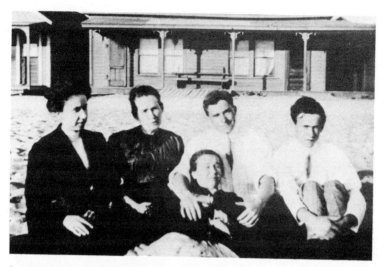

Lucey and family (*left to right*: his sisters Mary Ellen and Margaret Mary, his mother, and his brother Edmund) at home in California, ca. 1912. Photograph courtesy of the Archives of the Archdiocese of San Antonio.

Lucey (*center*, with false nose and moustache) and cast of St. Patrick's Seminary play (undated). Photograph courtesy of the Archives of the Archdiocese of San Antonio.

Lucey as a seminarian in Italy, visiting the town of Lulmona, September 1913. Photograph from his diary to his mother, courtesy of the Archives of the Archdiocese of San Antonio.

other hand, the letter helped establish him as the undisputed authority in the diocese. His action, necessary but harsh, gave a foretaste of what was to come.[28]

Soon after his arrival in Amarillo, Lucey began again to champion the cause of organized labor and the New Deal, now in company with other eminent churchmen like Cardinal Patrick Hayes of New York and Archbishop John T. McNicholas of Cincinnati.[29] Although the Catholic hierarchy unanimously accepted *Quadragesimo Anno* as official Church teaching, the bishops disagreed over its meaning and application, and especially over the role organized labor was to play in bringing about Pius XI's Christian social order. Some churchmen, like Cardinal William O'Connell of Boston, feared that stronger unions might seek their own interests at the expense of the labor-capital cooperation necessary for the success of the Pope's occupational group plan. Bishop Joseph Schrembs of Cleveland likewise called for cooperation, not competition, between labor and management as the surest way to social justice. Management's refusal to recognize unions and bargain with them in good faith did not sway conservative clerics from warning against militant unionism.[30]

Lucey, however, believed that the organization of the laboring classes lay at the heart of the papal program. He urged priests to "go to the labor temples" and "be dynamic for organized labor." He insisted, moreover, that the Church's commitment to labor go beyond mere endorsement of the *principle* of unionism. Workers had the right to expect something more concrete than rousing rhetoric. "When churches, hospitals and schools are built, organized labor has a right to be on the job—yes, exclusively on the job," he stated, "because today workingmen have a duty to join a labor union for their own good, the welfare of their families, and the peace and stability of human society." He went so far as to say that all Catholic dioceses ought to stipulate a union wage scale in their building contracts and use only union labor on their construction projects.[31]

Not one to preach what he did not practice, Lucey kept a watchful eye on his own backyard. In July, 1935, a pastor and members of the building committee of Sacred Heart Parish in Sweetwater, Texas, asked his permission to build a new church. The bid submitted by the contractor listed wages at $3.00 a day per man, but the diocesan building regulations, which Lucey himself had written, stipulated that skilled workers were to receive a wage of $1.00 an hour and unskilled ones $.66 an hour. When he saw the bid, Lucey wrote immediately to the building committee chairman:

> Mr. Balfanz [the contractor], it seems, did not intend to pay our wage scale when he submitted his bid. This can be explained either because he did not read the contract or intended to disregard it. If the former is true, he should have a guardian appointed to protect him, and if he intended knowingly to cut wages, he will get no contracts from the Diocese of Amarillo.[32]

To the pastor of Sacred Heart Church, he was even more direct:

> If I find that a wage less than that stipulated in the contract [the Diocesan Building Contract Regulations] is paid to any men on this job, both you and the contractor will be held to strict accountability. I am determined that the wage scale provided in the contract should be faithfully kept; and I shall question the men on the job to see that they receive the wage outlined in the contract. If I find that anyone is receiving less than the wage to which they are entitled, . . . you will be immediately removed from Sweetwater, and civil action will be taken against the contractor.[33]

In yet another letter to the building committee, he repeated his instruction that $1.00 an hour for skilled labor be paid for this project, adding that "if the parish cannot manage this or thinks the debt [cost] excessive, plans will be scrapped and a cheaper wooden church erected."[34]

Lucey was consistent in his policy of hiring only union labor or paying the union wage scale if union labor was unavailable. In April, 1936, he warned a church building committee in Rowena, Texas, that he would personally visit the job site to determine whether the workers were union men or were receiving the union wage scale. "We shall enforce without any exception [the diocesan building regulations]," he wrote, and "even though they appear strange to some, we shall enforce them nevertheless."[35]

It was with his endorsement of the Congress of Industrial Organizations that the Bishop of Amarillo took his strongest stand for labor and went farthest beyond mainline episcopal opinion. When John L. Lewis and Philip Murray began organizing the steel industry along industry-wide lines in the summer of 1936, Lucey backed them. "The industrial organization advocated by Mr. Lewis is quite a long step towards the occupational organization advocated by the Holy Father," he wrote. He hoped that industrial unionism would extend to worker participation in profit sharing and management and even complained to Lewis that the CIO's organizing drive did not "go far enough." Lewis agreed, but added that were he to advance such a proposal, "I would surely be put down as a communist."[36]

Lewis was right. From its inception the CIO had been tarred with the communist brush, and the sit-down strikes of 1937 hardened anti-CIO sentiment. Not a little of this hostility came from the Catholic press. Fearful of labor militancy and the communist presence in the CIO, the diocesan weekly *Brooklyn Tablet* accused the sit-down strikers of having "a definite link to communism." The Jesuit magazine *America*

regarded the sit-down tactic as unjust and immoral and ac-
cused Lewis of lusting after power and publicity. Father
Charles Coughlin, Detroit's famed "Radio Priest," used his
Social Justice magazine to smear Lewis as "an ally of the
reds." The *Catholic World* intimated that the CIO leader
might become an American Caesar with the legions of labor
at his command.[37] Hostility toward the CIO came from the
Catholic hierarchy as well. Bishop John F. Noll of Fort
Wayne, Indiana, editor of the mass-circulation *Our Sunday
Visitor*, charged that a strong communist influence permeated
the CIO and accused the CIO leader John Brophy, a Catholic, of being a communist sympathizer. Other prelates pre-
ferred more direct action. Archbishop Thomas J. Walsh of
Newark, New Jersey, discouraged Catholic participation in
CIO organizing drives in Jersey City, in effect joining forces
with Mayor Frank Hague and baptizing Hague's anti-labor
tactics as good Catholicism.[38]

During the labor turbulence of the thirties, the American
bishops issued no collective assessment of industrial unionism, but the view of Bishop Karl J. Alter of Toledo, Ohio, can
be taken as representative of the majority opinion. Writing in
Our Sunday Visitor in January, 1937, Alter expressed his fear
that the "old extreme of [economic] individualism" might be
replaced by a "similar irresponsibility on the part of labor."
While he supported labor's right to organize and bargain
collectively, he insisted that unions curb their use of the
strike, refrain from violence, and recognize that the public
interest always took precedence over any particular union
goal. Alter ruled out mass picketing as an acceptable labor
tactic because it inevitably led to violence and averred that
"the right to work was just as sacred as the right to quit
work," that is, to strike.[39]

Alter's cautious views were endorsed by the Catholic
hierarchy in November, 1937. In their pastoral letter the
bishops assured labor of continued Church support for unionism and collective bargaining, but once again admonished it

against coercion and violence, urging unions to "respect property rights" and "prove themselves worthy of the confidence of every community." A plea for the formation of occupational groups as the best means to industrial peace rounded out the hierarchy's middle-of-the-road program.[40]

The CIO also had its episcopal defenders. Cardinal George C. Mundelein of Chicago was the most eminent Church leader to stand with industrial unionism. His Auxiliary Bishop, Bernard J. Sheil, enthusiastically backed the CIO-led strike against the Hearst newspapers in 1939 and CIO organizing drives among Chicago meatpackers. Sheil also sponsored the publication of *Catholic Labor* magazine, which promoted union membership. In Detroit Archbishop Edward Mooney countered Coughlin's criticism by pointedly encouraging Catholic workers to join the CIO, and, like Sheil, spoke frequently in support of industrial unionism.[41]

Joining his counterparts from the Midwest, Lucey defended John L. Lewis and the CIO, pronouncing the labor leader "a patient man" whose program of industrial unionism was lifting thousands of unskilled and semiskilled workers from economic slavery. With praise for industrial unionism he mixed criticism for AFL conservatism. "Does the AFL leadership oppose Lewis because they fear he will unseat them?" asked the "Sentinel." For Catholic opponents of the CIO, particularly the Catholic press, Lucey had strong words. He cautioned against attacking "one who is looked upon as a Messiah by millions of workers." "The Church does not call any God-fearing laboring man a Communist," he wrote, and the "self-appointed defenders of the faith" were doing "immense harm" in attacking Lewis.[42]

Throughout the 1930s the Bishop of Amarillo was a full-fledged New Dealer, and, next to Cardinal Mundelein, the strongest voice in the Catholic hierarchy for Franklin D. Roosevelt. Lucey saw the New Deal as inaugurating Pius XI's Christian social order and the Roosevelt administration's interventionist role in the economy as corresponding to

Quadragesimo Anno's description of the role of government: "directing, watching, stimulating and restraining" whenever necessary.[43] Speaking in Texas and across the Southwest, Lucey praised the President's labor record, citing the National Industrial Recovery Act and the Wagner Act, which threw the weight of the federal government behind organized labor. He deprecated attempts by "so-called business leaders" to cast the socialist shadow over the New Deal and ridiculed these "stalwart Americans" for clinging to the belief that "socialism can be checked by Chamber of Commerce oratory." Unlike many of his fellow bishops, Lucey stood with Roosevelt in criticizing the Supreme Court's *Schechter* decision, which declared the NIRA unconstitutional, and encouraged the President to continue his battle against "reactionary judges" whose decisions "were the equivalent of anti-labor legislation."[44]

With Cardinal Mundelein and Archbishop Mooney, Lucey jumped to Roosevelt's defense when, in the months before the 1936 presidential election, Father Charles Coughlin broadsided the administration. Lucey scored the "Radio Priest" for his intemperate language (Coughlin denounced the President as a "great betrayer and liar" and "the dumbest man ever to occupy the White House")[45] and dissociated official Catholicism from Coughlin's National Union for Social Justice. "He represents no one but himself," Lucey stated flatly. "Least of all [does he] reflect the sane constructive social teaching of Pope Pius XI."[46]

Lucey's unshakable confidence in the New Deal even extended to Roosevelt's court-packing plan of 1937, which most Catholic leaders opposed. He called for an end to "the judicial dictatorship practiced by five old men" and for a new, liberal Court to protect the rights of workers and the democratic system. "In view of present day industrial standards a liberal court may be all that stands between us and chaos," he declared. "If anything will save democracy, it will be a Supreme Court that recognizes its own limitations, the prerogatives of Congress, and the rights of man."[47]

Catholic opposition to unionism and the New Deal gave Lucey many headaches. He lamented that "in the school of economic organization and economic morality most of our people are in the first grade and some have not yet reached kindergarten." Catholics were not united for social justice because opinion makers within the Church, especially the press, had misinterpreted the papal plan for social reconstruction and misled their fellow Catholics with anti-labor and anti–New Deal ideas.[48] Private devotion to a moral life and observance of the Ten Commandments were not adequate responses to the problems of industrial evils. "Moral reform is needed, true; but virtue alone will not build a new structure of economic life," he told a Catholic audience in Galveston. Social justice was the oil that lubricated the economic machine, and "if we discard the oil, the machine will break down."[49]

To inculcate liberal Catholic social doctrine, Lucey helped to organize the Summer Schools of Social Action for Priests, first in Milwaukee, Wisconsin, in July, 1937, and then in other cities, including New York, San Francisco, Los Angeles, Toledo, Pittsburgh, and Chicago, in subsequent years. These schools were to enable priests to study the social encyclicals, learn about industrial conditions, and review the principles and methods whereby they could involve themselves in the problems of industrial society. The school's faculty comprised a Who's Who of Catholic activists: John A. Ryan, Peter Dietz, Francis Haas, John Cronin, and, of course, Robert E. Lucey. Guest lecturers included John L. Brophy and Philip Murray of the CIO, lower-level officials of both AFL and CIO, George Donahue of the Association of Catholic Trade Unionists, and representatives of various state labor boards and the business community.[50]

The summer school consisted of four one-week sessions

with a recognized authority moderating each week. In the inaugural year Ryan began the program with "Economic Morality" as his subject, and Lucey spoke on the "Principles of Legislation." Other lectures dealt with women in industry, child labor, the sit-down strike, and company unions and unfair labor practices.[51]

It is difficult to evaluate the impact of these schools. They offered a forum for the dissemination of liberal Catholic social thought and continuing education in the social sciences for priests. On the other hand, they did not survive the war years and even in their heyday did not draw large numbers of priests. Lucey himself believed they were, on the whole, successful.[52]

As the threat of another international war became apparent by the mid-1930s, Lucey addressed the problem of world peace, and again found support for his views in papal teaching. During World War I, Pope Benedict XV issued "An Appeal to the Belligerent Nations," in which he called for a general reduction of armaments, compulsory arbitration of international disputes, and sanctions against all nations manifesting a militaristic spirit. The Pope pleaded for a league of nations in his encyclical *Pacem Dei munus*, issued in 1920. "It is much to be desired," Benedict wrote, "that all states, putting aside mutual suspicion, should unite in one league, or rather a family of peoples, calculated to maintain their own independence and safeguard the order of human society."[53] The Pope's message, however, went largely unheard in America, where isolationism prevailed throughout the 1920s and early 1930s.

As early as January, 1932, Lucey was arguing to a "Saint Anthony's Hour" audience that national security was just an excuse for building up arms. "Exaggerated nationalism"— Japan's dismemberment of China, for example—had to be countered by a strong League of Nations. By 1936, when the fighting broke out in Spain, however, Lucey had become convinced that the League, without American participation, could not forestall general war.[54]

Lucey's position on the Spanish Civil War was somewhere between the pro-Nationalist stance of the American Catholic hierarchy and the pro-Loyalist one of the American liberal community. About one month after General Francisco Franco's forces launched their revolt against the Republican government of Spain, the "Sentinel" suggested that war had come to Spain because the Spanish clergy had failed to teach social justice and wealthy Spanish Catholics had let their riches blind them to the fact that "poverty is fertile ground for Communism among the masses." They had "failed to read the signs of the times" and had not lived up to their duties as Christians in the field of social justice. Lucey admonished his Catholic countrymen not to "thwart the toiling masses in the name of the Church," as had happened in Spain. "Do not cause the Church to be called reactionary." Although an anti-communist, Lucey, taking his cue from Pius XI's encyclical *Divini Redemptoris* (1937), argued that anti-communist oratory must be balanced with social and economic reform. In particular, priests must "go to the working-man, learn his experience and stand by him."[55]

In November, 1937, at the annual meeting of the American Catholic hierarchy in Washington, D.C., the United States bishops issued a statement in the form of a letter to the Spanish hierarchy, declaring their sympathy and admiration for the Church in Spain caught in the throes of persecution. Signed by Bishop Emmet M. Walsh of Charleston and Cardinal Dennis Dougherty of Philadelphia in behalf of all the bishops, the letter expressed horror at religious persecution and deplored the "clever propaganda" of men "who before the world sought to appear in the role of vindicators of human rights." In the words of one historian, "almost to a man the hierarchy and the American Catholic press supported the Franco side, insisting that the Loyalist government was communist dominated, did not represent the will of the Spanish people and was bent on the destruction of the Church in Spain."[56]

Lucey, however, continued to stand apart from the majority. In an editorial in the *Texas Panhandle Register*, in July, 1938, he stated that although he was "dead against a *Communist* victory in Spain because of Communism's avowed hatred of religion," he was far from an avid supporter of Franco. The "Sentinel" called for an end to the killing and destruction in Spain and denounced the bombing of unfortified cities, adding that if Franco was guilty of atrocity, "we must be the first to condemn him. . . . General Franco, fighting for a noble objective, is not above the moral law."[57]

On the other hand, Lucey criticized liberals who overlooked the violations of the human rights of Spanish Catholics by the Republicans. When the *Nation* editorialized in behalf of the Loyalists, he accused the editors of whitewashing the communist persecution of Spanish priests and nuns. To the *Nation*'s charge that the Catholic Church in Spain was involved in a pro-fascist, anti-democratic campaign, Lucey replied that communism and democracy were not allied and that fighting communism "does not mean you are a Fascist." Pointing to Russia and Mexico, he argued that both countries were ruled by a "small group of ruthless men" who have "robbed the people of every right and liberty," and that in effect communism and fascism amounted to the same evil—totalitarianism. Thus the Church's fight against communism was a battle not for fascism, but for civil and religious liberty.[58]

As the world raced toward war, Lucey abandoned mainline episcopal isolationism in favor of collective security. He endorsed President Roosevelt's proposal to "quarantine" aggressor nations, opposed the appeasement of Hitler, and cautioned against Americans thinking themselves immune to international lawlessness. In 1939, when Roosevelt was criticized in the Catholic press for attempting to sell arms and ammunition to Britain and France, Lucey took to the radio to defend the President. Speaking in July, 1939, over Station KDKA in Pittsburgh, he declared that isolation and blind neutrality could not be reconciled with Catholic teaching and that the proper course for American foreign policy was toward collective international responsibility. He agreed that America ought not to police the world, but added that "unjust aggression must be recognized" and "international murderers" confined. "That is not policing the world; it is showing some self-respect."[59]

While Lucey was attacking isolationism, he also spoke out against anti-Semitism. In a 1940 editorial the "Sentinel" deplored the Nazi barbarism against Jews: "We as Christians, as citizens, as human beings must cry out against the horror of this debauchery." Addressing the National Conference of Christians and Jews in Dallas in December, 1940, he again denounced Hitler and insisted that "what is happening to the people of Europe is our business."[60]

Lucey's appointment in 1941 as Archbishop of San Antonio[61] led him to appraise conditions closer to home in the Amarillo diocese. He wrote with some pride that the diocese was now well organized and in a stable financial condition. The *Texas Panhandle Register* was running in the black, with the Catholic Action program and the Confraternity of Christian Doctrine operating in every parish.[62] Then he turned to the clergy.

Characterizing them as "too few and somewhat inferior," with only mediocre standards of learning, eloquence, and zeal, Lucey reported that of the twenty-seven priests serving in the diocese, three were of "very limited intelligence," two were "mental cases," one had "tuberculosis in both lungs," two were drunkards, and another was "feebleminded and absent without leave." The others, according to the Bishop, "are quite mediocre but are doing fairly well."[63]

Finally, Lucey reported that the condition of Mexican Catholics in the diocese was disturbing. "They are a people apart, ostracized and held in social and economic subjection," he wrote. "They are paid frightfully low wages . . . and barely manage to exist in poverty, disease and squalor. If a Mexican is murdered, the officials do little or nothing about it. The Mexicans in Texas, even if born here, are classed with Negroes."[64]

Bishop Lucey had become, by 1941, the leading Catholic voice in Texas for social justice and international relations. During his nearly seven years in Amarillo, he enhanced the image of the Church with a socially dynamic Catholicism that surprised as many Catholics as non-Catholics. But he did more than introduce Amarillo Catholics to social justice. He brought order and identity to the diocese, making it conscious of itself as a unified body with a sense of purpose and direction. He stretched the consciousness of Catholics beyond merely parish or even diocesan boundaries and involved them in the larger world.

Lucey also brought to Amarillo his peculiar style of episcopal leadership. He implemented his social justice gospel in an authoritarian manner, particularly in regard to the Church's position on organized labor, and used the full weight of his episcopal authority to put the social encyclicals into practice. His manner rubbed many the wrong way, but none would dare to question him for another twenty-five years.

4. San Antonio: The Bishops' Committee and the Migrant Farm Worker

When Archbishop Arthur J. Drossaerts of San Antonio died on September 8, 1940, there was little doubt that Robert E. Lucey would become the new Metropolitan of the San Antonio Province. In a few months his appointment was confirmed. The *San Antonio Express* called Lucey a "world peace advocate and a friend of the workingman," while the New Deal Mayor of the city, Maury Maverick, hailed the appointment as "the greatest single fortunate occurrence for San Antonio in a very, very long time." Maverick praised the new Archbishop as a "fellow soldier" who "will get in the trenches with us" to battle for the rights of workers. *Time* magazine described Lucey as "the most socially conscious New Dealer in the Roman Catholic hierarchy" and the "first out-and-out New Dealing archbishop since the death of Cardinal Mundelein of Chicago in 1939." It noted that the appointment was another indication of Pope Pius XII's desire to give American Catholicism "vigorous leaders" and predicted correctly that Lucey's liberalism would be directed toward the welfare of the Mexican American in Texas. Recognition came from still another source. To his staunch supporter in San Antonio, President Franklin D. Roosevelt sent his "hearty congratulations" and hoped that Lucey's new position would afford a larger opportunity for social activism.[1]

The formal installation ceremony took place in San Fernando Cathedral on March 27, 1941. The elaborate service was attended by so many prelates that a local newspaper had to notify Catholics several days in advance that "there will be no room in the Cathedral for lay persons," an unfortunate beginning to a long episcopal reign.[2]

Shortly after assuming his new responsibilities, Lucey resumed his stumping for the union movement. In St. Paul, Minnesota, he advised an audience of Catholic laymen to "think with the Church" on social as well as doctrinal matters: "If you claim that the American working man has no obligation to form or join a labor union, you are making a mockery of the most sublime social encyclical [*Quadragesimo Anno*] that the world has ever known."[3]

The laity were not the only ones exhorted to "think with the Church." The clergy, too, needed a refresher course on Catholic social doctrine. Accordingly, in August, 1941, Lucey sponsored a Summer School of Social Justice for Priests, modeled after those held in Milwaukee and elsewhere in the late 1930s, to familiarize clerics in the Southwest with labor and social problems. For two weeks 147 priests were instructed on such fundamentals as labor's right to organize, bargain collectively, and strike; the government's duty to intervene on labor's behalf; and the Church's obligation to assist unionism. *Time* magazine observed that "the spirit of the meeting was as far to the left as the thinking of the San Antonio Archdiocese had heretofore been far to the right."[4]

Lucey's leftist leanings provoked a reaction. "Alongside the names of Roosevelt and Wagner, . . . and other extremist 'friends' of labor," the *San Antonio Express* announced, "must now be entered the name of Robert E. Lucey, Archbishop of San Antonio." The newspaper accused the Archbishop of stirring up support for repeal of the state's anti-strike law and warned the Texas state legislature to keep "labor extremists" in their place.[5]

The salvo from the *Express* did not daunt Lucey. Addressing the state AFL convention in Houston in 1946, he reminded the delegates of their obligation to uphold the Church's teaching about the dignity of the worker, even while criticizing the AFL for excluding farm workers and blacks from its ranks. The following year he defended the CIO against charges of communist infiltration. Noting that he, too, had been smeared with the communist brush by a prominent San Antonio businessman, the Archbishop dismissed the label as "false propaganda."[6]

All his life Lucey had to deal with the charge that he was a meddler, and his work with organized labor provides a case in point. Writing in the Texas State Federation of Labor *Review*, he responded to those who advised him and all priests to stay in the sanctuary and mind their own business. "This is our business," he rejoined. "The Church must do more than help men pray on Sunday. [It] must help men live rightly all week long."[7]

By lending the labor movement his personal prestige and that of his office, as when he and Cardinal Mundelein threw their support behind John L. Lewis in 1935, Lucey gave it legitimacy, in Catholic circles at least. His support for labor also had internal consequences for the Church. It helps to explain why the National Catholic Welfare Conference, the administrative arm of the American hierarchy, consistently took a more liberal position on organized labor and New Deal reforms than that probably held by the majority of the American bishops.

By proclaiming the Church's social gospel, Lucey was exercising the teaching, prophetic office of the episcopacy and providing both a model for emulation and a measure of protection for clerical activists. Later, in the turbulent 1960s, Lucey's example was not lost on his priests, some of whom fought alongside their Archbishop for the poor and racially oppressed. Nor would Lucey's willingness to provide cover for his activist priests go uncontested by San Antonio civic and business leaders.

San Antonio was not only intensely anti-union; it was racially segregated. At a meeting of the National Conference of Catholic Charities in Houston in October, 1941, Lucey cried, "What a mockery of divine mercy to think that the Son of God died only for the white man." At a patriotic rally in Austin Memorial Stadium two weeks after Pearl Harbor, he stunned his audience by pointing out the contradiction between America's war against the "super-race" and discrimination against blacks and Mexicans. To a San Antonio seminar on inter-American relations in 1944, he suggested a new name for the "colored problem." "Who is it that condemns the 'master race stupidity' in Germany but makes a practice of it here?" he asked. "Who denies political rights to bonafide American citizens? Who has been guilty of lynching, torture and brutality? . . . We ought to be honest and call this thing the 'white problem.' "[8]

The Archbishop's words reflected the public stance of the American hierarchy, who in their wartime pastoral letters called for full constitutional rights for blacks. Unfortunately the bishops did not match their words with programs in major urban dioceses to relieve the acute racial tension of which they spoke, and little financial support followed their endorsement of racial equality. Even those Church organizations committed to black equality, such as diocesan interracial councils, were confined to the fringes of institutional power.[9]

In September, 1944, Lucey testified before the Senate Committee on Education and Labor, urging that the Fair Employment Practices Committee, created by President Roosevelt in mid-1941, be made permanent and given full statutory recognition. He expressed his conviction that

America's race problem could not be overcome without federal legislation. The same year Gunnar Myrdal's influential *An American Dilemma* was published, confirming Lucey's judgment about the urgency of the race problem. The following year he set up the San Antonio Catholic Interracial Council, one of the first councils organized in the postwar Southwest, and used it to address the issue of racism in his see city.[10]

In the late 1940s and early 1950s, Lucey carried his public denunciation of segregation throughout Texas and the South. In New Orleans he encouraged the Catholic Committee of the South to work toward inculcating the notion of racial equality in the national conscience. He rapped Southern labor leaders for maintaining segregated unions and pushed for the teaching of racial justice in public and private schools. In a speech to the National Council of Catholic Women in San Antonio, the Archbishop condemned Jim Crow laws, and at a meeting of the North Carolina Catholic Laymen's Association in Charlotte, he charged that "in the field of race relations, Christians are guilty of every crime from murder to restrictive covenants."[11]

The Supreme Court decision in *Brown* v. *Board of Education of Topeka*, handed down in May, 1954, confirmed one of the Archbishop's own decisions. Six weeks earlier, in a pastoral letter, he had announced that "henceforth no Catholic child may be refused admittance to any school maintained by the Archdiocese merely for reasons of color, race or poverty. . . '. In the field of social justice and social charity Catholics should lead, not follow."[12] Lucey's decision to make San Antonio the first Catholic diocese in Texas to integrate its schools was largely of symbolic importance because the number of black San Antonians has always been small, and at the time of the pastoral letter only 101 black students were enrolled in the elementary, secondary, collegiate, and graduate schools of the archdiocese. Nevertheless, some think Lucey's decision had a major influence on the successful, nonviolent desegregation of the San Antonio public school system after the Court's landmark ruling.[13]

After his decision to desegregate the Catholic school system, the Archbishop went after local political officials who were supporting racism in Bexar County, of which San Antonio is the county seat. In the spring of 1957, the Texas state legislature had before it a bill that would ban employment by state agencies of members of the National Association for the Advancement of Colored People. Five out of the seven Bexar County representatives voted for the bill, provoking Lucey to demand their resignations: "It is too late in the twentieth century for Texas legislators to act like hypocrites who talk democracy out of one side of their mouths and tyranny out of the other." His speech drew a predictable reaction. One state representative labeled him a "crackpot" with dangerous racial views. Another solon called him a "fuzzy-minded clergyman" and suggested that he not meddle in political affairs. Predictable, too, was the reaction of Lucey's religious peers. Speaking for the San Antonio Council of Churches, Dr. J. T. Morrow decried the personal attack on the Archbishop, but significantly, did not join him in his resignation demand.[14]

From his experience in Los Angeles and Amarillo, Archbishop Lucey understood the importance of an organized anti-poverty effort. Soon after his arrival in San Antonio, he made plans to establish a Catholic Welfare Bureau. Under Archbishop Drossaerts, Catholic charity had consisted largely of "giving a poor Mexican a quarter." No Catholic Charities program existed during his era. Early in 1941 Lucey rearranged diocesan priorities. He brought a professional social worker from California to set up the bureau and sent one of his priests, Father Paul Ehlinger, to Catholic University for advanced study in social work.[15] The new Archbishop had a broad vision of helping the poor, not only with Church funds but with city money as well. For three years he tried to win the Catholic Welfare Bureau a share in the San Antonio Community Chest, which was finally granted in 1944.[16]

In the midst of one fight with San Antonio Community Chest officials in 1943, Lucey got involved in another with the Bexar County Commissioners over funds earmarked for local, private charities. The commissioners had cut a promised $60,000 public assistance appropriation to $8,000, citing insufficient tax returns as the reason for the reduction. In a press conference at his chancery office, Lucey demanded that the commissioners restore the full appropriation and accused them of favoritism toward wealthy Bexar County landowners, whose delinquent taxes had gone uncollected for years. Angered by the charge, one of the commissioners demanded to know what the Church was doing for the county's poor.[17]

This was grist for Lucey's mill, and he proceeded to declare that the Catholic Welfare Bureau alone had a budget of $60,000, while Santa Rosa Hospital, a Catholic institution, contributed nearly $100,000 annually to charity patients in hospital care and clinical services. He produced statistics showing that Bexar County's $8,000 allocation compared poorly with other counties in Texas. Dallas County, for example, contributed nearly $70,000 for private charity, while Harris and Galveston counties allotted approximately $50,000 annually. The logic of Lucey's argument did not prevail. The commissioners kept the appropriation at $8,000.[18]

Health care was another form of public aid to the poor that Lucey defended. "Socialized medicine" was a scare phrase, he told delegates to the Texas Association of Catholic Hospitals convention in San Antonio in 1945. Government programs of health care and health insurance for the poor were not signs of creeping socialism but merely the demands of social justice. That same year Lucey informed San Antonio Catholics in a pastoral letter that it was their "solemn duty" to approve two tax propositions for the enlargement of tuberculosis facilities at a local city hospital. The city's tuberculosis death rate for Mexican Americans was nearly four times greater than that for Anglos, while Mexican American children died from diphtheria and whooping cough at similar disproportionately high rates.[19]

A final area of concern was public housing. Here Lucey had a predecessor, Father Carmine Tranchese, S.J., assistant pastor of Our Lady of Guadalupe Parish on San Antonio's west side. Through his connection with Eleanor Roosevelt, Tranchese brought to San Antonio one of the first federally funded public housing units in the country, Alazan-Apache Courts, begun in 1939 and completed three years later at a cost of more than five million dollars.[20] Lucey supported the Tranchese project and advocated similar ones. The city needed public housing desperately. The federal census of 1950 indicated that 41,000 dwellings, or 37 percent of San Antonio's housing, was substandard, but the City Council and the San Antonio Home Builders Association regularly opposed public housing projects. Lucey took up this problem as the keynote speaker at the Southwest Regional Conference of the National Association of Housing Officials in San Antonio in 1953. Responding to the tired charge that federal housing was socialism, he stated that for 1952 the federal government contributed only twenty-eight cents a month per family toward San Antonio's public housing units: "If that is socialism, it is frightfully cheap." He suggested that groups like the San Antonio Home Builders Association were to blame for condemning low-income people to "wretched, frustrated lives in dirty hovels."[21]

Lucey was no doubt correct about the opposition to public housing among local building interests, but his manner of dealing with the problem virtually ensured poor results. In the early 1950s he was invited to address the Housing Committee of the Texas state legislature. A Catholic layman who was a member of the committee at the time, and who later lobbied for the social programs of the Texas Catholic hierarchy, recalled the poor impression the Archbishop made in

Austin. "He was very authoritarian, talking to the committee as if he were giving orders to it. He was laying down the social doctrine of the Church, no question about that, but he was doing it in a very authoritarian manner. Telling, not asking." The Housing Committee member knew that Lucey's manner did not sit well with his fellow legislators. "I know I resented it . . . as a legislator, and that was one of the reasons I voted against him."[22]

Lucey suffered other defeats on the issue of public housing, but won recognition for the sincerity of his efforts. In 1957 he received the Distinguished Service Award from the Anti-Defamation League of B'nai B'rith for his crusades against slum housing, substandard working conditions, and segregation. Senate Majority Leader Lyndon B. Johnson spoke at the ceremony: "There is no need for advertising to recognize a truly pure heart and a truly pure mind. The finest recommendation that can be made for any man is that he is Archbishop Lucey's friend."[23]

The problems of unemployment, racism, and poverty came together in the Mexican American community. Of the estimated 195,000 Catholics in the San Antonio archdiocese in 1941, more than 65 percent were listed as "Mexicans," and during the war their numbers increased.[24] The presence of this sizable Spanish-speaking population had a great influence on the institutional Church in the Southwest, and on Lucey's career in San Antonio.

The clergy of the Southwest took a skeptical view of the Catholicism of Mexican Americans, whose institutional loyalties were loose and whose religious expression differed from officially sanctioned practices. In the clergy's eyes the typical Mexican immigrant in the early twentieth century was not a devout "Mass and sacraments" Catholic, and in fact the Mexican Revolution had weakened the bonds between the Church and Mexican Catholics. Where the Church's presence was weakest, a "folk" Catholicism emerged, a syncretic blend of Catholic and Indian ritualism that the immigrants brought with them as they moved north.[25]

Unlike the institutional Church in the East and Midwest, which the immigrant sought out for aid and consolation in adjusting to a new life in a foreign country, the Church in the Southwest had to seek out the immigrant in order to perform its religious function. Because of the acute shortage of priests, their inferior training, and a chronic dearth of funds, this outreach was not very effective.[26]

A comparison with the Catholic Church in the East and Midwest is instructive. By 1900 the Church from Boston to St. Louis was well established. Largely an urban organization, it had absorbed millions of Catholics from many countries, built churches and schools, and founded social welfare agencies to ease the immigrants' adjustment to the United States. Priests were present to provide leadership and mediate with the host culture. The predominantly Irish episcopacy, while protective of ethnic identity, insisted that the immigrants Americanize so that the Church would not only survive but develop into a fully accepted American institution.[27]

In the Southwest no such firmly structured Church existed to soften the confrontation between Mexicans and Anglos. Nor did the bishops of the Southwest, themselves mostly foreign-born, preside over compact urban communities. Instead, they were responsible for widely scattered patches of Catholics in rural areas.[28]

Lucey was faced in San Antonio with a nominally Catholic flock and meager institutional resources. He had frequently discussed with Father Raymond McGowan the possibility of forming a regional organization for the Spanish-speaking communities of the Southwest. When the Roosevelt administration launched its Good Neighbor policy with Latin America and sought the support of the Catholic church in smoothing relations with the countries south of the border, Lucey and McGowan capitalized on this interest. With State

Department funds they sponsored two seminars in 1943 and 1944 that brought together Catholic leaders working with the Spanish-speaking communities of the region. From these meetings emerged the framework of an organization that the Archbishop would use as his principal weapon in the fight for equal justice: the Bishops' Committee for the Spanish Speaking.[29]

The origin of the Bishops' Committee lay in Lucey's realization that the dioceses of the Southwest could no longer operate as autonomous units. To facilitate concerted action, he proposed that the bishops of the region cooperate in a program of "spiritual and temporal welfare work" for their Mexican American people. Lucey envisaged a multiservice program of religious instruction, health and medical care, adult education, and leadership training, and recommended that a committee of prelates from the Southwest oversee the project. He won approval and funding for his proposal from the American hierarchy, and in January, 1945, was elected executive chairman of the Bishops' Committee.[30]

The day-to-day work of the committee was handled by a regional office with an executive secretary and staff. As originally conceived, the regional office was to circulate throughout the seventeen dioceses of the Southwest, locating in each for a two-year period. During its stay the office would set up a "Catholic Council for the Spanish Speaking," which would continue the work after the office had moved on. It was a mark of Lucey's control of the committee that the regional office never left Texas in its nearly twenty-five-year existence. In fact, after several moves from diocese to diocese within Texas, the Archbishop had the office located permanently in San Antonio, from which he directed and coordinated all the committee's activities.[31]

Under Lucey's supervision the early work of the Bishops' Committee varied. In San Antonio it organized religious instruction classes for Mexican American children, set up child-care programs for their mothers, and constructed several clinics and community centers in the city's barrios. In El Paso it concentrated on youth work and public housing projects, while in the diocese of Corpus Christi it coordinated a successful unionization campaign for Corpus Christi bus drivers, 70 percent of whom were Spanish-speaking, and participated in voter registration drives and neighborhood self-help projects.[32]

Lucey's activities were causing a stir in San Antonio and drawing some attention in the nation's press. Local businessmen were uneasy about his advocacy of higher wages for all workers and equal pay for Mexican Americans. The *Washington Post* described him as "the sparkplug behind social progress" in the city and noted the anxious reaction of San Antonians to "this modern-minded, forceful prelate." The newspaper praised his attack on racism and his innovative use of the Bishops' Committee to develop local leadership among Mexican Americans.[33]

The *Washington Post* did not anticipate the new arena that Lucey would soon enter—the struggle for the rights of the migrant farm worker. Indeed, Lucey soon turned the Bishops' Committee into a virtual farm workers' organization, using it to expose the migrants' plight and broaden the Church's involvement in confronting this injustice. He dominated the committee, moreover, with his one-man style of leadership. Theoretically an organization of all the bishops of the seventeen dioceses of the Southwest, the committee would become in fact Lucey's personal instrument in the farm worker cause. When one thought of or heard about it, one would associate with it the name of Archbishop Robert E. Lucey.

It was in 1950 that Lucey first formally involved the Bishops' Committee in the migrant farm labor problem. In June of that year, President Truman asked him to serve on a blue ribbon panel investigating conditions among migratory workers in the United States and the problem created by the importation of foreign workers.[34] The commission held public hearings for twelve months. Lucey instructed Father Theodore Radtke, the executive secretary of the Bishops' Committee, to testify at the hearings in Brownsville, Texas. Radtke told of starvation wages, abominable food, filthy housing, and poor sanitation. Each season tens of thousands of domestic farm workers were forced onto the migrant trail in search of jobs. As they headed north from states like Texas, they could anticipate an average of 110 days of work with a corresponding annual wage of $350.00. Frequently housed in citrus groves or vegetable fields, farm workers regularly were victimized by growers who deducted exorbitant charges for food, clothing, water, and rent. Trapped by the cyclic pattern of their parents' work, whole generations of migrant children went without schooling and thus were locked into an identical fate.[35]

The President's Commission also studied the bracero and wetback labor systems. Due to labor shortages associated with both world wars, thousands of braceros, or legally contracted Mexican nationals, had entered the United States for temporary employment on American farms. After World War II, the bracero flow continued, an estimated two hundred thousand crossing the Rio Grande between 1948 and 1950 alone. The commission found that the braceros kept wages for domestic farm workers at extremely low levels and that the process whereby a domestic labor shortage was determined and the need for foreign labor certified was fraught with manipulation and corruption. Growers were discovered to have set wages at levels domestic farm workers could not afford to accept, and then to have claimed that a labor shortage demanded foreign workers.[36]

Wetbacks—Mexicans who entered the United States illegally allegedly by swimming across the Rio Grande—exacerbated the problem. At the time the commission was conducting public hearings, the *New York Times* correspondent Gladwyn Hill was investigating wetback labor in Texas. Hill's findings confirmed Radtke's testimony about the brutality of the wetback labor system. Comparing wetbacks to slave labor, Hill wrote of wetbacks toiling in the Rio Grande Valley for about twenty-five cents an hour, with this amount subject to deduction for meals, commissary purchases, even charges for the binding wire used in tying vegetable sacks. He described the complicity between growers and local law enforcement officials in maintaining the system.[37]

Hill confirmed the commission's findings that wetbacks undercut the domestic labor force. Unable to live on wetback wages, domestic workers migrated from Texas at an enormous rate, the Rio Grande Valley alone losing more than a hundred thousand annually. As for the growers' argument that wetbacks were used because local labor was unavailable, Hill summed up the situation with a biting parody of *Alice in Wonderland*:

> "What are these people doing?" asked Alice, surveying a vast, fertile southwestern valley.
> "They're cultivating surplus cotton and lettuce," replied the Red Queen.
> "Who are they?" asked Alice, tactfully ignoring the matter of why anyone should produce surplus crops.
> "They are Mexicans imported because of the labor shortage," explained the Red Queen.
> "Labor shortage?" asked Alice. "I thought we had 5,000,000 unemployed and a million or so migrant farm laborers who need work."
> "Obviously," retorted the Red Queen testily, "YOU don't understand the American agricultural system."[38]

In its final report the President's Commission recommended that bracero labor be discouraged, that the employment of wetbacks be prohibited by law, and that the domestic labor force be used more efficiently. The panel called for improvement in working conditions and length of employment and, most important, a minimum wage for America's agricultural workers. To carry out these recommendations the commission urged the establishment of a Federal Committee on Migratory Farm Labor appointed by and responsible to the President.[39]

Because of the strength of the farm lobby and the emergency created by the Korean War, President Truman ignored many of the recommendations of his own commission. On July 13, 1951, he signed Public Law 78, which provided the legal structure for bracero contracting for the fourteen-year life of the program. The law charged the Secretary of Labor with the contradictory duties of recruiting foreign workers and protecting domestic farm laborers from the adverse effects of such recruitment. Public Law 78 was extended by Congress until 1964, at the urging of the farm lobby, which exerted pressure through key congressional committees, and because of the compatibility of interests of American growers and the Mexican government and the weakness of the anti-bracero forces.[40] Despite repeated failures, the Archbishop continued to direct the activity of the Bishops' Committee against the bracero program for the next thirteen years.

Lucey divided his efforts on behalf of migrant farm workers between public opposition to their exploitation and a practical program of assistance. Writing in *America* magazine shortly after the President's Commission issued its report, he condemned the "scandal of migratory labor." In July he telegraphed President Truman, urging him to veto Public Law 78 because it failed to protect domestic farm workers. After the President signed the bill, Lucey testified before the Senate in favor of legislation to reduce the flow of illegal workers into the United States and provide a minimum wage for America's migrant farmers. Like the President, however, the Senate could not surmount political pressure and passed only a weak wetback bill.[41]

Lucey returned to Texas. In Dallas he told a convention of National Farm Union–AFL representatives that they could best fight the evils of migratory labor by lobbying for the creation of a federal migrant committee and for tougher enforcement of the child labor laws. In San Antonio he exhorted delegates to the American G.I. Forum of Texas to press for a federal minimum wage law for domestic farm workers. He also urged a "pay your poll tax" campaign so that a unified Mexican American electorate could "vote the high grade morons, idiots and imbeciles out of office."[42]

The Archbishop directed a steady barrage of criticism at Congress for the remainder of the decade. When the Senate finally began consideration of legislation to penalize growers who employed wetbacks and conspired in their illegal transportation across the border, Lucey sent the executive secretary of the Bishops' Committee, Father Matthew Kelly, to testify in favor of the bills. Although nothing substantial resulted from the Senate hearings, the Archbishop believed the effort was nonetheless worthwhile. He wrote to Kelly on July 20, 1954, "We cannot deny that in times past too many of our priests and practically all of our laymen were silent about the obvious crimes committed in our country in industry and agriculture. This sort of thing which you have done is good for the Church."[43]

Not all of the members of the Bishops' Committee agreed. Bishop Lawrence Fitzsimon of Amarillo disapproved of Kelly's testimony and accused Lucey of using the committee to advance his personal political views.[44] Writing to Kelly, the Archbishop explained away Fitzsimon: "The good bishop has recently had a blood clot on his brain, and his ideas regarding your duties must be interpreted in the light of his affliction."[45] When Fitzsimon complained to Cardinal Francis McIntyre of Los Angeles (Kelly's religious superior) about the secretary's testimony, Lucey again intervened to defend the priest and later assured Kelly of the Cardinal's continued high opinion of him.[46]

As executive chairman of the committee, Lucey brooked little opposition from anyone about his course of action and, as the Fitzsimon controversy reveals, quickly defended "his" people when they were attacked. He held a tight rein over the committee's executive secretaries, demanding, and getting, regular reports on their activities. When they spoke publicly, as Kelly had at the Senate hearings, they did so with the Archbishop's prior approval and blessing.[47]

The Archbishop and other opponents of the bracero program had few successes on Capitol Hill, and the victories they won were very small indeed. Working through Senator Lyndon B. Johnson, Lucey successfully pushed for a new bracero center at Hidalgo, Texas. Again with Johnson's help, Lucey lobbied for and won a $50,000 appropriation, which the Bureau of Labor Statistics divided among the "migrant" states in a cooperative effort to track the nation's migrating work force. But these were at best token accomplishments.[48]

Stymied by Congress, the anti-braceroists began pressuring the Secretary of Labor for help, and here their efforts had better success. When the Labor Department issued new minimum standards of housing for Mexican workers in early 1957, Lucey congratulated Secretary James P. Mitchell for his courageous leadership, even as the Texas legislature passed a joint resolution condemning the action as a "dictatorial exercise of bureaucratic authority" that placed an "unwarranted and unreasonable burden" on the growers.[49]

Lucey was not optimistic about the enforcement of the new regulations in Texas. To Monsignor George G. Higgins, the director of the Social Action Department of the National Catholic Welfare Conference, he wrote, "Some of the growers in Texas are voracious, and they see an opportunity to make big profits on the blood and sweat and tears of these unfortunate braceros. The growers will tolerate no interference with their game. I doubt if the code will be widely observed or enforced in the great state of Texas."[50]

Rather, Lucey hoped to organize Catholics in the

dioceses along the migrant trail. Local laity and clergy, after welcoming the arriving farm workers, were to use the parish facilities to distribute food, clothing, and toys and provide basic medical care. Classes in English and homemaking were to be conducted during the migrants' stay. Priests were to hold religious services at the camps, performing marriages and baptisms, saying mass, and hearing confessions. Further, representatives of the Bishops' Committee were to monitor the treatment of farm workers, visiting the camps regularly to check on food, housing, and health conditions and to ensure that the workers received their wages in full. Discovered abuses were to be reported to the state authorities. On departure days, Catholics in the next "migrant diocese" were to be alerted to expect the farm workers soon. This process was to be repeated as the migrants made their way from Texas to the North Central and Northwestern states during the harvest seasons.[51]

Lucey's plan for interdiocesan cooperation never materialized. Only to a very limited extent was the Bishops' Committee able to alleviate the hardships migrants encountered, and inadequate funds were not the only reason. The clergy and laity were indifferent to the migrant ministry, as Lucey evidently realized. In a letter to Father William O'Connor, the committee's executive secretary in 1956, he expressed his concern about locating concentrations of migrants and instructed O'Connor to obtain as much information as possible himself, because "if you leave all this to the pastors, they will do no more than they have done in the past, which is practically nothing."[52]

In December, 1964, the contracting of Mexican nationals for work on United States farms came to an end. Accelerated farm mechanization, Labor Department recognition of the adverse effect of imported labor on domestic wages, and presidential administrations promising all Americans a new frontier and a great society help account for the program's termination. The growing moralization of the bracero issue was also important in bringing down Public Law 78, and here Lucey deserves credit. In a speech delivered to a conference of anti-braceroist forces in Milwaukee in May, 1962, he had berated Congress for refusing to pass a minimum wage law for farm workers and challenged the Kennedy administration to end the bracero program. "What we do to Latin Americans every year is no secret," he said. "The American government has been a party to the program, and the foul stench of the whole miserable business is drifting across the land like a poisonous fallout." After the death of Public Law 78, the Archbishop could take some credit for the American public's realization that "a war on poverty and the bracero program could not be reconciled."[53]

The principal long-range accomplishment of the Bishops' Committee was its role in raising the public consciousness. It contributed to the political coming of age of the Mexican American in Texas and the Southwest at large by keeping before the public eye the prejudice and discrimination suffered by the Spanish-speaking. Cesar Chavez later used this visibility to great effect in his struggle against the exploitation of the nation's farm workers.[54] Moreover, the committee awakened not only national opinion but the American Catholic conscience as well. "I think we brought to the attention of the people of this country, and especially our own Catholic people, the scandal we had been hiding for years," Executive Secretary William O'Connor stated, "the scandal of exploiting the Spanish-speaking, . . . and the scandal of the Church ignoring their needs."[55] The committee pressured the institutional Church to meet its responsibilities to its Spanish-speaking members and succeeded in placing the American Catholic hierarchy squarely against the bracero program. At the same time, it fostered an indigenous Spanish-speaking leadership through the diocesan organizations it spawned.[56]

Those working closely with him in the Bishops' Committee saw Archbishop Lucey's accomplishments as substantial, but they described his style of leadership in less glowing terms. "Lucey was a man of action but not very personable or warm," William O'Connor stated in an interview. "He came on strong on social justice questions, but no one ever claimed that he felt comfortable in discussing matters with him." Father John McCarthy, who served as the executive secretary of the committee in 1966, observed that Lucey's style generated aloneness: "You couldn't question him. When you were at a meeting with Lucey, and he was the chairman, nobody talked. . . . He was not a team man; he couldn't consult. I mean, he operated off edict!"[57]

First impressions of Lucey were of a man who was "cold," "aloof," "very businesslike."[58] The Archbishop had little sense of people and was uneasy in informal settings. Some believed that he was arrogant and aloof; others say that he was simply shy and needed formality to feel comfortable. "Lucey was basically a very shy person," McCarthy said. "He didn't know how to make small talk. He'd have dinner, and he'd let everybody have two drinks, but you had to drink fast because he wanted to get to the table where he could preside and lecture."[59]

Lucey's style of leadership was very demanding, both on himself and on those under his supervision. The Archbishop "did not leave much room for human weakness," O'Connor noted. "He himself was strong, and he wanted others to be equally strong. He wanted others to back him without question. It was no secret that he could be ruthless with those who would not." A Mexican American labor leader, writing to a friend, said of Lucey: "If you know anything about the Archbishop, you will know that he never fools around, no holds barred."[60]

Another quality of Lucey's leadership was his distance from the poor. It was not his custom to invite them to his home, although he regularly entertained clergymen and prominent San Antonians, and he did not visit the poor or eat with them. His first and last trip to San Antonio's barrio came shortly after his installation. He explained that he went to the slum to "see my people and size up the situation." When pressed about why he never returned, he stated matter-of-factly that so long as "one of my priests was there, the Archbishop was there, too."[61] As one former official of the Bishops' Committee put it, Lucey preached social justice with much conviction but did not match it with a personal love for Mexican Americans and other minorities.[62]

The Archbishop's first home was a stately residence that he purchased on East King's Highway, situated in a quietly prosperous section of San Antonio. In 1957 he was presented with a ranch-style home in Hollywood Park, a well-to-do and largely Anglo housing development north of the city. Several years later Lucey moved the archdiocesan chancery office from its downtown location to its present site, also north of the city.[63] Thus the Archbishop lived and worked in areas of San Antonio where the poor rarely ventured. Mexican Americans "belonged" on the west side and the south side but were not seen along East King's Highway or in Hollywood Park. It is surprising that a man who battled much of his life for the poor would choose to remain remote from them, though, in fact, the tension between the Archbishop's commitment to the poor and his isolation from them is not entirely unique, as an examination of the impact of social class and race on Progressive reformers might reveal.[64] Lucey fought for the poor but never knew poor people personally. He labored for the masses, a favorite phrase of his, but never really identified with particular faces in that amorphous group.

In this respect Lucey's life differs from that of other Catholic social activists. The hallmark of Dorothy Day's Catholic Worker movement, for example, was its physical presence among the poor. Lucey sought justice for the poor not by personally identifying with them, but through legal and institutional means, such as federal legislation, unions, and the Bishops' Committee. The ecclesiastical office itself might help account for this distance. As a Roman-trained prelate,

Lucey lived according to his understanding of episcopal dignity, and while his personal habits were quite modest, he did not share the tradition of radical Catholics.

Closely related to his remoteness was the Archbishop's patronizing and dissembling administrative style. Lucey patted subordinates on the head for their services but found it difficult to acknowledge genuinely the value of their work. An incident typifying this tendency occurred in 1966 during a shake-up of the Bishops' Committee staff. After eight years of daily contact with the Archbishop as the committee's executive secretary, Father John Wagner was suddenly "retired." Lucey's letter to Wagner included the comment that "a memo on my desk has reminded me to write this letter to you." He then expressed his thanks for Wagner's "long years of devoted service." Writing to a mutual friend the next day, the Archbishop pleaded that he was too busy to throw a farewell party for Wagner. In another letter several weeks later, Lucey described the former secretary as "pretty well worn out" and patronizingly explained that "I decided to permit him to go back to parish work." The letter was less than candid, for Lucey had in fact fired Wagner over a policy dispute.[65]

Lucey never claimed to be, and indeed he was not, a sensitive man. His need for personal relationships stopped at the level of acquaintance. Concerned about his personal image, he demanded the spotlight in his archdiocese and refused to share center stage with subordinates. The Archbishop was also, however, deeply conscious of the image of the Church. His total dedication to the institution led him to place it before all else and to expect such absolute devotion from others. Lucey believed that preaching the social gospel was the priestly vocation and thus felt no compulsion to extend his personal gratitude to those who worked with him. Those who expected warmth and accolades in return for their dedication found him unresponsive.

5. The Confraternity of Christian Doctrine and Operation Latin America

The Confraternity of Christian Doctrine is the Church's official association devoted to religious education. It received papal recognition in 1560 when Pope Pius IV established the first society in Rome. The development of scientific thought and the spread of secularism in the late nineteenth and early twentieth centuries occasioned a decline in religious knowledge and prompted Pope Pius X to write his encyclical *Acerbo Nimis* (1905). Lamenting the growing indifference toward the Christian message, the Pope ordered the establishment of the Confraternity in every parish throughout the Catholic world. His decree was incorporated in the code of canon law in 1919, and under Pope Pius XI, Confraternity work came to be regarded as an essential apostolic concern. In the United States the Confraternity's principal thrust was a program of religious instruction for Catholic children and adolescents not attending parochial schools, for adult Catholics, and for non-Catholics inquiring about the faith.[1]

Robert Lucey's first contact with the Confraternity came in the early 1920s in conjunction with his work in the Bureau of Catholic Charities in Los Angeles. Mexican and Italian immigrants on the east side of the city received material assistance from the bureau but were offered no religious education. Encouraged by bureau social workers, in particular Miss Verona Spellmire, Lucey pressed Bishop Cantwell for an "immigrant-oriented" Confraternity along the lines of those already functioning in New York and Pittsburgh. Cantwell approved the idea and established the Confraternity in March, 1922. As Spellmire saw it, Lucey was the driving force behind the creation of the Los Angeles Confraternity. "Father Lucey was like the match that causes the bonfire to blaze," she wrote.[2]

Annual bureau reports and minutes of Confraternity meetings reveal that Lucey's concern in these years was simply to provide a minimum of religious instruction for neglected Catholic souls. He would deal later with the task of drawing the laity toward social Catholicism. For now he stressed that the Confraternity's first objective was to establish and maintain contact with immigrants, especially children. Accordingly, he recruited Spanish- and Italian-speaking volunteers to visit immigrant homes, enroll children in catechism classes, and encourage them and their parents to receive the sacraments. Lucey was not unaware, however, of the Confraternity's social contribution. At a meeting of members in 1923, he noted the tendency of Confraternity work to "lessen delinquency among Catholic children" and congratulated them on the success of their "Americanization" efforts.[3]

The social environment of Amarillo differed markedly from that of Los Angeles, and consequently Bishop Lucey shifted the Confraternity's emphasis from settlement work and instruction of immigrant children to religious education for adults. Work now focused on the establishment throughout the diocese of adult study clubs, which Lucey envisioned as the building blocks of social Catholicism and the training ground for lay leaders. Meeting weekly under the direction of selected leaders, the clubs would encourage cooperative study and gradually fashion an active and informed Catholic laity.[4]

The Bishop saw his vision of the study club partly realized

at Sacred Heart Parish in Amarillo. Surviving minutes of meetings indicate that the club met weekly for ninety-minute sessions and discussed topics ranging from the life of Christ to the New Deal and organized labor. Books from a circulating library were distributed, along with newspaper and magazine articles, and "very interesting conversations followed." This study group was so advanced that it invited Protestants to attend the meetings, which for the time and place was quite unusual.[5]

It goes without saying that not all study clubs were successful; some parishes could not even organize one. Much of the Amarillo diocese was rural, and as one pastor told Lucey, organizing study clubs was nearly impossible. "My people didn't come to study clubs this fall," he wrote, "because they say it was just too much to pick cotton twelve to fourteen hours a day and study." When another pastor mentioned a similar difficulty in his farm parish, the Bishop replied that the farmers should hold the study club first, then do their chores, advice that clearly betrays Lucey's city background.[6] Nonetheless, he remained set in his determination about religious education and was publicly critical of pastors who were not enthusiastic about the work. "Show me a parish where study clubs do not flourish, and I will show you a pastor who is not doing the work of God properly," he wrote in the *Texas Panhandle Register.*[7]

The Confraternity of Christian Doctrine ranked high on Lucey's agenda when he arrived in San Antonio in 1941. Prior to his coming, it had been at best a scattered and sporadic effort at providing religious instruction for Catholic children enrolled in public schools. The new Archbishop soon announced different priorities. He ordered that the Confraternity be established in every parish, decreed that "a definite and progressive course of study" be set up for Catholic schoolchildren, and informed his pastors that adult discussion clubs were to become part of regular parish life.[8]

In the postwar decade Archbishop Lucey broadened his

vision of the possibilities of Confraternity work. He saw the Church in the Southwest, with its paucity of priests and parochial schools, as in need of vitalization and the Confraternity as a means of injecting this new life. With a sound program operating in his own archdiocese, Lucey reached toward the task of getting the Confraternity organized throughout the Southwest. As a member of the American hierarchy's Episcopal Committee for the Confraternity of Christian Doctrine, he designed and supervised the establishment of leadership training courses in San Antonio. These institutes trained priests and lay people from the Southwest in Confraternity theory, helped standardize teaching methods, and greatly improved the quality of religious instruction offered by the program. Graduates of the San Antonio institutes were to apply their training in their home dioceses.[9]

Lucey's underlying objective was the formation of a Catholic social conscience. Addressing a Confraternity audience in Austin, he challenged them to oppose racial discrimination in their diocese. To a group of lay and clerical leaders meeting in Albuquerque, he spoke of the need for continuing religious education for adult Catholics, especially "half-Catholics," those who accepted only Church teachings that suited their convenience. He told a Confraternity gathering in Oklahoma City that social justice lay at the core of religious instruction, and until Catholics realized this, their faith was inadequate. "A Catholic might sing the Introit Psalm beautifully and still be opposed to good housing for the poor," Lucey lamented; he or she "might enjoy the *Missa de Angelis* and still think that all labor leaders were doing the work of satan."[10]

The Archbishop's zeal led him to carry out his program with a heavy hand. In a steady stream of pastoral letters, he demanded detailed statistical information on the progress of parish Confraternities. He also used monthly clergy conferences and spiritual retreats to outline his plans and criticize publicly pastors who were negligent in Confraternity work.

As a number of priests stated in interviews, the Archbishop's performances on such occasions were notorious.[11]

Lucey used threats and "truth squads" to keep tabs on the program. For example, when he learned that some pastors intended to hold parish bazaars and festivals on dates that conflicted with a scheduled Confraternity meeting, the Archbishop told them in a letter that "any pastor who interferes with this Inter-American [Catechetical] Congress will be expected to endure the consequences of such an act." Sensing that some of his pastors' reports were bogus, Lucey organized "flying squadrons" of investigators, teams of priests and lay people who would arrive unannounced at parishes throughout the archdiocese to investigate the condition of the local Confraternity program.[12]

A related issue equally illustrates Lucey's authoritarian style. In accord with standard practice in the pre–Vatican II Church, he commanded Catholic parents to send their children to parochial schools or be judged unworthy to receive the sacraments. The manner in which he enforced the law and the language he used in dealing with Catholic parents were far from standard. In a 1936 sermon at Sacred Heart Cathedral in Amarillo, for instance, Lucey stated that Catholic parents who disregarded their obligation to give their children a parochial school education must be ready "to answer to heaven for a crime against childhood and disloyalty to God." Addressing Catholic parents in the *Texas Panhandle Register* in 1939, he warned, "The price they will have to pay through all eternity for this crime against childhood is dreadful to contemplate."[13]

Lucey brought his campaign to San Antonio. He published annual warnings about the ecclesiastical censure awaiting negligent Catholic parents and reserved to himself all decisions regarding applications for exemption from the Church law mandating parochial school education.[14] His attitude and style are summarized in a pastoral letter of 1953. "Parents who fail to give their children a Christian [Catholic] education will answer to God for the consequences." Furthermore, "the excuses given by parents are as unconvincing as they are stupid." The "shipwreck of faith" was the inevitable consequence of "godless education." In the end, he thundered, "the laws of the Church, the pronouncements of the popes and bitter experience tell us that education is either for God or against God—there is no neutrality, no middle."[15]

Archbishop Lucey was not content to confine his religious education work to San Antonio or even the United States. His desire that Catholics better understand and thus better live their faith drove him to undertake spreading the gospel in Latin America.

Operation Latin America had its origin in a Confraternity seminar held in Kansas City, Missouri, in 1942. Sponsored by the United States Episcopal Committee for the Confraternity of Christian Doctrine, the seminar was designed to improve relations between the hierarchies of the United States and Latin America. After the war these seminars continued under Lucey's direction as chairman of the American hierarchy's Inter-American Relations Committee.[16]

In September, 1956, at an Inter-American Relations Committee meeting in Buffalo, the Latin American Bishops' Council (CELAM) requested aid from the United States hierarchy to begin a program of religious education in their countries. The Latin American prelates were interested primarily in monetary assistance, with which they would direct the creation and operation of the program. Lucey suggested, however, that instead of an outright gift, the United States hierarchy funnel funds to CELAM through his committee. He was openly skeptical of a carte blanche grant, fearing that the money would be used for other than Confraternity purposes.[17]

Writing to a Confraternity official in Washington in October, 1956, Lucey noted a letter he had received from the Cardinal of São Paulo, Brazil, announcing the construction of a tremendous basilica in Aparecida. He then referred to the minutes of the Buffalo meeting, in which the Auxiliary Bishop of São Paulo, Paulo Laureiro, had requested American aid for a religious instruction program. Why was there money for basilicas but none for religious education?[18]

The Archbishop was also convinced that the only way to get the Confraternity going in Latin America was to organize and direct the program from the United States.[19] He offered a plan: CELAM's Confraternity Secretariat, located in Bogotá, Colombia, was to accept an American priest as a liaison from the Confraternity committee of the United States bishops. This priest would contact Latin American prelates, persuade them of the need for the program in their dioceses, and ask them to send clergy to San Antonio for training in method and organization. After a short, intensive course of instruction (called a "cursillo"), these leaders would return to their respective countries and train other priests in Confraternity work. The goal was to establish a national Confraternity office in every Latin American country, which, in turn, would set up diocesan offices and thus bring the program to the local level. Transportation, tuition, and other costs would be defrayed by Lucey's Inter-American Relations Committee.[20]

It was a grand plan. According to one insider, the Latin American bishops almost choked on it. Although they eventually agreed to Lucey's terms, they were wary of North American dominance and of Lucey's penchant for running the show. As one Colombian prelate characterized him, the Archbishop had the capacity to see and bring about big things, but he was also rigid and domineering. It was "his way all the way."[21]

Operation Latin America began in early 1957 after Lucey succeeded in placing Father James McNiff, M.M., in the catechetical office in Bogotá.[22] The start had been anything but smooth. CELAM officials were not enthusiastic about Lucey's proposal and procrastinated on McNiff's appointment. Incensed, the Archbishop went straight to the top. In January he wrote to Cardinal Domenico Tardini, Secretary of State for the Vatican, and requested that the Holy See pressure CELAM to act. A few weeks later he told McNiff's religious superior that he had "made it clear to the Holy See that if we do not get an American priest into the Bogotá Secretariat, the organization of the Confraternity in Latin America will be indeed a long drawn out job."[23]

The Archbishop got what he wanted. On April 9, 1957, Monsignor Julian Mendoza, secretary general of CELAM, informed Lucey in a letter that CELAM had "no objection" to McNiff's "rendering service" at Bogotá, provided that his expenses for the first year were covered. (CELAM's budget for 1957 had already been approved.) Lucey responded quickly. He agreed to fund McNiff for 1957 but demanded in turn that CELAM extend its "cordial approval and enthusiastic support" to McNiff. Mere tolerance was not enough. Mendoza replied diplomatically that because CELAM could not meet McNiff's expenses for the year, it had hesitated to express a great desire for his help. But now that this matter had been clarified, Mendoza promised to receive the liaison "with open arms and the greatest enthusiasm."[24]

Thus the program began, not exactly a model for the future, but significant for that time as one of the first cooperative efforts between the North American Catholic Church and its Latin American counterpart. And Lucey was the link between the two. "Lucey was like a bulldog," McNiff recalled. "He got [this] thing in his teeth and ran with it. He blocked down the opposition and didn't care too much about whom he hurt."[25]

From 1957 to 1960 McNiff, a veteran of missionary work in Peru, traveled extensively throughout the continent, trying to win support for Confraternity cursillos. In the summer of 1957 the Archbishop began the first Six Week Confraternity Leadership Course in San Antonio and was excited about the program's possibilities. But the early going was difficult. During the first four years McNiff met with some rebuffs, and Lucey could claim only fifty-nine "experts" trained in his San Antonio program. The Archbishop vented his impatience. In correspondence with U.S. Confraternity officials, he complained that the bishops below the border were "utterly impossible" to deal with because "they don't answer letters." In a memo to Father Joseph Till, his archdiocesan Confraternity director, he remarked in disgust that "the Latin Americans, as you know, are children" and were wasting precious time by their refusal to accept his program completely. To the secretary general of the Holy See's Pontifical Commission for Latin America, he reported the foot-dragging and ill-will he and McNiff had experienced.[26]

Despite all this, however, some progress had been made. At their annual meeting in 1958, the Latin American prelates agreed in principle to the establishment of the Confraternity throughout the continent and the appointment of national Confraternity episcopal committees. In April, 1959, the Cardinal-Archbishop of Bogotá ordered the establishment of the Confraternity in every parish in the diocese.[27] The first real breakthrough came in the fall of 1960, when part of a National Catholic Welfare Conference multimillion-dollar grant to the Church in Latin America was earmarked for a catechetical program. The money, approximately a quarter of a million dollars, was intended to spur the creation of a continental Confraternity training center. In place of the San Antonio leadership courses and to supplement McNiff's traveling cursillo operation, a permanent center for catechetical instruction was to be established in Latin America itself.[28] Lucey was pleased with this development but rightly feared that McNiff would be named as the center's permanent director. "I think that the move would be most unfortunate," he wrote to McNiff in December, 1960. "Our work would be set back at least three years, and we just can't take that sort of disaster at the present time." Lucey argued that McNiff's knowledge of the Confraternity structure and his good relations with Latin

American bishops were about to pay handsome dividends in getting the program widely established across the continent. He allowed McNiff to accept a temporary assignment at the new center but made it clear that field work was still his most important job. "The big job, as I see it, is to contact dozens of Bishops and keep at it until we get the Confraternity moving in a great many dioceses," he wrote.[29]

When the Latin American bishops met in November, 1960, they chose Santiago, Chile, as the site of the first Instituto Catequistico Latinoamericano (ICLA) and persuaded McNiff to become its first director. McNiff accepted a one-year term of office, and in May, 1961, the institute opened its doors.[30] The founding of the Instituto Catequistico gave Operation Latin America an element of permanence. Its location made the Confraternity more available physically and psychologically to priests and catechists in Latin America. The Confraternity was becoming less a North American product and increasingly a program shaped and defined by Latin Americans themselves.

Two years later, 1962 brought out into the open a power struggle that had plagued the catechetical venture from the beginning. The president of CELAM, Archbishop Dario Miranda of Mexico City, and Julian Mendoza, its general secretary, had gone to Rome that summer to protest against Lucey's domineering attitude. They told Archbishop Antonio Samoré, head of the Pontifical Commission for Latin America, that Lucey was "temperamental" and was pushing his catechetical project without regard for Latin American sensitivities. They also charged him with trying to operate the Confraternity independently of CELAM.[31]

Lucey was angered by the protest and, as he told McNiff, intended to challenge those who were "knocking us in Rome."[32] Both sides came to the Vatican in the fall of 1962 armed with arguments. In separate meetings with Archbishop Samoré, the Latin American bishops represented by Miranda and Mendoza complained about Lucey's self-appointed supervisory role as well as his attempts at unilateral action. Lucey in turn cited repeated instances of deliberate procrastination, lack of communication, and outright ill-will. He charged that Archbishop Miranda's way of sabotaging the program was simply not answering his letters, while he accused Mendoza of seeking absolute control of Vatican Confraternity funds so that he could divert the money to other projects. He complained also that "plenty of resolutions have been passed" by CELAM, but little had actually been done. In contrast to this inactivity, he pointed to the work of his "team" of priests who were setting up national and diocesan Confraternity offices (some twenty in Colombia alone), giving leadership cursillos, and directing the continental institute in Santiago.[33]

Apparently Lucey won the battle, for in the months following the meeting in Rome the catechetical department of CELAM was reorganized. In the shake-up, however, Lucey lost influence, and CELAM officials took firm control of the reorganized Confraternity.[34] Operation Latin America was now a genuinely indigenous program, and the shift in leadership occasioned a change in direction. In the wake of the Second Vatican Council (1962–1965), Third World theologians began talking about "profundization" and *conscientizaçāo*, by which they meant the process of stimulating a revitalized spiritual and socioeconomic awareness among the "People of God."[35] Consequently the work of the Confraternity there changed. In place of cursillos, "Study Weeks" were sponsored at which international catechetical experts assembled to discuss the radicalization of the Confraternity message.[36] The original objectives of Lucey's program—sensitizing the Latin American hierarchy to the need for the Confraternity and training leaders—had been accomplished. The new direction of the program was toward promoting a more critical examination of the meaning of the gospel for the Third World. This new initiative, moreover, came from Latin Americans themselves.

The changes in leadership and direction did not occur entirely with the Archbishop's blessing. As the Latin American bishops took control of "his" program after 1965, Lucey felt that his work and personal financial contributions were unappreciated. In a fit of pique he wrote to one member of his team: "We must always remember that the Latin Americans do not like us, although they like our money. . . . Beyond that, they wish that we would go home." To another he complained of the shabby treatment he and they were receiving in the leadership transition and reorganization of the Confraternity.[37] But Lucey realized that Operation Latin America had passed on to other hands and acknowledged as much in his report to the United States hierarchy at their annual meeting in Washington in 1967. Summarizing his ten years of work, he stated that nearly seventy thousand people had been trained in Confraternity work and that another catechetical institute had been founded in Latin America, this one in Manizales, Colombia, in 1966. He noted the shift toward Study Weeks and international convocations and graciously characterized the greater role of Latin Americans in the religious education program as "a gratifying breakthrough."[38]

Lucey's work for religious education in Latin America had no explicit social action component, unlike his Confraternity work in the United States. His efforts were focused instead on creating an organizational framework from which the gospel could be preached. The Latin American hierarchy gradually appropriated that framework and used it for a radicalized catechesis that analyzed the problems and tensions of contemporary Latin American society. Current liberation theology, especially that associated with the names of Gustavo Gutierrez and Juan Luis Segundo, springs from this catechetical movement.[39]

As in other areas, the Archbishop's accomplishments were substantial and his methods high-handed. Intent on *his*

Confraternity program, he bullied Latin American prelates and rode roughshod over cultural sensitivities. Increasingly out of step with the style of Church leadership encouraged by the Second Vatican Council, Lucey was simply pushed aside in Latin America when he refused to adapt to changing times and realities. In San Antonio, however, his domineering and intractable personality led to unavoidable conflict.

6. New Life and a Renewed Church

Two major developments of the 1960s were to affect Archbishop Lucey's social justice program and episcopal career. The first was the maturing of the civil rights movement, which heightened the political consciousness of black Americans and later Mexican Americans. The second was Vatican Council II, which, with Pope John XXIII's encyclical *Pacem in Terris*, occasioned a new approach to authority in the Church.

Pacem in Terris, issued in the spring of 1963, spoke of respect for personal rights as a civil obligation, not only as a matter of individual moral duty. The papal message resonated well with the civil rights movement. The black revolution, like Vatican II and *Pacem in Terris*, seemed to confirm Lucey's lifelong commitment to social justice, but like them it contained the seeds of a general challenge to authority that would have far-reaching consequences for him.[1]

San Antonio's theaters and restaurants reflected the pattern of segregation prevalent throughout the South in the early 1960s. To combat this problem Archbishop Lucey created the Archdiocesan Department of Social Action and appointed Father Sherrill Smith to head the office. Smith had come to San Antonio from Chicago to study for the priesthood because he knew of Lucey's liberal reputation. At first, the priest was Lucey's troubleshooter and the apple of his eye.[2]

Early in 1960, Smith planned and led the assault on segregation in San Antonio. The prime target was the "colored balcony" of the Majestic Theater, a moviehouse located in the downtown shopping area. Operating with Lucey's full approval and support, Smith adapted a tactic of the sit-in movement and organized a stand-in, whereby Sunday after Sunday for nearly a year "patrons," mostly college students, lined up two by two, one white and one black, and tried to purchase tickets together. By circling the building with lines of "theater-goers," Smith forced the eventual integration of the Majestic. Once it was desegregated, local restaurants and cafes in the downtown area, fearing the same treatment, quickly and quietly integrated.[3]

While Smith was on the picket line, Lucey continued preaching the gospel of racial justice. Speaking at a seminar on interracial relations at Texas Christian University, he called for federal protection for the "freedom riders" who were challenging segregation in the Deep South. Back home in San Antonio, he took aim at local construction unions for discriminating against blacks and Mexican Americans in their apprenticeship programs. After receiving reports from Smith confirming these practices, he ordered the inclusion of a nondiscriminatory clause in all future archdiocesan contracts.[4]

In the spring of 1964, support had mounted for a proposed national civil rights bill. Several months earlier the American Catholic bishops had announced that it was time to "go beyond slogans and generalizations" and get specific about removing racial barriers.[5] Lucey himself took direct action. He urged his clergy to take an interest in civil rights demonstrations, for when the oppressed and exploited demand equality and self-determination, a priest "cannot be silent, neutral, afraid to raise his voice." Turning to the laity, he told them that it was "a moral imperative" to support civil rights legislation:

> But even as we encourage immediate support, we urge something more: that we look beyond passage of the

bill now to its compliance in the future; that we welcome in our minds and hearts now what is right and just, so that we may, in the months ahead, welcome our brothers in the places where we eat and vote and work and learn and take our recreation. We expect more than justice; we expect love. For the Christian, satisfying Caesar's wife is never enough. . . . Justice alone can divide us according to our separate rights and duties, but love can unite us. Justice may be difficult; love can make it easier. H.R. 7152, currently before the Senate, is a means of justice; it is also an act of love.[6]

This pastoral letter was surely one of the most eloquent Lucey ever wrote. But the Archbishop was always too practical to be satisfied merely with eloquence. He sent his priests detailed sermon outlines for Sunday, May 24, and ordered them to preach in favor of the civil rights bill. Pastors were told to post the names and addresses of Senators Yarborough and Tower on their church bulletin boards to encourage the laity to write or wire them. Finally, Catholics entering and leaving churches that Sunday were handed literature asking them to support the controversial legislation. Reaction to "Civil Rights Sunday" in the archdiocese was not entirely favorable, but the Archbishop remained unswayed.[7]

The focal point of the civil rights struggle shifted from Washington to Selma, Alabama, in the spring of 1965. Lucey responded enthusiastically to a request from Sherrill Smith to take part in a planned march. "I am delighted that you are prepared to witness the faith that is in you," he wrote to Smith. When the Selma confrontation began building in early March, Smith and another San Antonio priest, Father Lawrence Murtagh, went to Alabama with Lucey's permission.[8]

Smith was one of two dozen whites chosen by the march leaders to make the trip from Selma to Montgomery and was Lucey's personal representative at the funeral of James Reeb, the Unitarian minister killed during the Selma violence. In the archdiocesan *Alamo Messenger*, in a black-bannered editorial entitled "Murder in Alabama," Lucey insisted that the demonstrators had marched peacefully; "it was state troopers, mounted police and white neurotics who did the rioting."[9]

Local San Antonio newspapers criticized the participation of Lucey's clergy in the Selma march. The Archbishop at once defended his priests for having "rightly placed the law of God above the laws of man." He compared their protests to Christ's driving the moneychangers out of the temple and praised all the priests and nuns who "marched down the streets of Selma giving testimony to the charity of Christ in deed and truth."[10]

In Alabama, meanwhile, Thomas J. Toolen, the Roman Catholic Archbishop of Mobile-Birmingham, strongly criticized the priests and nuns from other dioceses who had marched in Selma. He labeled them "outside crusaders" ignorant of conditions in the South, and indicated that these "eager beavers" were most unwelcome in his diocese.[11]

The Lucey-Toolen dispute was widely publicized in the Catholic press.[12] Lucey never publicly responded to Toolen's charges of meddling, but wrote to Smith upon his return to San Antonio after the march: "Welcome home to a good soldier from the warfare in Alabama. . . . What has the Catholic Church been doing in Alabama for the last quarter of a century? Alabama is a cesspool of iniquity, and the Church should do something about it."[13]

The Selma demonstrations concluded the interracial phase of the civil rights movement. The emergence of Black Power as an organizing principle was only a year away—on the other side of the Watts riot in Los Angeles and the Meredith march from Memphis to Jackson. For Lucey the Selma march had another significance. From his public statements it must be concluded that he saw opposition to racism as a moral question, one that transcended issues of canonical jurisdiction, diocesan boundaries, and canon law. Toolen's complaint about priests coming from other dioceses and ignoring his ecclesiastical jurisdiction was dismissed as irrelevant. Not more than fifteen months later, the farm workers' strike in the Rio Grande Valley raised a similar question of whether a moral issue was larger than ecclesiastical law.

In the aftermath of the Selma protests, Lucey unveiled "Project Equality" in August, 1965. It was a program designed to use the Church's buying power to promote fair employment practices in businesses supplying the San Antonio archdiocese with goods and services. Under the program's guidelines suppliers were required to provide equal job opportunities for blacks and Mexican Americans and take affirmative steps to hire and promote minorities in their companies. Significantly, the Archbishop appointed Sherrill Smith as administrator of the program.[14]

Project Equality was bitterly resented in San Antonio. Local businessmen saw it as a pressure tactic to further the Archbishop's pet project. "A good many of those who wrote letters to the editor would like to take me for a ride," Lucey commented to a friend.[15] One critic asked for public prayers to keep Lucey out of hell, for which the Archbishop expressed his gratitude.[16] The appointment of Smith as the program's director was another cause for criticism, for by this time Smith had at least a local reputation as a social activist, a union sympathizer, a civil rights advocate, and all-around troublemaker. In other words, Smith and his Archbishop were two of a kind.

From his friend in the White House, however, Lucey received a letter of appreciation for Project Equality. He relied on this friendship with President Lyndon Johnson to funnel federal dollars to San Antonio. Between 1965 and 1967 the San Antonio Neighborhood Youth Organization (SANYO), an agency created and supervised by Father John Yanta, received over six million dollars, more than one-third of all the federal poverty money sent to San Antonio in those years. Employing nearly two hundred full- and part-time workers to operate its thirty multipurpose neighborhood centers and National Youth Corps job-training programs, SANYO was soon the biggest and most active anti-poverty agency in the Southwest. As one local reporter put it, "the anti-poverty crusade has become big business, and San Antonio is the Detroit of the industry." Through his priest at SANYO, Lucey disbursed approximately nine million dollars of federal anti-poverty funds by January, 1968.[17]

By the mid-1960s, the Archbishop was working with rejuvenated vigor, and President Johnson paid him a personal honor in signing the Medicare registration extension bill in San Antonio. Lucey had been shunted to the side by local politicians eager to capitalize on the President's visit, but Johnson went out of his way to bring him into the spotlight. Discarding his prepared remarks at the signing ceremony, the President reminisced about his relationship with Lucey. "I remember Archbishop Lucey in the 1930s," Johnson told the crowd. "He wasn't nearly as respectable then as he is now. He was kind of a bolshevik in the minds of a lot of people when he came down here."[18]

It seemed fitting that 1966 should mark a watershed in the Archbishop's career. On May 10 of that year Lucey celebrated his triple jubilee: he was seventy-five years old, fifty years a priest, and twenty-five years Archbishop of San Antonio. At a huge banquet Lucey received congratulations from Pope Paul VI. President Johnson telegraphed his tribute to the Archbishop for his "long search . . . for more education for more people, more jobs, more hope, more decency, more dedication to God and country." Sargent Shriver, director of the Office of Economic Opportunity, observed that while the War on Poverty was only two years old, for the Archbishop it had begun long ago. "The voice of Archbishop Lucey has been particularly eloquent in support of our most forgotten and most neglected Americans, the Indians and the Mexican

Americans and the Negroes of the Southwest," Shriver added. "His voice on their behalf now is registered in the highest councils of the government's official program."[19]

It was a grand moment, and as many commented years later, it would have been a perfect time for Lucey to retire. Lucey, however, was not the type who retired from anything. He had developed a small coterie of social action priests, such as John Wagner and Henry Casso at the Bishops' Committee, John Yanta at SANYO, Sherrill Smith at the Social Action Department, and William Killian, the fiery editor of the *Alamo Messenger*. These priests were generally younger and more liberal politically than the clerical old guard, from whom Lucey had never received enthusiastic support. The Archbishop delighted in these hard-pushing activists and luxuriated in the growing publicity he was receiving as the man in charge of the revitalized Church in San Antonio.

Retirement was also unlikely while his friend Lyndon Johnson was President and while the Johnson administration was promoting some of the most extensive civil rights and anti-poverty legislation in one hundred years. Lucey was participating vicariously in the accomplishment of some of his most cherished goals. He was optimistic that the cause of the poor had finally become the cause of the nation, and the Church, especially the Church in San Antonio, was doing its share in making the gospel come alive.

The principal reason why the Archbishop remained in office was the Second Vatican Council. The renewal of the Church, begun by the Council, had antecedants in the post-1945 United States, where Catholics were freeing themselves from a self-imposed ghetto mentality to posit a whole new set of questions about the quality of American Catholic life. What was the nature of authority and obedience in the Church? What did it mean to be a Catholic in the modern world?[20]

A similar theological debate was in full swing in Europe by 1950. Led by such scholars as Karl Rahner and Henri de

Lubac, the "new theology" urged an existentialist inquiry into the mystery of the Church. With modern historical consciousness influencing its methodology, the new theology rejected an understanding of man derived from ahistorical first principles in favor of a study of man in human history. Accompanied by a renewal of Catholic biblical studies and a movement for liturgical reform, the new theology announced a full-scale re-examination of Catholic ecclesiology.[21]

All of these powerful elements were stirring in the postwar Catholic world, but they had not yet coalesced. For that to happen, an age, an institution, and a person would have to merge at just the right time. In 1958, when the papacy became vacant with the death of Pius XII, the right time was at hand. The Catholic Church was on the verge of an unexpected revolution. Flexibility, a collegial spirit, and a high tolerance for uncertainty would be demanded of Church officials, as bishops, priests, and lay people struggled to discover what it meant to be a Catholic in the modern world.

The story of how Pope John XXIII decided to call the Second Vatican Council is well known and has been told elsewhere in detail.[22] When the conclave of cardinals elected seventy-seven-year-old Angelo Roncalli as the successor of Pius XII, it was widely believed that they had intended to choose an interim pope. To the surprise of all and the alarm of some, this *Papa di passaggio* called the Church to define itself anew in the context of the modern world and created an atmosphere within the Church in which this redefinition could occur. Instead of stressing final answers, Pope John asked questions and encouraged others to do the same. Were old ways of thinking and customary ways of acting necessarily the best ways for the modern Church? What in the Church's tradition represented the accumulated wisdom of human experience and therefore must be preserved? What, on the other hand, were merely the encrustations of time?[23]

The Church fathers issued sixteen documents on their deliberations at Vatican II.[24] These documents announced enormous transformations, particularly in regard to the operation of authority within the Church. The Council presented the notion of authority in terms of service rather than domination. Pope Paul VI in his closing speech to the bishops on December 7, 1965, stressed this theme. "The Church has . . . declared herself the servant of humanity," the Pope said. Throughout the conciliar discussions, "the idea of service has been central."[25]

Archbishop Lucey spoke enthusiastically about the work of the Council.[26] Two events put to the test his understanding of and willingness to adapt to the post–Vatican II Church. The first was the formation of the Priests' Senate in San Antonio; the second was the Rio Grande Valley farm workers' strike. His response to these events previewed the trouble that was soon to come.

The beginning of the Archdiocesan Priests' Senate can be dated from a homily given by Monsignor Roy Rihn in May, 1966. Taking as his theme the priesthood of Christ, Rihn noted that the Vatican II "Decree on the Ministry and Life of Priests" stressed the uniqueness and oneness of the priesthood, realized in the person of Jesus Christ. It followed that although hierarchically graded, bishop and priests fundamentally were brothers because both shared in the one priesthood of Christ, not as "monarch and subject" but as "colleagues and co-workers."[27]

Because no guidelines had been laid down for translating collegiality on the diocesan level, "bold experimentation" was in order. Rihn urged the formation of a senate of priests that would effectively assist Lucey in the government of the diocese. While priests must recognize their subordination to the bishop, they must not be asked to "sacrifice their manhood to a merely authoritarian system" or be expected to "forfeit their human dignity to something which parades as 'obedience.' " In a ringing conclusion he called for a deepening of the unity between the Archbishop and his priests:

United in one priesthood, rooted in one faith, impelled by one charity, . . . and not without hope, let us set ourselves to the glorious challenge: to incarnate collegiality. Let us together make the Church of San Antonio the Church envisioned by Vatican II: where obedience and respect for God-given authority exist side-by-side with freedom and the opportunity just to be a man.[28]

Lucey's reaction to the homily was an uneasy one, for he sensed the threatening nature of Rihn's proposal, but in the next few weeks the Archbishop was persuaded to turn the idea of a senate into fact. In a pastoral letter dated July 8, 1966, he announced the creation of the Archdiocesan Priests' Senate with elections of the twelve-member body to held in the fall.[29] It was a significant step toward implementing the spirit of Vatican II, but ironically it was a step that began the final act in the Archbishop's career.

The Rio Grande Valley farm workers' strike, Lucey's second test, had an unusual beginning. In the fall of 1965, Cesar Chavez and the National Farm Workers Association struck the grape growers in Delano, California. The following February, as part of a nation-wide campaign, Chavez dispatched Eugene Nelson, an assistant, to Houston to organize a boycott against Schenley Industries. When Schenley unexpectedly agreed to negotiate with the NFWA, Nelson's task was completed and his authority to represent the NFWA ended. Convinced of the need for a union in south Texas but unauthorized to speak for Chavez, Nelson formed the Independent Workers Association and left for the Valley. Within a short time he had organized several hundred farm workers in Rio Grande City, and on June 1 the association struck La Casita Farms, seeking an hourly wage of $1.25 and recognition of their union. The battle was on.[30]

It was a dubious decision to strike in an area close to the

Mexican border and its endless supply of foreign labor, but the farm workers of the Rio Grande Valley had little to lose. The focus of the strike was Starr County, the poorest county in Texas and one of the poorest in the nation. Dominated by several large agricultural businesses, such as La Casita Farms, Starr County's median family income hovered around $3,000 a year, below the federal poverty level. Ninety percent of its 20,000 people were Mexican Americans, many of whom depended upon farm work for income. Each year domestic workers were forced to migrate from Texas in search of employment because Valley growers preferred to hire cheaper foreign labor. Those who chose to stay in the Valley and work at La Casita Farms could expect wages of 50 to 85 cents an hour.[31]

Soon after the strike began, the Catholic Church became deeply involved. On June 6 two of Lucey's priests, Sherrill Smith and William Killian, went to Rio Grande City, with the Archbishop's permission, to participate in a rally for the strikers. In the town square the priests celebrated mass and spoke in support of the strike. The following week, Smith, Killian, and Father Henry Casso, executive secretary of the Bishops' Committee for the Spanish Speaking, returned to Rio Grande City and led a march through the town to the Court House steps. With county officials looking on, Killian attacked "the power structure of Starr County" for forcing people to take to the streets for justice.[32]

In addition to words, the priests brought food and financial aid. With Lucey's approval Casso had organized "Operation Foodstuff" and by the middle of June had shipped about ten thousand pounds of groceries to the strikers. The Bishops' Committee thus provided crucial support to sustain the strike in its early stage.[33]

When Smith and Killian first went to the Valley, the diocese of Brownsville had no bishop. The Most Reverend Adolph Marx, the first Bishop of Brownsville, had died on November 1, 1965. Several months later the news arrived that

Monsignor Humberto Medeiros, a priest of the Fall River Diocese in Massachusetts, was to be the new Bishop. Medeiros was consecrated on June 9 in Fall River and scheduled to be installed in Brownsville on June 29. Thus Medeiros himself did not arrive in Brownsville until nearly one month after the strike had begun.

Lucey was not consulted on Medeiros' appointment, even though the diocese of Brownsville is located in the San Antonio Province and Lucey, as Archbishop of San Antonio, was the Metropolitan for the region. The Archbishop merely received official notice from the Apostolic Delegate that Medeiros had been appointed.[34] It was a strange procedure. Previously, Lucey had had a lot to say about who would become the new bishops in Texas. His influence was apparent in the appointments of the bishops of Corpus Christi, Amarillo, San Angelo, and Galveston-Houston, and Adolph Marx had been his choice for Brownsville. To add to the confusion, shortly after he got official word of the appointment, the Archbishop received a letter from Pope Paul VI, congratulating him on his triple jubilee celebration. "It is especially to your praise," the Pope wrote, "that you have gone out to and aided Mexican workers who migrate in great numbers throughout the United States, and that you have shown them every type of loving kindness."[35]

Was the Pope's letter merely a gesture, a polite expression of gratitude for Lucey's lifelong work, with the real direction of Vatican thinking appearing in the Delegate's letter? Was Lucey being told gently by the Vatican that his time in Texas was drawing to a close and that it would be well for him to prepare for retirement? If so, the sign was much too subtle for a man like the Archbishop. He proceeded full steam ahead in his support for the migrant farm workers and for the participation of his priests in this national issue.

After their two-day stay in the Valley, Smith and Killian returned to San Antonio and reported to Lucey. Meanwhile the press was giving the strike much publicity. The *Houston*

Post characterized the Rio Grande Valley situation as potentially a "major social revolution" and pictured Smith and Killian as in the center of the controversy. Killian himself began a series of editorials in the *Alamo Messenger* that was to win him a national journalism award and lose substantial financial support for the newspaper in the archdiocese. In his first "Valley" editorial on June 17, 1966, he applauded the courage of the farm workers and expressed the hope that the strike was but "a first stirring" that eventually would spread across the state. "God forgive us," he concluded, "if we bury our middle class heads in the sand and withhold support to our brothers."[36]

Not everyone viewed the issue as Killian did. From the Valley, Monsignor Daniel Laning of Mission, Texas, charged in a Sunday sermon that Smith and Killian were "imposters" and "intruders" who did not represent the Catholic Church. To Laning, the strike was a civil affair, not a religious one, and the Catholic Church did *not* support it. He suggested that Archbishop Lucey "clean out his own dirty cellar in San Antonio" and let the Valley people solve their problems for themselves.[37]

Laning's remarks were scooped by the local press and served up the following day as editorial opinion. In its June 20 edition, the *Valley Evening Monitor* (part of the Freedom Newspaper chain that exercised a virtual monopoly over the Rio Grande Valley) commended Laning for dissociating the Church from the farm workers' action. The editorial tagged the strike "a sort of traveling road show—a Huelga portable—with the principal actors arriving from some far-off point, script in hand, to cast the local rubes in the role of supporting players." It noted the arrival of "some of Archbishop Lucey's firebrands," characterizing them as the Archbishop's personal representatives and Lucey himself as "the most liberal, politically, of any prelate, who is always found mixed up in political matters of far left sympathies."[38]

Lucey immediately issued a statement defending Smith

and Killian, and to an AFL-CIO representative who was unnerved by Laning's remarks, he wrote: "You must not be too disturbed by this incident. . . . When I get to Brownsville next week, *Deo volente*, I shall straighten out this matter."[39] He was referring to the installation of Bishop Medeiros on June 29.

The installation came close to being a free-for-all. Tension between strikers and growers was high. Smith and Killian had entered the bishopless Brownsville diocese and openly sided with the strikers, implicitly indicting Valley priests for their negligence in preaching the social gospel. A predictably sharp reaction had come from the Valley clergy, in turn provoking Lucey's public approval of his priests' activities in Brownsville. Medeiros had just arrived from Massachusetts, thoroughly uninformed about the strike, but resolved to placate both sides.

The installation ceremony, held in the cathedral, was crowded with strikers, growers, editors, and clergy. In his homily Bishop Thomas Drury of Corpus Christi, a Lucey protégé, upbraided "the persons in high places who have not heard the good news that slavery was outlawed in this land more than a century ago."[40] Near the end of the mass, it was Lucey's turn to speak. He directed pointed words at the Valley growers and clergy in a paraphrase of the gospel:

> I was a campesino near Rio Grande City, working ten hours a day under the burning sun for starvation wages. I was tired and weary, and you did not comfort me. My children were hungry, and you brought us no food, although you yourself were well-fed. Three priests came from afar; they walked with Me and talked with Me; they offered Me their love and loyalty, and you called them imposters. Some laymen came to visit Me; . . . they gave Me sympathy and food. Other friends of mine, living at a distance, col-

lected money and brought food, that my children should not go hungry. You called them agitators.[41]

Monsignor Laning barely contained his outrage at the closing remarks and demanded equal time "to get back at everybody," but Medeiros intervened. The new Bishop refused to let Laning speak at the installation banquet and instead took the podium himself. Recognizing the tense and difficult struggle that lay ahead, Medeiros prayed for justice and divine direction. With that, the ceremony ended.[42]

Although Medeiros' installation fueled the controversy, the strike itself was making little headway. Court injunctions against picketing at La Casita Farms, Mexican strikebreakers, a reduced demand for workers due to rain-damaged crops, and the annual migration northward were breaking the back of the strike. Strike leaders decided at this point to stage a march on Austin to publicize their cause. As the plan developed, the march was to begin on July 4 in the Valley and end with a rally in the state capital on Labor Day. Its purpose was to pressure for a state law setting the minimum wage at $1.25 an hour and management recognition of Local 2 of the National Farm Workers Association.[43]

In the steaming Texas heat, the marchers set out on their 500-mile pilgrimage, and on August 26 they reached San Antonio. At San Fernando Cathedral Lucey reluctantly endorsed their demand for an hourly wage of $1.25, characterizing it as "ghastly recompense" for their exhausting labor.[44]

After an unproductive meeting with Texas Governor Connally on the highway about forty miles outside Austin, the 6,500 marchers reached the capital on September 5 and were met by several thousand supporters. At the Labor Day rally they heard speeches from Cesar Chavez and State Senator Barbara Jordan and received promises from Senator Robert Kennedy of continued federal support for all farm workers. Buoyed by the march, the farm workers returned to the Valley determined to continue their fight.[45]

President Truman and members of the Commission on Migratory Labor at the White House, April 7, 1951. *Seated with Truman*: Maurice T. Van Hecke, chairman. *Left to right*: Robert E. Lucey, Peter H. Odegard, William E. Leisenson, and Noble Clark. Photograph courtesy of the Archives of the Archdiocese of San Antonio.

Left to right: Lucey with Rev. John Gorham, Rev. Virgil Elizondo and Rev Msgr. Ramon Garcia, during International Catechetical Week (August 11–17, 1968) in Medellin, Colombia. Photograph courtesy of the Archives of the Archdiocese of San Antonio.

President Johnson presenting pen to Lucey after signing the Medicare Extension Bill in San Antonio, 1966. Photograph courtesy of *Today's Catholic* and the Archives of The Archdiocese of San Antonio.

Archbishop Lucey viewed the Delano and Austin marches as turning points in the history of the Southwest. In a letter to Monsignor George Higgins, he said, "The Mexican-Americans are learning at long last that docility in the face of brutality is lovely but doesn't get you anywhere, and that they can achieve liberty and justice if they stand up and fight."[46] The irony of these words would become apparent when Mexican Americans began directing their new-found militancy against the Archbishop.

After the Austin rally the changing concept of authority in the Church began to exert its influence on Lucey's commitment to social justice. The controversy focused initially on the Archbishop's social action priests, particularly Sherrill Smith. No other priest in the archdiocese embodied Lucey's social ideals more clearly than Smith. None had received such unwavering support from the Archbishop as Smith had. Yet when the confrontation between social justice and authority occurred, it came first between Lucey and Smith.

Ever since he became Lucey's social action trouble-shooter, Sherrill Smith had worked closely with San Antonio's labor organizations. Early in 1959, for example, he walked the picket lines with members of the International Ladies Garment Workers Union, which had struck Tex-Son Company, a San Antonio textile firm. In a letter to him after the strike began, Lucey expressed his delight at Smith's actions. In the sixties, Smith intensified his labor activities. In the summer of 1964 the vice-president of George C. Vaughan and Sons Building Materials, a local construction supplies firm, complained to Lucey that Smith was trying to unionize his employees. The Archbishop defended Smith and accused company executives of exercising "paternalistic authority, sometimes known as domination," to scare off unionization. In March, 1966, Lucey learned that a group of San Antonio Catholic businessmen had confronted Smith at a luncheon and attempted to intimidate him. The Archbishop was flabbergasted that "Catholic business and professional men [had been] so bold as to argue with a priest about the social teaching of the Church."[47] But more than anything else, it was Project Equality that galled the city's business community and tested Lucey's support for Smith.

In April 1966, Smith testified before the San Antonio City Council in support of a fifty-cent-an-hour wage increase for members of the City, County and Municipal Employees, Local 1095. He was asked whether church property ought not be taxed to help pay for the wage increase and replied that the suggestion was at least debatable. Smith went on to criticize the Church's own low wage scale and mentioned specifically the poor wages paid employees of Santa Rosa Hospital, a Catholic institution. Within a day Lucey received an angry letter from John E. Coughlin, director of public relations at the Santa Rosa Medical Center, charging that Smith's remarks showed a complete lack of judgment and accusing him of ineptitude in interpreting and implementing "certain programs" (Project Equality) that had "created confusion, indignation and outright animosity" in the San Antonio business community. On April 25 Lucey fired off a memo to Smith, admonishing him to be better prepared the next time he testified in public and warning him against being derailed from the topic of bad city wages to those paid by Catholic institutions. "Frankly, if the newspaper reports were accurate, you did not fare very well," the Archbishop said.[48]

The Santa Rosa Medical Center was not the only institution complaining about Project Equality. That same week Lucey heard from Albert T. Range, vice-president of the Pearl Brewing Company. In a letter sent to Smith and forwarded to the Archbishop, Range protested bitterly about receiving a Project Equality fair employment practices form: "Writing such a letter to this company is almost like asking the President of the United Sates if he is a good citizen or asking the Pope if he is a practicing Catholic!" He stated that Pearl's employment practices were fair and equal and that the company was an annual donor to Santa Rosa Hospital. The implication was clear.[49]

More pressure was brought to bear on Lucey as a result of Sherrill Smith's highly publicized activities on behalf of members of the International Union of Electrical, Radio and Machine Workers, AFL-CIO, Local 1012, who went on strike in August, 1966, against the Marshall Steves Sash and Door Company, a building materials supply firm owned and managed by a wealthy San Antonio family. Steves had vigorously resisted an IUE organizing campaign, and despite complaints from the National Labor Relations Board, continued to fire workers attempting to unionize his company. After months of futile negotiations, the workers walked out.[50]

Predictably, Smith was soon on the picket line with the strikers, and Steves was at the chancery office demanding to see the Archbishop. On Tuesday, September 1, Steves had his visit. In a memo to himself written after the meeting, Lucey first reminded himself to see Smith regarding "unwise remarks damaging his influence in Texas—causing criticism of the Archbishop, and he already has plenty of this—irritating some of the Bishops and hurting the image of Catholicism." The Archbishop recorded Marshall Steves's statement that his employees had been on strike for ten months "and only Father Smith prevents a settlement." After noting that Steves "does not wish to win the battle" and would like "to give the workers what they want," Lucey repeated that "the only obstacle to a settlement is Father Smith."[51]

There was more to the visit than the memo reveals. Steves, a friend of President and Mrs. Johnson, was at the time president of "Hemisfair 68," an international exposition that was scheduled to open in San Antonio in a little more than a year. Preparations for this world's fair were well under way, and San Antonio would soon be in the international spotlight. How would it look to the world if the city, and the president of Hemisfair in particular, were entangled in an ugly labor dispute? Furthermore, with a priest leading the strikers, the Church and the Archbishop would likewise suffer public discredit and embarrassment.

Concerned with his image and that of the Church, the Archbishop apparently gave in to the pressure. On October 10 he addressed a two-page memo to Smith in which he sharply reprimanded him for becoming involved in strike negotiations with Marshall Steves's company "as a union representative." In a particularly revealing passage, the Archbishop instructed Smith to tell the International Union of Electrical Workers that "if they have no representative in Bexar County, they should get in touch with the Central Labor Council who might furnish them a representative. . . ."[52]

Lucey reminded Smith of his "unwise remarks to City Council about taxing churches" and his dangerous course of action. "When you bring yourself to the point in public estimation at which honest men and good friends of ours are disappointed, if not disgusted, then you are not following the right track. You have hurt the Archbishop of San Antonio by throwing yourself too passionately into labor controversies." Lucey admitted that one could not preach social justice without making enemies, "but making enemies of good men and good friends is most unwise. . . . It is one thing to preach social justice and make reactionaries mad. It is quite another thing to take over a layman's job and act as a representative of a labor union. That is not papal teaching."[53]

Smith took a month to reply. Then, in a fifteen-page letter, he shredded the Archbishop's argument. Speaking "as a priest to his bishop but also man to man," Smith charged Lucey with impugning his intelligence and with listening too readily to so-called men of good will. He expressed surprise at Lucey's sudden interest in his involvement with the Steves strike and denied being the obstacle to a settlement. According to Smith, Steves was "basically no different than any other owner around here: anti-union, paternalistic, and subjectively convinced that he's been a real good employer all these years."

Here's an employer who has some fifty unfair labor practice charges filed against him, who has dragged out negotiations for months, . . . who pays a worker . . . after twenty-five years employ[ment] only $1.25 an hour, something you called a ghastly recompense; who sets up a TV-watcher system in his plant to spy on his workers; here's a man who symbolizes management's attitude in San Antonio—yes, even contempt—toward labor, organized or not. I confess, Your Excellency, to being a bit confused by your criticism of me in all this.[54]

Smith next tore into Lucey's suggestion that the IUE contact the Central Labor Council for a bargaining agent. "Can you be serious as late as 1966 wondering if the International Union of Electrical, Radio, and Machine Workers (350,000 members) . . . knows how to run itself? Can you be serious in doubting that after almost ten years' experience and association with unions that I should lack even a basic understanding of union structure and my own limitations in relation to it?"[55]

Smith hammered at the Archbishop's inconsistency. "One minute I'm a champion; the next, I'm reproved—for doing nothing really different from the past," he wrote. Noting that he had walked picket lines before and publicly criticized exploitative employers, he asked what had suddenly made his activities imprudent and unwise.[56]

Finally, Smith suggested that the root of the problem was that Lucey's authoritarian approach to social action was outdated. He asked about the freedom to make errors. "Is Vatican Council concern for freedom in the Church merely matter for quotation? . . . Is authority like a sharp-pointed pencil, producing from one end a packaged party line and with the eraser-end rubbing out errors?" Smith accused Lucey of pulling back from the social justice fight: "so many bold gestures followed too quickly by meek retreat into the security of papal encyclicals, . . . so many eloquent words about JUSTICE and yet so little of it established."[57]

That same month tensions in the Valley rose when striking farm workers were charged with setting fire to the only railroad bridge into Rio Grande City, seriously hampering the shipment of farm produce. At this point Cesar Chavez telegraphed Lucey: "Request Father Smith and Father Killiken [*sic*] have permission to go to strike area. Their presence is Insurance for peaceful progress."[58]

The next day Lucey directed one of his chancery officials to telephone Bishop Medeiros for permission for Smith and Killian to enter his diocese. Medeiros, however, feared that the two priests would worsen matters and asked Lucey to keep them out of the Brownsville diocese. On that same day, November 10, 1966, Smith and Killian requested permission from Lucey to go to Rio Grande City and asked the Archbishop to "clear the way with Bishop Medeiros." In their letter the two requested that Lucey surmount canonical protocol, which "may end up being the enemy of progress instead of its promoter and protector." Playing on Lucey's ego, they reminded him that people like Cesar Chavez looked to his leadership, not in terms of "diocese" but rather in terms of "Church." "It's known to the world that the Church is opposed to [exploitation] on principle, but it's not sufficiently evident what the Church wants to do about it," they said. "Principles that don't get into practice are meaningless to the world. . . . How do we get the Church's alliance with the poor out of rhetoric and into reality?"[59]

Several days later Lucey responded. He told the priests about the telegram from Chavez and Medeiros' response. Noting that Medeiros had decided to use one of his own priests as a mediator, and expressing doubts about the effectiveness of that priest, Lucey told Smith and Killian that "this emphasizes the fact that . . . we should try to hold the confidence of the Texas Bishops in order to conserve some remnant of good influence in the state."[60]

Meanwhile the labor situation in San Antonio was also deteriorating. The strike against the Steves plant continued, and a strike against the Pioneer Flour Mill Company had just begun. Once again Smith very publicly supported the workers. On December 3 prominent Catholic businessmen of the city met with Lucey. In strong language they protested against Smith's direction of Project Equality and the damage he was allegedly doing to the image of the Archbishop and the Church in San Antonio.[61]

Apparently they got to Lucey. Little more than a week later, when Smith led a three-mile "March for Justice" through the streets of San Antonio against the Steves Company, the Archbishop made a decision. He notified Smith that because of his lack of prudence and discretion, he would be transferred in the near future to another parish. Lucey accused Smith of having embarrassed him by the march and made it clear that he would not tolerate Smith's agitation against Marshall Steves. The transfer was the last warning Smith would get, he wrote; the next time, "I shall take appropriate action."[62]

The Archbishop informed Smith on January 13, 1967, that he was being transferred to Saint Lawrence Church, located at the farthest edge of San Antonio, and that he had five days to take up his new assignment. In an extraordinary breach of protocol, Lucey sent advance word of the transfer to Mr. Edward Sullivan, a Catholic business leader, and asked Sullivan to keep the news of the transfer "quite confidential" until he had made his move.[63]

Smith was not the only one to get the ax. On the same day, Lucey fired Henry Casso from the Bishops' Committee. The dismissal was announced as a transfer from the active committee position to a new post as Archdiocesan Episcopal

Vicar for Urban Ministry. Ostensibly concerned with problems of health, employment, and inner city housing, the new position had no office and no budget. Obviously the transfer was Lucey's way of putting Casso on the sidelines. Dismissed with Casso was Erasmus Andrade, a militant Bishops' Committee field representative whom Casso had hired. Casso had become deeply involved in the Rio Grande Valley farm workers' strike, and Andrade had marched with Smith against Steves. Both men had become troublesome and threatening to the Archbishop's authority.[64]

Lucey was pulling back on his activist priests, in part because he was losing control of the social justice movement, in part because of the shadow allegedly cast over his image and that of the Church by Smith's actions. He might also have been concerned about his own position within the ecclesiastical establishment, reflected in the appointment of Medeiros and the growing criticism of Smith by other Texas bishops. There were additional pressures as well. Father Charles Herzig, finance secretary for the Archbishop, reported to Lucey in October, 1966, that pledges for the Archdiocesan Development Fund, a money pool used to subsidize various diocesan programs, were down considerably. For 1966 only $454,800 had been received out of $733,724 pledged, and the deadline for pledges was fast approaching. Herzig also reported that since the ADF drive had begun in the spring, some cancellations had been received because of the Archbishop's social action program. Many of the cancellations were coming from the rural areas of the archdiocese, where opposition to the Church's involvement in the Valley strike and march was strong. Finally, the *Alamo Messenger*'s strong editorial support for Smith's labor activities and the Valley strike had provoked many Catholics. Subscriptions were being canceled and threats of more nonrenewals were running high.[65]

The final act in the Valley farm workers' strike, at least from Lucey's point of view, was about to unfold. By January, 1967, the strike was going badly for the farm workers. The growers charged them with repeated acts of vandalism, and many arrests were made. Borrowing another tactic from the Delano strike, the United Farm Workers Organizing Committee began using sound equipment to coax workers out of the fields and announced a nationwide boycott of La Casita Farm products. When one of the union officials asked Smith to come to the Valley and help in the new offensive, he went, despite Lucey's refusal of permission.[66]

The day Smith arrived in Rio Grande City, January 29, Medeiros telephoned Lucey. He had told Lucey previously that the economic system of the Valley needed to be reformed but that "cool heads and brilliant minds" alone could perform that task. Now Medeiros told Lucey in unequivocal terms to keep Smith out.[67]

On February 1, Smith, along with Killian and three other San Antonio priests, returned to Rio Grande City. While urging La Casita farm workers to quit their jobs and leave the lettuce fields, the five priests were arrested by Starr County sheriffs for disturbing the peace. Later they and five activists also arrested were released on bond.[68]

"Five San Antonio Priests Arrested in Rio Grande City"—the banner headline in the *San Antonio News* screamed at Lucey, and the Archbishop screamed at Smith and Killian. "Because you have defied my instructions to you I have made arrangements for both of you to go to Via Coeli, Jemez, New Mexico, on Monday, February 6. You will remain there until further instructions are given to you. I need not add that the injury you have done to the priests of this archdiocese and to the good name of the Archbishop is beyond measure."[69] Lucey had chosen the medieval punishment of banishment from the diocese for his disobedient priests. Via Coeli was a place for priests who suffered from alcoholism, sexual difficulties, drug abuse, and the like.

Lucey later defended his treatment of Smith and Killian on two grounds. He insisted first that the priests had offended protocol by their unauthorized trip to Rio Grande City, and second that they had violated canon law and therefore had to be punished.[70] Neither reason is persuasive. If the priests had merely been discourteous, then their punishment was out of proportion to the offense. If they had violated canon law by entering Medeiros' jurisdiction against his explicit wishes, then Lucey's response was inconsistent. After all, he had allowed Smith and another San Antonio priest to go to Selma in 1965 against the explicit wishes of Archbishop Toolen. A more plausible explanation of the heavy-handed punishment of Smith and Killian is that Lucey feared a confrontation with Medeiros over the consequences of disregarding the Bishop's ecclesiastical jurisdiction. The diocese of Mobile had been a long way from home, but Brownsville was in the Archbishop's backyard. He was vulnerable there and had to protect himself.

Lucey apologized to Medeiros on February 2. "It was a source of very deep regret to me to learn that five of my young Turks had invaded your jurisdiction. . . . I can give Your Excellency two assurances: one is that I shall take care of these five priests in due time, and the other is that if they ever enter your jurisdiction again without your approval and mine, they will be suspended. I add my humble apologies to you for the disastrous conduct of the San Antonio clergymen. The so-called liberal cause of the United States and my good name have been severely damaged."[71]

Local San Antonio newspapers gave front page coverage to the arrest and banishment of Smith and Killian. On February 3, Roy Evans, executive secretary of the Texas AFL-CIO, urged Lucey to reconsider his action. "Texas working people have too few friends now who are willing to sacrifice for the cause against legalized slavery," he said. "The loss of these two men will be a severe blow to gaining human dignity in South Texas." Hank Brown, the Texas AFL-CIO president, expressed his hope that the disciplining of the priests did not reflect a change in the Archbishop's philosophy.[72]

For a champion of organized labor and the poor to receive

such advice must have been angering, but the letters were mild in comparison with what came next. On Saturday, February 4, the Valley Farm Workers Assistance Committee, headed by Erasmo Andrade, voted against the advice of Smith and Casso to picket the Catholic chancery and Archbishop Lucey's home to protest against the banishment of Smith and Killian. The next day the pickets appeared in front of the closed chancery office and later traveled to Lucey's Hollywood Park residence. Carrying placards that read "Medeiros and Lucey: How Many Pieces of Silver?" "Lucey, Betrayer of Mexican Americans," and "Lucey, Unfair to Priests," the protestors never saw the Archbishop but did receive extensive press and media coverage.[73] The protest hurt and angered Lucey. "This was a fraud—this marching," the Archbishop said. "Why would the Mexicans march against me? I was the only friend they had. I'm sorry to say it's typical of the Spanish speaking that they knock off their best friends."[74]

The pickets and protestors muddied Lucey's public image but were beyond his power to control or punish. This was not true of another group of protestors, nine priests who went to him in a body. As reported in the *San Antonio Express*, a group of thirty to forty San Antonio priests met at Saint Joseph Church, Downtown, on Friday, February 3, to discuss a response to Lucey's banishment of Smith and Killian. The result of the meeting was that nine of them, plus four members of the Priests' Senate, met with the Archbishop at the chancery on Monday, February 6, "to discuss the crisis of authority in the Church and the place of personal freedom and liberties of priests." At the meeting Lucey listened as the spokesman for the group accused him of abusing his episcopal authority and turning away from the social idealism he had spawned in them. An eyewitness reported that the Archbishop turned white with anger, asked each priest individually whether he agreed with what the spokesman had said, and, after hearing that they all did, had them say an Our

Father and then dismissed them.[75] Within a short time these protestors were either suspended or transferred to parishes outside the city limits.

Even while Lucey was meeting with this group of protestors, a dramatic scene was transpiring at the San Antonio International Airport. Approximately one hundred supporters saw Smith and Killian off on their flight to Via Coeli. It was one more embarrassing scene for the Archbishop. But if the send-off was embarrassing, the hero's welcome the two priests received on their return from their one-week banishment was nothing less than infuriating. They were met at the airport on Saturday, February 11, by an even larger crowd. Killian made no statement, but Smith said that while he did not approve of the picketing of Archbishop Lucey, he did see it as an expression of the people's right to speak out, something Lucey and the Church had long supported.[76] Lucey, however, construed Smith's remarks as a sign of his lack of repentance.[77]

Smith's days in the Social Action Department were numbered. On March 8, 1967, Lucey had Father Erwin Juraschek, the archdiocesan moderator of Catholic Action, under whose supervision Smith allegedly operated, fire him. "You are hereby authorized to take temporary rest from the tension and strife of the Social Action Department so that you can comply more fully with your duties as assistant pastor at Saint Lawrence," Juraschek wrote. When asked later whether the Archbishop had ordered Smith's removal, Juraschek denied it, saying he had made the decision on his own.[78] His answer was unconvincing. One man hired and fired in the San Antonio archdiocese—Robert E. Lucey.

Smith's dismissal angered Mexican American leaders, who, after a meeting with the Archbishop on February 8, had believed that they had Lucey's promise "that Father Sherrill Smith would remain in his position as Moderator of the Social Action Department."[79] A chancery official now informed them that "he [Lucey] did not say that Father Sherrill Smith could continue in his position forever, because he did not know what Father Smith's behavior would be when he got back." To this reference to Smith's airport remarks, the official added: "Some of you are now going to be told that the Archbishop has managed this Archdiocese for twenty-six years and with the help of God he continues to [do so]."[80]

Things would get much worse. As Smith put it, "When you were on his side, and you were saying all the things that happened to coincide with the things he said, then it was great. But whenever he found that you had a mind of your own or some convictions of your own, then you were running up against that brick wall."[81]

The strained relations between Lucey and his activist priests grew out of the Archbishop's authoritarianism. Social justice was the cause to which he had given his life, but it was always to be *his* cause, with him alone in unquestioned control. Others could participate under his direction but were forbidden independent judgment and autonomous action. The latter Lucey considered an assault on his authority that had to be defeated. Unfortunately the 1960s could not abide such an absolute style of leadership, and confrontation became inevitable.

7. Coming Apart

In the midst of Lucey's estrangement from his social action priests, one more issue burst onto the scene: the war in Vietnam. The Archbishop had long supported the idea of collective security and international sanctions against aggressor nations. He expressed his understanding of America's role in the world in the inaugural invocation he delivered for President Johnson in 1965: "In Thy divine Providence, Oh Heavenly Father, the moral leadership of the world has been entrusted to us; the fate of humanity is in our hands; the nations look to us for survival; western civilization stands or falls with America."[1]

It was not surprising that Lucey defended President Johnson when he intensified American involvement in Vietnam. In a homily given in San Fernando Cathedral on April 2, 1967, the Archbishop told the congregation, which included President and Mrs. Johnson and twenty-nine Latin American ambassadors being feted to promote Hemisfair 68, that the United States had a "sad and heavy obligation" to halt the "unjust aggression" of the Communists in Vietnam. Curiously ignoring Pope Paul VI's repeated pleas for a ceasefire, he praised Johnson's peace initiatives as, "in view of the fact that the Communists cannot win," both "historic and magnificent." Ho Chi Minh's "scornful, arrogant and brutal" rejection of an American offer to halt the bombing was just another proof that the Communists did not want peace.[2]

The homily was widely quoted in the nation's newspapers. The *New York Times* commented that President Johnson dropped twenty dollars in the collection basket and left the church in high spirits. The *Los Angeles Times* reported that the homily upheld American war aims in Vietnam, and the Washington, D.C., *Evening Star* noted the ambassadors' delight with their Texas visit, except for Lucey's homily, which "more closely resembled a foreign policy address aimed at the envoys"—A "hawkish speech," delivered by "a frustrated Secretary of State," as one of them put it.[3]

In San Antonio, the Saint Mary's University *Rattler* charged Lucey with avoiding the "essential moral problems" of the war, including the morality of bombing North Vietnam and the destruction of people and land in the South. "It is ironic," the *Rattler* noted, "that the man who supposedly is our spiritual leader is also one of the leading exponents of the 'balance of terror.' Perhaps *frightening* is a more appropriate word. . . ."[4]

The sharpest attack on Lucey's homily came from the *National Catholic Reporter*, which likened the sermon to the Italian bishops' blessing of Mussolini's tanks on their way to Ethiopia. Besides chastizing the Archbishop for his lack of sympathy with the Pope's plea for "no more war," the news-paper regretted that Lucey did not *come* to conclusions—he simply stated them. Agreeing that the papal program con-demned unjust aggression, the editorial pointed out that "that's where the argument starts, not where it ends." The war in Vietnam might be a clearcut case of unjust aggression, but who was the aggressor?[5]

In August, 1967, President Johnson asked the Arch-bishop to go to Saigon as an observer of the Vietnamese presidential elections. Writing to Senator Ralph Yarborough a few days before his departure, Lucey admitted that he did not understand domestic anti-war sentiment but said that he hoped to discover in Vietnam "additional evidence" that American foreign policy there was sound.[6]

After his return from Southeast Asia, Lucey accompan-ied Johnson back to Texas aboard Air Force One and urged him to "stay on the beam" in Vietnam. Later, at a press conference, he assured reporters that the voting in Vietnam was fair and rejected as a "tremendous cruelty" and a "great stupidity" any suggestion that the administration withdraw troops. "If the doves would just shut their mouths, we'd be OK," he concluded.[7]

Catholic doves, especially those among the American hierarchy, were particularly bothersome to Lucey. Writing to Cardinal Francis Spellman, he trained his guns on Bishop Fulton J. Sheen, denouncing Sheen's "highly emotional" appeal to Johnson to withdraw American troops from Southeast Asia. Such an appeal caused "immense embarrassment to Catholics" in Vietnam and did "grave damage to the United States" by giving "aid and comfort to the enemy." In a letter to the Apostolic Delegate, Lucey branded Sheen an insatiable publicity hound with "the vanity of a woman."[8]

Lucey never subjected his support for American involvement in Vietnam to a critical examination. Instead, he proceeded from a priori assumptions about communist aggression and America's obligation to contain it. He would reason the same way in the emerging conflict over eccelesiastical authority.

Following Lucey's confrontation with nine of his priests on February 6, the issue of his use of episcopal authority smoldered for a while and then flared into a conflagration. On April 30 an article appeared in the *San Antonio Express* entitled "Young Priests Speak Out."[9] Four of the priests who had been present at the February meeting had given an interview to an *Express* reporter in which they accused the Archbishop of abuse of his episcopal authority. Lucey had learned of the interview but not what the priests had said. He warned them, nonetheless, that if a story was published, they would automatically be suspended. The priests tried to prevent the publication of the interview and informed the newspaper that they would be suspended if it appeared. They were told that it was too late.[10]

It may have been too late to cut the story, but it was not too late to add to it. Thus, on Sunday, April 30, when the interview was published, another article ran alongside it, announcing that the priests had been suspended. The suspensions "only verify the article and our thoughts in the interview," one priest said. Another referred to the Archbishop's sermon on the Vietnam War and observed that although Lucey himself was outspoken, he denied others the right to criticize.[11]

The local press pounced on Lucey. The *San Antonio News* sided with the priests and supported their right to question Church authority. The *San Antonio Express* commented that "if he [Lucey] has had second thoughts about the scope of the revolution triggered by Vatican Council II, they came too late." The *San Antonio Sun* recalled Lucey's defense of American action in Southeast Asia in the face of Pope Paul VI's pleas to end the bombing of North Vietnam. If the Archbishop could publicly disagree with the Pope, the *Sun* inquired, why couldn't Lucey's priests publicly disagree with him?[12] In criticizing the Archbishop's attempt to quash the interview, the conservative San Antonio press found itself defending Lucey's radical priests.

On May 4 about four hundred people attended a rally in downtown San Antonio in support of the suspended priests. The equal opportunity director of the Texas AFL-CIO spoke against Lucey, saying that the priests had been suspended "for the simple reason of aiding and preaching the plight of the working poor, the agricultural worker, the Negro and Latino."[13]

The press continued to remind its readers of Lucey's "strange brand of liberalism," which condemned before it knew the facts, defended the Vietnam War from the protection of the sanctuary, and exercised authority with no accounting to anyone. "Those liberal wings don't shine so brightly these days," one reader gloated. The Archbishop himself continued to be preoccupied with the February 6 confrontation. In a self-addressed memo, he recalled his "indictment" by "young Turks" who "slandered the Archbishop and maligned the Church. The scandal was unprecedented and inconceivable. . . ."[14]

Forgiveness did not come easily to Archbishop Lucey. Within weeks after the May rally, he began his reprisals. In June three of the nine protestors were transferred out of San Antonio, and a fourth was given an unprecedented six-year leave of absence to work in Cuernavaca, Mexico. Another priest was transferred in early September, and yet another was refused incardination into the archdiocese and sent packing. One protestor retained his position at Assumption Seminary only after the rector personally intervened. Another member of the February 6 delegation would soon be transferred in disgrace, and the ninth priest escaped censure only because Lucey reportedly could not remember his name.[15]

Spurred by the reassignments of the first group of protestors, the Priests' Senate late in June proposed the creation of personnel committees to advise the Archbishop. As reported by the *San Antonio Express-News*, the formation of the placement committees reflected the dissatisfaction of archdiocesan clergy with Lucey's transfer policy.[16]

From the very beginning Lucey had been wary of the Senate. After the first meeting on December 6, 1966, he instructed its secretary, Father Robert Walden, to send him the minutes of the meeting "for my inspection and approval before they are sent to anyone else." Lucey was angered by the Senate's complaints about pastoral assignments and told Walden to include the "nasty statements" in the minutes "because if they continue, it may be necessary to drop the whole program."[17] Now he complained to the Senate of being "slandered in the public press." He admitted delaying the announcement of the recent transfers until the last moment in order to reduce as much as possible the scandal that the "Young Turks" would cause when they learned of their reassignments. The "garbage" that these young priests were "spewing out" in the press, radio, and television constituted "an immense scandal," the likes of which he had not seen in his thirty-three years in Texas, and one that "will not be forgotten for a quarter of a century." He accused the Senate of "distorting the truth" to the newspapers and warned again that since "the idea of a Senate is on probation," it "must earn the approval of the bishops in the years to come."[18]

Next fall Lucey and the Senate were once more at odds over the issue of authority. On October 30, 1967, the Senate distributed to all the priests of the archdiocese a "white paper" on authority and obedience. Based largely on John F. McKenzie's *Authority in the Church*, the document represented an introductory probe into the complex and highly sensitive area of bishop-priest relations.[19]

The probe hit a nerve. In a twelve-page single-spaced rebuttal, Lucey accused the Senate and McKenzie of two very serious errors. First, it was "obvious heresy" to claim as McKenzie did that "authority in the Church belongs to the whole Church and not to particular officers." The Archbishop stated flatly that "the authority of the Pope is supreme" and that the bishop was charged by Christ with the mandate to teach, govern, and sanctify. "The clergy and laity who will not believe the Bishop shall be condemned," he added.[20]

The second error was McKenzie's statement that "love is the only power which the New Testament knows," a notion Lucey called "openly heretical." "In the Church, authority is not subject to love," he declared. Ecclesiastical authority "is the power to rule, to teach, to punish"; McKenzie, however, "confused authority which is power, . . . with love, which is not power." As the possessor of power and authority in the Church, the bishop had Christ's solemn assurance that "if one of the faithful rejects the Bishop's teaching, he rejects Christ and . . . our heavenly Father." After passing on the rumor that McKenzie would soon leave the Society of Jesus, the

Archbishop stated that "it might have been better all around if he had left the community, willingly or otherwise, before he wrote [this] very dangerous book."[21]

The chairman of the Senate, Father Clarence Leopold, responded that the white paper had been designed to open the door on the subject of authority, not slam it shut with definitive declarations. The Senate was not attempting to teach or deny any Church doctrine, he insisted.[22] But by this time the affair had passed the point of no return. Someone had sent the *National Catholic Reporter* a copy of the Archbishop's letter to the Senate. On November 29, the newspaper published excerpts from the letter and observed that the book Lucey was attacking had just won the 1967 Cardinal Spellman Award of the Catholic Theological Society of America for outstanding work in the field of theology.[23]

In a later issue, McKenzie himself regretted that the Archbishop had not contacted him directly about his writings but instead "chose to come blasting out like John Wayne defending the Alamo." He clarified two statements that Lucey had denounced as heretical. Authority "does belong to the Church and is vested in particular officers, not, of course, in the same grade and degree," McKenzie insisted. He denied having said that the Pope and the bishops have no more authority than anyone else. According to McKenzie, Vatican II recommended a broader participation in authority, as evidenced in its recommendation of priests' senates and parish councils. "These have been understood as a sharing of authority, not a diminution of the same," he stated. "My thesis . . . is that clergy and laity, by their membership in the Church and by sacramental character, have received something which makes them apt and able to share in Church authority." Lucey, however, seemed to believe that "Jesus instituted an apostolic college and committed to the college the task of founding a church." McKenzie implied that such a church would not be of divine origin and suggested that "if the word *heresy* is to be tossed about carelessly, perhaps the Archbishop's thesis deserves closer study."[24]

As for the statement that "love is the only power the New Testament knows," McKenzie agreed to rephrase it to read that "love is the supreme power which the New Testament knows." Whatever the adjective, he emphasized that the New Testament "knows no ecclesiastical act which is not a fulfillment of love." However, "if I read the Archbishop correctly, he seems to say that authority and love have nothing to do with each other." If this is what Lucey meant, McKenzie observed, then "the rest of us can only be grateful that we are not within the ecclesiastical jurisdiction of San Antonio." In conclusion, he challenged Lucey either to press formal heresy charges or retract his accusations.[25]

The Archbishop counterattacked. He contended that the *National Catholic Reporter* had distorted his letter of October 30, and so he had his own newspaper, the *Alamo Messenger*, print what purported to be the original letter. The *Messenger* in fact published a sanitized version, eliminating most of the Archbishop's epithets and excising the rumor about McKenzie's leaving the Jesuits. To many of the local clergy, such deception exemplified the tactics Lucey employed to protect his power.[26]

Even after the McKenzie affair had blown over, the Senate continued to be a source of consternation for Lucey. In November it began a series of discussions about the personal development of priests and their need to remain person-oriented in their ministry. Lucey did not understand the new personalism and decided to expose this "solemnly proclaimed theological nonsense." He examined a Senate discussion question that read: "Is the primary object of a priest's love God, or His people, or God and His people?" One priest suggested that initially he must make God's people the center of his love because they were the means to God himself. To which Lucey responded:

This is certainly a new kind of theology. It is strange that a man can get into the holy priesthood without having learned to love God above all the creatures of God. It would be quite an achievement to study in a Catholic elementary school, a Catholic high school, and a major seminary without learning how to observe the first and greatest commandment. And if on the day of his ordination, he actually loves his Creator above all creatures, how does it happen that the sacrament of the priesthood reverses his love for God and causes him to love creatures above the Creator?[27]

In February, 1968, the secretary of the Priests' Senate resigned in protest over Lucey's screening of the minutes of every meeting. At the same time the Senate passed a resolution stating that it wanted to study transfers and promotions in the archdiocese and requested that no personnel changes be made until it had an opportunity to investigate the circumstances.[28] All these actions indicated how far apart Lucey and the Senate were.

Disturbed by the increasing intransigence of their Archbishop and the ineffectiveness of the Senate, forty-one priests assembled in Saint Ann's Parish Hall on March 3, 1968, and formed the "Priests' Association of the Archdiocese of San Antonio." The association defined itself as a "brotherhood and fellowship of the presbyterate, diocesan and religious priests, in union with the Archbishop, who freely and responsibly collaborate in the common purpose of advancing collectively and personally the professional, human, and spiritual fulfillment of all priests." A letter to the Archbishop dated March 3 informed him of the association's existence and announced a general meeting for March 21 to which Lucey and all archdiocesan priests were invited. The letter was signed by the association's steering committee: Fathers James Brandes, Roy Rihn, Sherrill Smith, Joseph Till, Joseph Nowak, and Paul Search.[29] Depending on one's point of view, the association was either a patent attempt to overthrow the established ecclesiastical authority of the Archbishop or a sign of hope, despite the failure of the Priests' Senate, that lines of communication between Lucey and his priests could still be established.

Less than three weeks after its formation, the association took up the case of Father Marion Swize, a priest of the San Antonio archdiocese assigned to Saint Rose of Lima Parish in Schulenburg, Texas. By general agreement, Swize was an intelligent and dedicated priest. He was also one of the "Young Turks" who had confronted Lucey on February 6 at the chancery office. On March 12, Swize was informed that he would be transferred shortly because of complaints about his activities at Bishop Forest High School in Schulenburg, where he taught religion. The accusations against him were not specified but had something to do with a sex education course he was offering. His accusers were also unnamed.[30]

Swize wrote to Lucey on March 16 that he was not contesting the Archbishop's *right* to transfer him, but only the timing of the transfer, which appeared to justify the complaints leveled against him. He then requested a meeting with Lucey "to find out what there is about me that is so unpriestly in my behavior and teaching at Bishop Forest High School."[31] At the same time Swize appealed to the Senate for due process. But it was all to no avail. Swize was notified again that he would be transferred as of March 20.[32]

A day after the transfer, the Priests' Senate objected to Lucey. Swize's letter of appointment stated that his reassignment was made "upon consultation with the Senate," implying that the Senate had approved the transfer, when in fact it had not. Rather, the Senate had urged that the charges against Swize be made in his presence so that he would have a chance to defend himself. The Senate further had recommended that no action be taken until Swize's innocence or guilt was proved.[33] Lucey ignored the Senate's objection; Swize's transfer remained in effect.

The Priests' Association, now with approximately 125 members out of a total of 427 archdiocesan priests, continued to press Lucey for a resolution of the Swize case and for the establishment of a permanent archdiocesan grievance and personnel board. On April 6 the association resolved to work out the problems "here at home, if this be possible" and pledged to avoid publicity "so long as there is hope that our internal problems are actually tending toward resolution." The association informed Lucey, however, that in order to keep their hope alive, they needed a sign of good faith. It therefore requested some positive action on the Swize case and on the proposal for a grievance board before their next general meeting on April 25, 1968.[34]

Lucey interpreted the resolution as an ultimatum. "If they don't like his good faith, they will carry their garbage to the public press, to television studios and radio stations," he wrote in a memo. A "little group of willful men" who "hate divine authority" was now threatening "immense scandal" to the Church. If it was a fight they wanted, he would give them one.[35]

The April 25 meeting was stormy. Lucey's tactics were condemned, and the Priests' Association resolved to continue its support of Marion Swize. After the meeting Father Joseph Till, the association's press secretary, told an *Express* reporter that Swize had never been able to learn the precise accusations made against him. "This type of thing has happened before," Till stated. "In other cases frustration was involved because there was no group to stand behind the person." With the creation of the Priests' Association, however, that had changed. On April 28 the Sunday *San Antonio Express-News* reported Till's remarks.[36] Thus, while the Swize affair was still smoldering, a new personality came to occupy center stage—Joseph R. Till, pastor of Saint Agnes Parish. Till was one of the few San Antonio priests whose inflexible spirit could match Lucey's. Conservative in his politics and theology (he had consistently disapproved of Smith's and Killian's social activism), Till had joined the association because it seemed the only way of protecting himself from the Archbishop's arbitrariness. His position as press secretary made him both hot copy among San Antonio newspaper reporters and the object of Lucey's anger.

Till's printed remarks about the injustice done to Swize and others rankled. Then another issue brought down the Archbishop's wrath on Till's head. In December, 1967, at the urging of the Senate, an archdiocesan tithing system was introduced to replace a very unpopular Development Fund campaign. According to the plan, by the tenth of each month each parish was to send to the chancery 10 percent of its ordinary monthly income. The first four hundred dollars of regular parish monthly income was not subject to the tithe. In mid-May, 1968, Lucey suspended the tithing system when it fell short of its projected 1968 quarterly goal. In its stead he imposed a quota system that assessed each of the 144 archdiocesan parishes a certain amount based on the individual church's net taxable income for 1967. The Priests' Association immediately protested against the change. In a May 21 letter to Lucey, Till stated that the parish tithing plan had been the product of the general consensus of priests and laity in the archdiocese and that the Archbishop had not given it "a fair and sufficient time to prove its worth." As for the parish quota system, he termed it "unjust, burdensome, repressive, and a system which no one seems able to fathom mathematically." Till informed Lucey of the association's resolution and was quoted extensively in the next day's newspaper.[37]

On June 11 Till was officially summoned to the chancery and informed that his press releases of April 28 and May 22 were "offensive, insulting and slanderous" to the person of the Archbishop and as such constituted a violation of canon law. In a letter to Till three days later, Lucey informed him that he was initiating formal proceedings "to determine whether or not you have been guilty of the crime condemned by Canon 2344, and if such be true, the gravity of the offense." The Archbishop warned Till that the "evidence in this case is abundant" and assured him that "the Holy See means to defend the authority of bishops."[38]

Two days after the Till monitum, the *San Antonio News* reported that Father James Brandes, director of the Catholic Welfare Bureau, would soon be fired and transferred out of the city.[39] Brandes was a charter member of the Priests' Association and a vociferous critic of archdiocesan personnel assignments. He had chaired several association meetings and at the crucial April 25 gathering had excoriated Lucey's vicar general, Monsignor Leroy Manning, for his criticism of dissident priests. Shortly after the *News* story appeared, Brandes was removed from the Bureau and transferred to Victoria, Texas. His June 18 letter of appointment from Lucey gave no reason for the move.[40]

On July 25, 1968, Pope Paul VI reaffirmed the Church's traditional ban on artificial means of birth control in his controversial encyclical *Humanae Vitae*. In an August pastoral letter, Archbishop Lucey attacked the "specious arguments" of "alleged theologians" who had criticized *Humanae Vitae*. Such critics "were fighting the Holy Spirit and the wisdom of the ages," and thus "they never had a chance."[41]

An index of the frustration and anger present in the archdiocese is the letter Brandes sent to the *San Antonio Express-News* in response to Lucey's pastoral. The priest deplored the way "the senile Archbishop of San Antonio," as Brandes described him, was "rant[ing] callously" over a sensitive moral issue. He pointed out Lucey's use of the past tense when speaking of anyone who disagreed with his judgment that the Pope's encyclical had permanently settled the contraception question. To Brandes this "outburst of triumphalism" showed Lucey's "appalling lack of contact with the present state of the Church."[42]

Fall came and with it more trouble. On September 4, Lucey wrote to Joseph Till, informing him that "for the good of souls and the welfare of the Church" he was being transferred to Saint Michael Parish in Cuero, Texas, effective September 18. "If you have any objections to this transfer," Lucey stated, "you are to submit them to this office according to Canon 2159 by Tuesday, September 10, 1968."[43] Lucey anticipated some objection from Till and had a plan for dealing with him. Following closely the procedure of canon law as outlined in a memo from Monsignor Manning, Lucey first was to tell Till of his transfer and inform him of his right to submit any objections in writing. Next the Archbishop was to submit these objections to two of his consultors and discuss the transfer with them. Then a second letter was to be sent to Till, "advising him that the discussion has taken place and that the reasons which he submitted do not outweigh the reasons for the transfer; hence it is still in effect." A third letter was to follow, "confirming the transfer, setting a specific date and informing him that as of that date the parish is *ipso facto* vacant."[44]

On September 8 Till responded that the reassignment had come as a "profound shock." He noted the reason given for the transfer, "the good of souls and the welfare of the Church," and surmised that his continued presence at Saint Agnes was considered "harmful to souls and detrimental to the welfare of the Church," serious accusations against his priestly discharge of parochial duties and his personal moral conduct and deportment. He demanded specific canonical reasons for the contemplated transfer and sufficient time to study them, and he insisted on a personal meeting with Lucey because in the transfer "there is something specially unmentioned that needs to be brought into the light of day." Anything less than a full open discussion, Till said, would be a "monstrous breach of good faith."[45]

Pausing only long enough to transfer another antagonist, Father Clarence Leopold, Lucey replied to Till on September 10. Because Till had given no reasons why the transfer should not take place, it remained in effect. Furthermore, Lucey refused to see Till before September 18 because his calendar was too crowded.[46]

A sharp retort came from Till. The priest termed the reason for his transfer "none other than your vindictiveness to 'get me' because of my relationship to PAASA [the Priests' Association]." A blind man could not fail to see the pattern of repression associated with the transfer, Till declared. He castigated Lucey for hiding behind canon law, "making yourself believe that whatever you do is always lily-white, righteous and absolutely infallible," and warned him that "the day is coming when this façade is going to come crumbling down." On that note Till stated that he was taking a leave of absence as of September 19 for as long as was necessary "either to detect a change in heart on your part or to await the day when another bishop, more benign, understanding and sympathetic, will come along here to San Antonio."[47]

Beneath the pattern of repression evidenced in the string of transfers lay the trampled expectations of the San Antonio clergy. They had had reasons to anticipate exciting advances for the Church in San Antonio after Vatican II. The Council had encouraged bishops to share their authority in a collegial spirit, and Lucey's enthusiasm for the Council and his long, liberal record on social issues heightened expectations of shared responsibility. But more than this, the Archbishop's personality had seemed to stimulate optimism. As one priest remarked, "Even his enemies would have to admit that Lucey stood for something. He spoke out. He was fearless and articulate and eloquent. He not only said good things, but he said them in a way that swept you up into the fervor of it."[48] Such optimism, however, was unfounded, for when the issue of authority emerged, clerical expectations ran into episcopal intransigence. A rapid erosion of traditional priestly docility followed.

From Archbishop Lucey's vantage point, the Priests' Association threatened his personal authority and the entire episcopal structure. What made the confrontation especially painful was the fact that it came not from outsiders but from the very ones who ought to have been most loyal—his own priests. Something diabolical had taken hold of his archdiocese. Never the hireling, Lucey was not about to desert the sheep. He was determined to stay and fight.

For the executive board of the Priests' Association, however, the Leopold and Till transfers were the last straw, and on September 11 it began the process that would culminate in Lucey's retirement. At a meeting at Assumption Seminary, the board decided to send a letter to Pope Paul VI requesting the resignation of Archbishop Lucey. Written by Sherrill Smith and Roy Rihn, rector of the seminary, copies of the letter were sent to Lucey, the Apostolic Delegate, Luigi Raimondi, and several other high Church officials.[49]

"We the undersigned priests, serving in the Archdiocese of San Antonio, Texas, seek the resignation of Archbishop Robert E. Lucey as Ordinary of this place," the letter began. Pointing out that the signers represented a broad spectrum of age and diocesan responsibility, the letter summarized the situation: "There is an atmosphere of fear, alienation and dissatisfaction on the part of many priests in this Archdiocese," an atmosphere "currently intensified" by the latest in "a long line of vindictive and repressive transfers" of priests. "The occasion is current but the history of such happenings here is long."[50]

Contending that a pattern of "aloofness, repression and paternalism" on Lucey's part had frustrated their efforts to promote the spiritual well-being of the archdiocese, the priests advanced a solution. In addition to Lucey's resignation, they requested the creation of an outside fact-finding commission to visit the archdiocese and investigate local conditions. Finally, the priests hoped that they would be "realistically and honestly consulted" in the naming of Lucey's successor in order to "help forestall the appointment of another Ordinary who is unable to bring a true collegial spirit to his relationship with clergy and faithful."[51]

The letter closed with a warning. Promising not to publicize their protest and to remain silent so long as there was hope that their appeal was being seriously heard, the priests declared: "We want you to know that we are so determined that if we shall not have received within thirty days some positive sign of action on our requests, we will make this letter public to the news media, and we will involve the Catholic laity in our appeal."[52]

Dated September 16, 1968, the letter was made available for signing at an emergency meeting of the Priests' Association at Assumption Seminary. It was read aloud by Charles Herzig, and the members in attendance had the option of signing or not signing. Fifty-one priests of the more than one hundred present signed the letter, and all the priests at the meeting pledged themselves to secrecy regarding its contents.[53]

Lucey's reaction to the letter was quick and bitter. To the Apostolic Delegate he wrote on September 20 of the "incredible and fantastic charges" made against him by a "dozen hard-core troublemakers," two of whom, Roy Rihn and Joseph Till, he named specifically. He accused Rihn of engineering the scandal and Till of spreading it in the press. Lucey was greatly embarrassed by the affair and particularly incensed by the thirty-day ultimatum to the Holy See. In his fifty-two years of priestly life, he said, "I have never read anything so insolent and so arrogant."[54]

In another letter to the Delegate six days later, Lucey again condemned his priests' "clumsy adventure in ecclesiastical blackmail." Charging them with "reckless hypocrisy," he denied being vindictive and uncommunicative and accused the Priests' Association of disgracing his clergy. Furthermore, calling for an outside fact-finding commission had been "a desperate gamble" for the "51." "Our loyal priests would welcome any sort of canonical trial for the conspirators," he insisted.[55]

In view of his confidence that an investigation would

make a shambles of his opponents' case and elicit a loyal response from the archdiocesan clergy, it is puzzling that Lucey made no effort to promote one. In fact, as events would soon reveal, he dragged his feet over just such an investigation.

Time was beginning to run out for both sides. Having sent the letter to the Apostolic Delegate in mid-September, the "51" had no response until October 10, when the Delegate urged Roy Rihn to use his influence with the priests "to pacify them and encourage them to have confidence that the Holy See is vitally interested in the situation." Stating that he wrote "at the direction of the Holy See" and to Rihn as rector of the major seminary, the Delegate asked him to "discreetly emphasize to your fellow priests the delicacy of this matter and seek to induce them to patience and confidence."[56]

Meanwhile Lucey was planning his counterattack. In mid-October he reported to the Delegate that none of the addressees had responded to the September 16 letter and that the "51" were getting "quite desperate." The Archbishop revealed that he had made copies of the notorious letter and distributed them to some loyal priests and laymen, along with his rebuttal. In the event that "the rebels publish their garbage," thirty laymen would speak over the radio and television and in the newspapers in the Archbishop's defense.[57]

Another part of the Archbishop's strategy for dealing with the "51" focused on Assumption Seminary personnel: Roy Rihn, the rector; Robert Walden, the vice-rector and former secretary of the Priests' Senate; Louis Michalski, dean of men and board member of the Priests' Association; and Raymond Henke, spiritual director at the seminary and one of the "Young Turks" of February 6. All of these priests had signed the resignation petition; all had to be fired. Lucey laid out his strategy on October 17. In a letter to a loyal priest he proposed to create a "special three-priest committee" that would go to Assumption Seminary and interview "key witnesses" early the following week so that "by perhaps

Wednesday or Thursday a decision can be conveyed to those involved . . . if all goes well." Having synchronized the procedures so that everything could be done "in an appropriate manner at the proper time," he addressed a crisp letter to Rihn: "Reports indicate unfavorable developments among the faculty and student body of Assumption Seminary. I have appointed a committee to get the facts immediately. . . . I am instructing these priests [the committee] to interview key persons in the seminary at the earliest possible date and give me an immediate report."[58]

Rihn welcomed the announcement. "All of us here are praying and working for the kind of Church in which nothing will have to be done in secrecy or in darkness," he wrote. He observed that it was "supremely ironic" that the Archbishop was so "exquisitely conscientious" about appointing a fact-finding committee for the seminary "when you have so aggressively resisted the appointment of a fact-finding committee to come to your archdiocese." Rihn welcomed the committee, "but I do not welcome the real reason behind it." Aware that the investigation was designed to furnish evidence to make his dismissal and that of the others "look good and ever so righteous," Rihn had "no doubt that you will have your pretext—the window dressing will be just great, the smoke screen will be a masterpiece—I am saddened but unafraid, because I am confident the truth will out—perhaps not now but eventually."[59]

The investigation at Assumption Seminary came off on "Black Monday," October 21, 1968. At one o'clock in the afternoon, the Archbishop, with four priests and four laymen in tow, made an unannounced visit to the seminary. With one priest guarding a group of seminarians waiting to be questioned, and another priest standing in front of the interrogation room, Lucey's committee grilled individual students on seminary discipline, including reports of drinking, dating, and disregard for traditional spirituality. The inquisition ended only with Rihn's arrival and a sharp exchange with the Archbishop.[60]

The time limit stated in the resignation letter had run out before Black Monday. On October 17, Louis Michalski of the Priests' Association telegraphed the Apostolic Delegate in Washington: "The thirty days have passed. We have received no response to any of the requests. We reiterate the pressing urgency of the situation." Dismissing the Delegate's correspondence with Rihn as unclear, Michalski asked him for an "unambiguous" reply to the priests' requests: "Has any positive action been initiated concerning the resignation of Archbishop Lucey—yes or no? Is a fact-finding commission being constituted by you to come here as soon as possible— yes or no? Will the clergy and responsible laity be realistically and honestly consulted in the naming of the successor to Archbishop Lucey—yes or no?" Michalski indicated again that the crisis was now nearly impossible to contain but promised to wait until midnight on Tuesday, October 22 for the Delegate's reply.[61]

The first sign that Lucey was losing the battle came on October 21. The Apostolic Delegate had an aide deliver a letter to the Archbishop in which Raimondi first assured Lucey of his sympathy regarding the state of affairs in San Antonio and then got to the point:

> In view of the trend of events it occurred to me that it may be helpful if you took the initiative and requested the Holy See to appoint some competent person to examine the situation in the Archdiocese. The record of your ministry is so splendid that there would be nothing to fear from this. You would be vindicated in the public opinion.
>
> Your Excellency may propose the name of one or another Prelate who could be assigned for this purpose. You understand, of course, that this is a sugges-

tion advanced with the desire of easing the situation and avoiding serious consequences.[62]

Lucey knew enough about Church politics to recognize an offer he could not refuse, and so he dutifully followed the Delegate's advice. On October 22 he hand-delivered a letter announcing a new course of action to Father Eustace Struckoff, O.F.M., the recently elected chairman of the Priests' Senate: "All of us are aware that the unrest and controversy among some of the clergy of our country are harmful to the Church. Our archdiocese has experienced some of these difficulties. For that reason I have requested the Holy See to appoint a neutral observer who will come here to review the situation." Lucey asked Struckoff to convey the contents of the letter to key members of the Priests' Association.[63]

The response of Rihn, Walden, Michalski, and Monsignor Joseph Nowak was a product of the enormous tension and suspicion of the times. Clearly this was a "positive sign" from the Delegate that some action was being taken, but it came wrapped in ecclesiastical protocol. According to canon law, no "outside observer," bishop, or commission may come into the diocese of another bishop without the explicit permission of the resident ordinary. Lucey had refused to consider any of the three demands in the September 16 letter; now he was permitting, even calling in, an observer to review the archdiocesan situation. Surely the "51" and their leaders ought to have perceived that the Archbishop would never have taken this step unless tremendous pressure had been brought on him, and the only authority capable of that kind of pressure was the Holy See. But the association leaders came away with a different interpretation of the October 22 letter; they concluded that the Holy See had ignored their request. Rihn and the others found nothing in the letter "to indicate that Rome or Washington had responded by requiring Archbishop Lucey to make this request for a neutral observer."[64]

Admitting that they were amateurs in deciphering ecclesiastical protocol, the four priests urged Struckoff to contact the Apostolic Delegate and have Raimondi call Michalski by midnight, October 22, "if he wished to convey to us that Archbishop Lucey's letter had not been written on his own initiative, and that it did indeed signal the 'positive sign of action' we awaited." The four told Struckoff that such an assurance from the Delegate would be sufficient to prevent publication of the letter. Struckoff called the Delegate that afternoon, October 22, but was told that he was unavailable. He delivered the message and urged the Delegate to return his call. About 9:30 P.M. Raimondi's secretary called Struckoff with a message from the Delegate: "Tell the priests to accept the Archbishop's letter."[65]

The "51" were true to their word. On October 24 they called a press conference in the Renaissance Room of the Menger Hotel in downtown San Antonio and announced the contents of their September 16 letter. In a statement read by Louis Michalski, the "51" regretted having to make the letter public, but said that the official silence of the hierarchy had forced the issue. They lamented the "defensive posture" of Church officials, whose prime concern appeared to be avoiding publicity. Deploring the communication impasse and the "unbearable lack of rapport" with Lucey, they called for an end to the Archbishop's style of unilateral decisionmaking, and, in fact, an end to Lucey's career: "We feel it is time for him to step aside so that the 500,000 Roman Catholics in San Antonio may have the kind of responsive leadership that this age requires."[66]

The Apostolic Delegate was becoming alarmed by the situation. One hundred and twenty-seven of the 160 students at Assumption Seminary informed Raimondi of their "deep regret and amazement" at the lack of response from the official Church to the priests' requests and unequivocally endorsed the "51." He received from the Parents' Club of Assumption Seminary a telegram that strongly protested against Lucey's actions and gave its full support to the faculty and program. He may also have gotten wind of plans by Catholic laity for a huge rally in support of the priests. Moreover, petitions calling for Lucey's resignation were circulating among the laity, while numerous priests throughout the archdiocese were defending the "51" from their pulpits.[67] Raimondi expressed his concern about all this to Lucey. Referring to the letter from the Assumption students, he observed that it was all the more "surprising and distressing" because "twenty or more dioceses are represented there." "Does Your Excellency have some intentions with regard to it?" he asked. "I will be pleased for further information about this situation."[68]

On October 30 Lucey fired Rihn, Walden, Michalski, and Henke from Assumption Seminary. When word of the firings got out late that afternoon, a large number of priests went to the Archbishop's residence to protest, but Lucey refused to meet with them. That evening when he arrived at Saint Pius X Church for confirmation services, Lucey was confronted with a "pray-in" rally, organized by local parishioners. On top of all this, another letter to Pope Paul VI was drafted and signed by seventeen more priests. The letter noted that the predicted reprisals had begun and that conditions in the archdiocese were deteriorating rapidly. In the next day's newspaper, there were banner headlines describing the events of "Black Monday" and front page pictures of the priests standing on Lucey's lawn.[69]

Clearly the situation was out of control. The Archbishop needed help. The older conservative clergy, with whom he had never had much rapport, could not provide the brilliant rear guard action that was demanded. But fortunately for Lucey, there was one man who could and did, William Killian, the radical priest and editor of the *Alamo Messenger*. Killian stepped into Lucey's corner and evened up the fight.

Killian had made something of an about-face after his

banishment to Via Coeli in February, 1967. He had returned from the New Mexico retreat and made his peace with Lucey, accepting, in effect, the primacy of episcopal authority. While he maintained his support for the Valley farm workers' movement throughout 1967 and 1968, he never challenged Lucey's retreat from the issue. Nor did he support Smith as vigorously as before. When Smith became persona non grata, the *Alamo Messenger* dropped all editorial support for his labor activities. Killian was deeply loyal to the Archbishop, as a son to a father, and now began to engineer the necessary rear guard action.

In a memo to the Archbishop dated October 30, Killian outlined the strategy that Lucey would use to fight the dissidents. First, the Archbishop should call together a select group of pastors and inform them of the personnel changes at Assumption Seminary, explaining some of the reasons for the faculty changes confidentially. "This is communication at its best," Killian said. "It also gives a positive tone to the meeting." He next advised Lucey to strive to enlist his pastors' support against the critical sermons and resignation petitions circulating throughout the archdiocese. "We are now down to nut cracking time," he explained, "and not one of us can afford the luxury of sitting comfortably on well-padded fences well away from the fray." Killian told the Archbishop to exhort his pastors to act like pastors; "the subtle threat here should be that fidelity to the episcopacy is a requisite qualification for a pastor."[70]

Anticipating resistance from the eight pastors who had signed the September 16 letter, Killian said that "it is Monsignor Manning's chore to program some of the loyalists to react firmly, swiftly and spontaneously to such a possible outburst." In closing, he reiterated his main point: the Archbishop should stress supportive pastoral action, not just elicit a pledge of loyalty from these men. Specifically, he wanted Lucey to get the pastors to squelch any petition drives against the Archbishop and have them read personally from the pulpit the next Sunday a letter from Lucey that Killian would write.[71]

Following the advice, Lucey called in sixty selected pastors the next day, introduced them to the new Assumption Seminary faculty, and asked to forbid the use of Church property for resignation petitions (a reversal of Lucey's position on the 1964 Civil Rights Act). Finally, he requested that the pastors use the pulpit to calm the people; and "if you can't trust the assistant [pastor], read the pastoral letter at all masses yourself."[72]

A second part of Killian's strategy followed from Lucey's meeting with the pastors. Opposed to any open-ended mediation of the dispute, he told the Archbishop that the task now was "to get the spotlight off of you, try to settle the troops down and search realistically for a solution." To that end he proposed that as a result of Lucey's meeting with the pastors, a number of them "be induced to decide to form a board of inquiry" that would examine the statements and actions of the "68." The pastors would empanel such a board, Killian went on, secure Lucey's approval, and then begin investigating. This approach would get the Archbishop off the hook and get ten or fifteen pastors to "share the steam." The board of inquiry would appear as a genuine attempt by the Church to get at the root of the problem, Killian said, and if the "68" did not cooperate, "we have the lever of making these legitimate charges against them. It will give us the upper hand."[73]

The editor suggested that Monsignor Manning and another Lucey loyalist be given the job of "spontaneously getting this thing going in the next twenty-four to thirty-six hours." Such a step would be "putting the Church [i.e., Lucey] in an offensive position." Killian warned, however, that Manning must be very careful about the loyalty of the board. "When the fact-finding board has been established and Monsignor Martin [a loyalist] has been elected chairman," he wrote, the board would then ask the dissidents to "substantiate or retract the charges" in their letter. This would "blow the vague generalities about inability to communicate sky high." Finally, during the six or eight weeks needed for the fact-finding committee to do its work, a policy of total silence should be followed.[74] Killian was convinced that this positive, head-on approach to the problem would impress the Apostolic Delegate. In a memo dated November 4, the Archbishop agreed to the whole program.[75]

Meanwhile, Lucey continued his correspondence with the Apostolic Delegate. In an October 31 letter, he informed the Delegate of his firing of the four members of the seminary faculty. He also relayed his decision to establish an archdiocesan board of mediation and closed his letter with this comment:

> I am not unmindful of the generous offer which Your Excellency made to me a couple of weeks ago regarding a review of the situation here by a responsible party, but since the Association has adamantly refused to accept any investigation on a high level, I think that for the moment we might allow our priests to study everything that has happened for possibly three or four weeks and then reveal the truth to everybody who will read it.[76]

The Archbishop was convinced that the tide had turned.

On Sunday, November 3, Lucey's pastoral letter was read from every pulpit in the San Antonio archdiocese. Quoting from Hebrews 13:17, "obey your superiors and be subject to them," the Archbishop told how the Church in San Antonio was "wounded publicly" by the "hostility, dissension and controversy" of the recent days. He called on his co-workers in Christ to "renew the ideals of the priesthood" and work together with him in "mutual respect and friendship." But his words were ineffective. That evening more than two thousand supporters of the "68" jammed the San Antonio

Convention Center to demonstrate their opposition to the Archbishop's leadership.[77]

Tension in San Antonio remained high. The day after the rally, Rihn, Michalski, Walden, and Henke announced that they were taking indefinite leaves of absence from Lucey's jurisdiction. Resignation petitions gathered more names daily, while local and national newspapers and magazines continued to publicize the controversy. *Newsweek* magazine ran a story on "The Priests' Rebellion," as did the *Washington Post*. The *New York Times* did a couple of articles on dissent within the Catholic Church in general and the San Antonio affair in particular. Both the *San Antonio Express-News* and the *Light* provided daily coverage of the dispute.[78]

All this did not escape the attention of the Apostolic Delegate, who informed Lucey that an observer had been designated and would arrive in San Antonio on November 29. Bishop William G. Connare of Greensburg, Pennsylvania, Raimondi's personal friend, would conduct interviews with all interested parties from Monday, December 2, to Sunday, December 8.[79] There is no indication that Lucey had specifically asked for Connare as the Holy See's neutral observer.

Bishop Connare was a stranger to virtually everyone in San Antonio, including Lucey, although the two prelates had had limited contact at the annual meeting of the American hierarchy in Washington. To the priests Connare was completely unknown, and due to the secrecy of his arrival, he was quickly dubbed the "Phantom of Greensburg." Members of the Priests' Association intended to meet Connare at the San Antonio Airport, but apparently the Bishop took the more indirect route suggested in a letter from Lucey to his protégé, Thomas Drury, Bishop of Corpus Christ. At Drury's direction, Connare flew to Corpus Christi, Texas, and was driven the 150 miles to San Antonio.[80] In any event, the first evidence that the outside observer had arrived in San Antonio came in a letter from Connare to the priests dated Monday, December 2, 1968. The Bishop announced that he was staying at the Incarnate Word Guest House in the city and was ready to listen to any and all who wished to discuss the problem at hand.[81]

Events now took a new turn. In a letter to Lucey from the Delegate dated November 29—the day Connare arrived in San Antonio and three days before he began his investigation—the hard facts of ecclesiastical life surfaced. "Quite independently of the current developments in the archdiocese," Raimondi said,

> I am requested to recall to Your Excellency the desire of the Holy See to implement the dispositions of the decree, "Christus Dominus" (N. 21) of the Second Vatican Council and the motu proprio "Ecclesiae Sanctae" (I, n.11) regarding the resignation of Prelates with the care of souls at the age of seventy-five.
>
> Although the Holy Father reserves to himself the decision on the petition, Prelates are expected to submit their resignation when the limit is reached.
>
> Apart from the general discipline in this matter, as I had the opportunity to tell Your Excellency on the occasion of your recent visit to the Apostolic Delegation, there is also the desire of the Holy See to avoid embarrassment to Your Excellency and to protect the good of souls. Public polemics and discussions of the conciliar norms are unfavorable to this.
>
> I am sure Your Excellency is fully aware of the present delicate situation. I know too that you earnestly desire to avoid any blemish on your splendid record as well as anything that would place you in an untenable position with the people

to whom you have given such splendid example of devotion to the Church and her discipline.

While the Holy See awaits your petition, she assures you that the esteem and consideration you have enjoyed in her eyes remain undiminished. The present action stems from the desire to put into practice what the Vatican Council has judged to be most convenient for all concerned.

Finally, I repeat my personal sentiments of true devotion and admiration for your zeal, courage and dedication. I desire to be of every possible help to Your Excellency.

While recommending myself to your good prayers, I remain,

Luigi Raimondi[82]

It is difficult to avoid the conclusion that the decision about Lucey's fate had been made prior to any observations by the Vatican's neutral party, and thus that the whole Connare episode was a charade. Connare himself stated in an interview that when he returned to Greensburg, he submitted no formal report to the Apostolic Delegate because "no report was ever asked for."[83]

Lucey was angered by the Delegate's request for his resignation. "I would be less than frank," he wrote to Raimondi five days later, "if I did not assure Your Excellency that when procedures in this case become publicly known, they will be a source of utmost embarrassment to me, to my relatives and to my friends. When a prelate must resign under fire, it is profoundly humiliating, particularly if he has done no wrong."[84]

On that same day Lucey wrote to his old friend Cardinal Amleto Giovanni Cicognani, Secretary of State for the Vatican, asking him to intervene. He insisted that the request for his resignation be delayed until more favorable circumstances prevailed; otherwise "my good name will be unjustly tarnished." Aware that Raimondi might demand his resignation, he asked Cicognani to help avert "an unfortunate situation."[85]

Lucey's attempt to secure Vatican intercession failed. The Delegate again asked for his resignation, and on December 10 the Archbishop complied.

> Your Holiness:
>
> By this letter I offer Your Holiness my resignation as Archbishop of San Antonio, Texas. I am seventy-seven years of age.
>
> With continued prayers that God will give your Holiness strength and courage, I remain
>
> > Sincerely yours in Christ,
> >
> > + Robert E. Lucey
> > Archbishop of San Antonio[86]

Lucey wrote out the letter, and his vicar general typed and mailed it that day. No one else knew of the Delegate's pressure on him or of his resignation.[87]

Lucey vented some of his feelings about his forced resignation to Cicognani. "It seems strange that Archbishop Raimondi should send a busy Bishop to Texas on a fact-finding mission and then make a fatal decision before the Bishop could return to the Delegate with the facts. I hesitate to believe that the Holy See was putting so much pressure on the Apostolic Delegate to hasten my retirement." Accepting the situation, Lucey suggested that a period of "several months, if not a year," be allowed to pass before his resignation was accepted in order to "prevent astonishment on the part of the Bishops of our country. . . ." Insisting again that

the charges against him were "completely without foundation," he warned of great harm to the Church if the Holy See
buckled under pressure from a small group of rebel priests.[88]

In San Antonio, meanwhile, Bishop Connare completed
his probe and asked the archdiocesan priests for their prayers
as he "studied the facts you have so graciously shared with
me." The Killian-inspired archdiocesan fact-finding committee also completed its work after more than three weeks of
hearings.[89] And there the matter stood. Connare submitted
his notes to the Apostolic Delegate but made no public statement or report to the San Antonio priests. The fact-finding
committee's transcript of hearings was buried in a chancery
safe, to be recovered by a researcher nearly ten years later.
Lucey himself, obviously undisposed to reveal that he had
submitted his resignation, was instructed by the Delegate to
continue the normal work of the archdiocese and make "no
outer indication that anything is in the offing" until his resignation was accepted and made public.[90]

The impasse between Lucey and his priests continued
through the spring of 1969. In January representatives of the
"68" met with him to attempt some reconciliation. The meeting was a disaster. Lucey told the priests that they had caused
grave scandal and were traitors to the Church. They promptly
denied the charge, after which the Archbishop stated that it
was useless to talk further about the matter.[91]

Whatever hope for resolving the situation the priests entertained now rested with Bishop Connare. In Mid-March the
Priests' Association asked for a report of his findings. "At the
moment we are waiting on you," they wrote. "We cannot
believe that you would come all the way down here and listen
and read through our testimony without coming to some
conclusions. We are anxious for some kind of report. . . . Are
we unreasonable to expect a response from you soon?"[92]
There is no record of a response from Bishop Connare.

The breakdown in communication had become complete.
Lucey was marking time until his resignation was publicly

acknowledged. Rome was likewise waiting for a sufficient number of months to pass so that Lucey could be removed with a modicum of dignity. Connare had long ago passed out of the scene. The only people left to suffer the agony of not knowing their fate were the priests, most of whom remained in their pastoral assignments under a cloud of suspicion and doubt.

On May 23, 1969, the Archbishop received the "health and apostolic benediction" of Pope Paul VI, who in his letter stated that he reluctantly accepted Lucey's resignation. Twelve days later Lucey formally announced his retirement in San Antonio.[93]

Letters of congratulations followed the announcement. At a testimonial dinner in July, former President Lyndon Johnson had kind words for his old friend. "No servant of God has worked with greater devotion for the peace and progress of God's people," he said. "All of us who have known him will proudly carry the badge of that friendship throughout our lives." Hubert Humphrey characterized Lucey as "a tower of strength for decency and human dignity." In response, the Archbishop said that he regretted that he was unable to retire several times: "I didn't realize what a good person I have been."[94] Later in the fall Pope Paul saluted Lucey's "generous spirit and greatness of soul . . . and undying spirit of sacrifice." From Bishop Connare, Lucey heard assurances that his "valiant struggle to maintain discipline and order" would long be appreciated by his brother bishops.[95]

And what of Lucey himself? What was his reaction to the events of 1968 and 1969? After many months of interviews, the Archbishop admitted that he had been deeply hurt by what he felt was an almost diabolical attack on the Church. But he managed his personal pain privately, refusing to share it with anyone. His anger at the priests never entirely subsided, nor did he modify his categorization of them as ecclesiastical turncoats. As for his treatment at the hands of the

Apostolic Delegate, he eventually admitted that he thought that Raimondi's behavior had been "most peculiar" and that in his "quiet quarrel" with the Delegate, he had been treated unfairly.[96] Nevertheless, Lucey never made any public protest against his forced retirement. To do so might have damaged the Church, and the Church was his life.

Epilogue

"Fighting for the poor leaves no room for regret," Archbishop Lucey said as he reminisced about his life. Sitting in a rocking chair in his study, Lucey admitted that at first retirement had been difficult. Twenty-eight years as Archbishop had ended in an ignominious conflict. Yet on balance he managed his remaining years well. Accepting his forced resignation with stoic loyalty, he cooperated fully in the transition to power of his successor, Archbishop Francis J. Furey, and never interfered in archdiocesan affairs. From 1969 to 1972 he worked with Werner von Braun and other scientists on a telecommunications project designed to study the feasibility of using space satellites for global catechetical programs. Unfortunately a serious illness in 1972 curtailed his participation in the discussions.[1]

As for the events of 1968–1969, the Archbishop gradually put aside bitterness. For the most part, he was reconciled with his priests before his death on August 1, 1977, but to the end remained convinced that their rebellion was unjustified and that history would vindicate him. He strenuously denied being vindictive or unforgiving and admitted only to a lack of gentleness in dealing with people.[2]

Those of the "68" who were willing to initiate a reconciliation with Lucey found him receptive. Roy Rihn and Sherrill Smith, for example, visited the Archbishop regularly after his retirement, and both retain great admiration for him as they continue their ministries in the San Antonio archdiocese. Joseph Till, on the other hand, remained bitter and had nothing to do with Lucey after 1969. While Till is still active in priestly work, others, including Louis Michalski, Robert Walden, Marion Swize, and Henry Casso, resigned from the priesthood to pursue professional careers. For William Killian, Lucey's retirement brought a special pain. Having stood by the Archbishop during the crisis, Killian found that his deep affection for Lucey went unreciprocated after 1969. More and more cut off from his fellow priests and saddened by the Archbishop's distant attitude, Killian died in an automobile accident in 1974.[3]

There is one final irony in Archbishop Lucey's story. With his departure from San Antonio there came also a de-emphasis on social action, suggesting the possibility that a more democratically governed Church preaches a weaker social gospel. Pope John Paul II appears currently to be reaffirming a style of leadership that mixes an insistence on human rights outside the Church with a retrenchment on matters of internal Church discipline. In 1979, for example, the Vatican in a declaration of censure announced that Hans Küng could no longer be considered a Catholic theologian because of his writings on the meaning of Catholic identity. Father Robert Drinan quietly acceded to Vatican pressure to relinquish his political career in the United States Congress, while William Callahan, a Jesuit, was silenced for has advocacy of the ordination of women. Contemporary papal leadership, then, suggests that the Church's authoritarian structure is well suited to a liberal social gospel. If this proves true, the old Archbishop can rest in peace.

Notes

Abbreviations

AALA	Archives of the Archdiocese of Los Angeles
AASA	Archives of the Archdiocese of San Antonio
ADA	Archives of the Diocese of Amarillo
AMM	Archives of the Maryknoll Missionaries, Maryknoll, New York
BUL	Baylor University Library, Waco, Texas
CATA	Catholic Archives of Texas at Austin
CMLLUC	Cudahy Memorial Library, Loyola University of Chicago
FDRL	Franklin Delano Roosevelt Library, Hyde Park, New York
LBJL	Lyndon B. Johnson Library, Austin, Texas
UTARL	University of Texas at Arlington Library

Chapter 1

1. Bronder interview with Robert E. Lucey, March 1, 1977; Bronder interview with Msgr. Joseph Truxaw, August 10, 1976; Baylor University Oral History Project (cited hereafter as BUOH Project), BUL, interview with R. E. Lucey, September 15, 1972.

2. Bronder interview with Truxaw, August 10, 1976; Kuehler interview with Marguerite and Esperanza Batz, n.d.; Bronder interview with R. E. Lucey, January 18, 1977.

3. Bronder interview with Truxaw, August 10, 1976; Bronder interview with R. E. Lucey, January 18, 1977; Kuehler interview with R. E. Lucey, October 26, 1972.

4. Los Angeles County, Cal., coroner's record for John J. Lucey, June 25, 1900.

5. Bronder interview with R. E. Lucey, June 22, 1976.

6. For a sampling of the literature on the Progressive movement, see Richard Hofstadter, *The Age of Reform* (New York: Harper and Row, 1955); Samuel Hays, *The Response to Industrialism, 1885–1914* (Chicago: University of Chicago Press, 1957); Robert Wiebe, *The Search for Order, 1877–1920* (New York: Hill and Wang, 1967); and Robert H. Bremner, *From the Depths: The Discovery of Poverty in the United States* (New York: New York University Press, 1956).

7. The San Antonio archdiocesan archives contain several albums of Lucey family photographs, on which the above description is based.

8. Letter from R. E. Lucey to Mrs. L. D. Hist, December 9, 1952, R. E. Lucey Papers, AASA; Saint Patrick Church, Brasher Falls, N.Y., marriage record, 1879; Saint Patrick Church, baptismal records, 1880, 1883; Saint Augustine Cathedral, Tucson, Ariz., certificate of baptism, 1888; Arizona Department of Health Services, Vital Records Section, certificate of birth, 1888.

9. George E. Mowry, *The California Progressives* (Berkeley: University of California Press, 1951), p. 38; Robert M. Fogelson, *The Fragmented Metropolis: Los Angeles, 1850–1930* (Cambridge: Harvard University Press, 1967), pp. 63–84.

10. Mowry, *California Progressives*, pp. 9–23.

11. Letter from R. E. Lucey to Edmund Lucey, September 17, 1941, R. E. Lucey Papers, AASA.

12. Los Angeles County, Cal., Registrar Records, 1890–1894.

13. Bronder interview with R. E. Lucey, June 17, 1976; BUOH Project, September 15, 1972.

14. Sacred Heart Church, Los Angeles, Cal., baptismal records, 1894, 1897.

15. Bronder interviews with R. E. Lucey, January 11 and 25, 1977; Kuehler interview with Rev. John Devlin, n.d.; BUOH Project, September 15, 1972.

16. Kuehler interview with R. E. Lucey, October 23, 1972; BUOH Project, September 15, 1972.

17. Kuehler interview with R. E. Lucey, October 23, 1972.

18. Bronder interviews with R. E. Lucey, January 18 and 25, 1977; BUOH Project, September 15, 1972.

19. Kuehler interview with Julia May, Genevieve, and Florence Kelly, n.d.

20. Bronder interview with Truxaw, August 10, 1976; Kuehler interview with R. E. Lucey, October 30, 1972; Kuehler interview with Sister Angela Clare Lucey, December 28, 1972; Kuehler interview with Kelly sisters, n.d.; BUOH Project, September 15, 1972.

21. Bronder interview with R. E. Lucey, January 18, 1977; Kuehler interview with R. E. Lucey, October 23, 1972; BUOH Project, September 15, 1972.

22. Kuehler interview with R. E. Lucey, November 10, 1972; BUOH Project, September 15, 1972.

23. Bronder interviews with R. E. Lucey, January 18 and 25, 1977; Francis J. Weber, "What Ever Happened to Saint Vincent's College," *Pacific Historian* 14 (1970): 76–90.

24. "The Church and the Labor Question," *Saint Vincent College Student* 7 (1904): 237–41; Marshall Winnie, Bachelor's Oration, "The Dignity of Labor," *Saint Vincent College Student* 10 (Commencement Issue, 1907): 373–75.

25. *Saint Vincent College Student* 9 (Commencement Issue, 1906): 253.

26. Francis J. Weber, "Saint Patrick's, Source of Spiritual Life," *Tidings*, December 23, 1966.

27. Ibid.

28. Bronder interview with Truxaw, August 10, 1976; Bronder interview with R. E. Lucey, January 18, 1977; Kuehler interview with Truxaw, n.d.

29. Kuehler interview with Truxaw, n.d.

30. Joseph Truxaw, *Diary of a Seminarian, 1907–1917* (Los Angeles: Privately published, n.d.), p. 183.

31. Ibid., pp. 102, 208, 219, 234, 241, 268.

32. Ibid., p. 223.

33. Bronder interview with R. E. Lucey, January 18, 1977; Truxaw, *Diary*, pp. 205, 210–12, 256–57, 263, 268.

34. Kuehler interview with Truxaw, n.d.

35. Bronder interview with R. E. Lucey, January 18, 1977. See Joseph S. Brusher, *Consecrated Thunderbolt: Father Yorke of San Francisco* (Hawthorne, N.J.: Joseph F. Wagner, 1973).

36. See John A. Ryan, *A Living Wage* (New York: Macmillan, 1906), and Francis L. Broderick, *Right Reverend New Dealer: John A. Ryan* (New York: Macmillan, 1963).

37. Letter from Most Rev. Thomas Conaty to Rt. Rev. Thomas F. Kennedy, September 14, 1912, R. E. Lucey Papers, AASA; *Tidings*, n.d.

38. R. E. Lucey, address to the First Annual Raymond A. McGowan Award Dinner, Kansas City, Mo., February 23, 1963, R. E. Lucey Papers, AASA.

39. Bronder interview with R. E. Lucey, January 25, 1977.

40. John Tracy Ellis, "The Formation of the American Priest: An Historical Perspective," in *The Catholic Priest in the United States: Historical Investigations*, ed. John Tracy Ellis (Collegeville, Minn.: Saint John's University Press, 1971), p. 65.

41. Michael V. Gannon, "Before and After Modernism: The Intellectual Isolation of the American Priest," in Ellis, *The Catholic Priest*, p. 335. See also "Pascendi Dominici Gregis," in *Readings in Church History*, ed. Colman Barry, 3 vols. (Westminster, Md.: Newman press, 1965), 3:112–14. For an account of modernism, see John Ratte, *Three Modernists: Alfred Loisy, George Tyrell, William L. Sullivan* (New York: Sheed and Ward, 1967).

42. Gannon, "Before and After Modernism," pp. 335–36.

43. "Pascendi Dominici Gregis," p. 113.

44. Quoted from "Pascendi" in J. B. Lemius, *Catechism on Modernism: Founded on the Encyclical "Pascendi Dominici Gregis" of His Holiness, Pius X* (New York: Society for the Propagation of the Faith, 1908), pp. 122–23.

45. Ellis, "Formation of the American Priest," pp. 61–62; Gannon, "Before and after Modernism," pp. 333–37.

46. E. E. Y. Hales, "The Americanist Controversy," *Month* 31 (1964): 36.

47. Gannon, "Before and After Modernism," pp. 341–43. For the story of the *New York Review*, see Michael J. DeVito, *The New York Review, 1905–1908* (New York: United States Catholic Historical Society, 1977).

48. Gannon, "Before and After Modernism," p. 352.

49. Ibid., pp. 355–56. See also John Tracy Ellis, *Essays in Seminary Education* (Notre Dame, Ind.: Fides Publishers, 1967).

50. Robert F. McNamara, *The American College in Rome, 1855–1955* (Rochester, N.Y.: Christopher Press, 1956), pp. 16–88.

51. BUOH Project, September 15, 1972; McNamara, *The American College*, pp. 94–105; Bronder interview with R. E. Lucey, January 25, 1977; grades of R. E. Lucey at the Pontificia Universitas Urbaniana, 1912–1916, R. E. Lucey Papers, AASA.

52. Kuehler interview with R. E. Lucey, November 22, 1972; BUOH Project, September 15, 1972.

53. Records of orders for R. E. Lucey at the Pontificia Universitas Urbaniana, 1912–1916, R. E. Lucey Papers, AASA.

54. Kuehler interviews with R. E. Lucey, October 27, 1972, and September 25, 1973.

Chapter 2

1. Letter from Msgr. John Cawley to Newton Baker, U.S. Secretary of War, July 24, 1917, AALA; BUOH Project, September 15, 1972.

2. Letter from Cawley to R. E. Lucey, November 29, 1920, AALA; letter from Cawley to R. E. Lucey, October 31, 1921, AALA; Bronder interview with R. E. Lucey, July 6, 1976.

3. Bronder interview with R. E. Lucey, July 6, 1976; Donald Gavin, *The National Conference of Catholic Charities* (Milwaukee: Bruce Press, 1962), p. 62.

4. Bronder interview with R. E. Lucey, July 6, 1976; Kuehler interview with R. E. Lucey, October 23, 1972.

5. There are a number of good translations of the social encyclicals; particularly good are those published by the Paulist Press and the National Catholic Welfare Conference. References cited in this book are from Gerald C. Treacy, ed., *Five Great Encyclicals*, (New York: Paulist Press, 1939).

6. "Rerum Novarum," in Treacy, *Five Great Encyclicals*, pp. 1–9.

7. Ibid., pp. 2, 17, 22–23.

8. David J. O'Brien, "The American Priest and Social Action," in *The Catholic Priest in the United States: Historical Investigations*, ed. John Tracy Ellis (Collegeville, Minn.: Saint John's University Press, 1971), p. 440.

9. John A. Ryan, "The Study of Social Problems in the Seminary," *American Ecclesiastical Review* 39 (1908): 117.

10. Report of the Bureau of Catholic Charities, Los Angeles diocese, 1919, pp. 1–12, AALA. See also Hugh J. Nolan, ed., *Pastoral Letters of the American Hierarchy, 1792–1970* (Huntington, Ind.: Our Sunday Visitor, Inc., 1971), pp. 262–86.

11. Bronder interview with Msgr. Augustine O'Dea, August 12, 1976.

12. Report of the Bureau of Catholic Charities, Los Angeles diocese, 1921, pp. 3–4.

13. For a discussion of this linkage, see Leo Grebler, Joan Moore, and Ralph Guzman, *The Mexican-American People: The Nation's Second Largest Minority* (New York: Free Press, 1970), pp. 453–57.

14. See reports of the Bureau of Catholic Charities, Los Angeles diocese, 1919–1926.

15. Ibid.

16. BUOH Project, September 15, 1972; Kuehler interview with R. E. Lucey, November 29, 1972.

17. O'Brien, "The American Priest," pp. 440–41; Gavin, *Catholic Charities*, pp. 27–70.

18. Bronder interview with R. E. Lucey, February 1, 1977; letter from R. E. Lucey to Most Rev. John J. Cantwell, August 18, 1926, AALA.

19. R. E. Lucey, address to the Catholic Conference on Industrial Problems, Los Angeles, 1928, AALA.

20. *United States Supreme Court Reports*, 67 Lawyers' ed., U.S. 260–62, October term, 1922 (Rochester, N.Y.: Lawyers' Cooperative Publishing Company, 1924), pp. 785–802.

21. R. E. Lucey, "The Living Wage: Our Present Problem," *Tidings*, August 24, 1928.

22. R. E. Lucey, "The Living Wage: The Church and Industry," *Tidings*, July 27, 1928.

23. R. E. Lucey, "The Living Wage: Remedies Proposed for Poverty," *Tidings*, August 3, 1928.

24. R. E. Lucey, "The Living Wage: Evils of Bare Subsistence Wage," *Tidings*, August 10, 1928.

25. R. E. Lucey, presidential address to the California Conference of Social Workers, Los Angeles, June 15, 1928, AALA.

26. R. E. Lucey, "The Living Wage: The Fair Standard of Living," *Tidings*, August 17, 1928.

27. R. E. Lucey, presidential address.

28. R. E. Lucey, "The Living Wage: Our Present Problem."

29. Bronder interview with R. E. Lucey, June 29, 1976.

30. Bronder interviews with Msgr. John Dunne, August 13, 1976; O'Dea, August 12, 1976; Most Rev. Joseph McGucken, August 23, 1976.

31. For an account of the United States in the roaring decade, see William E. Leuchtenburg, *The Perils of Prosperity, 1914–1932* (Chicago: University of Chicago Press, 1958).

32. O'Brien, "The American Priest," p. 443. See also Wilfrid Parsons, "The Social Thought of the American Hierarchy: Our Bishops Speak," *Social Order* (1952): 259–78; Thomas T. McAvoy, "The Catholic Church in the United States between Two Wars," *Review of Politics* (1942): 409–31; D. W. Brogan, *The American Character* (New York: Alfred A. Knopf, 1944); and Edmund Moore, *A Catholic Runs for President: The Campaign of 1928* (New York: Ronald Press, 1956).

33. "Quadragesimo Anno," in Treacy, *Five Great Encyclicals*, pp. 125–43.

34. Ibid., pp. 143–68.

35. Thomas E. Blantz, "Francis J. Hass: Priest in Public Service," (Ph.D. diss., Columbia University, 1968), p. 48; David J. O'Brien, *American Catholics and Social Reform: The New Deal Years* (New York: Oxford University Press, 1968), pp. 133–35.

36. Letter from Cawley to R. E. Lucey, April 23, 1929, AALA; Bronder interview with R. E. Lucey, June 22, 1976; Bronder interview with McGucken, August 23, 1976; R. E. Lucey, transcripts from broadcasts of "Saint Anthony's Hour," September 9, 1930, to January 29, 1933 (cited hereafter as SAH transcripts), AASA.

37. SAH transcripts, January 31, 1932, and October 18, 1931, AASA.

38. SAH transcripts, January 31, February 7, 14, 21, 1932, AASA.

39. SAH transcripts, May 1 and December 4, 1932, AASA.

40. SAH transcripts, March 13 and May 15, 1932, AASA.

41. SAH transcripts, February 7, 1932, AASA.

42. SAH transcripts, February 14, 1932, AASA.

43. SAH transcripts, February 21, 1932, AASA.

44. SAH transcripts, February 29, 1932, AASA.

45. SAH transcripts, October 9, 1932, AASA.

46. Bronder interview with McGucken, August 23, 1976; letter from Cantwell to R. E. Lucey, December 29, 1932, AASA.

47. Bronder interview with R. E. Lucey, January 25, 1977; Kuehler interviews with R. E. Lucey, November 22 and December 29, 1972.

48. R. E. Lucey, "Catholic Social Teaching and the Open Shop," *Tidings*, September 9, 1933.

49. Bronder interview with McGucken, August 23, 1976; letter from Most Rev. Amleto Giovanni Cicognani, Apostolic Delegate, to R. E. Lucey, January 29, 1934, AASA.

50. Letter from E. B. Webb, secretary of the Long Beach Building Trades Council–AFL, to R. E. Lucey, February 23, 1934, AASA; letter from Louise Drury, executive secretary of the Children's Protective Association of Los Angeles, to R. E. Lucey, February 16, 1934, AASA; letter from D. C. MacWatters, secretary and general manager of the Los Angeles Community Welfare Federation Community Chest, to R. E. Lucey, February 13, 1934, AASA.

51. Letter from Rabbi Edgar F. Magnin, Wilshire Boulevard Temple, Los Angeles, to R. E. Lucey, February 13, 1934, AASA; letter from Rev. C. Rankin Barnes, executive secretary of the National Council of the Protestant Episcopal Church, to R. E. Lucey, February 14, 1934, AASA; letter from Frank L. Shaw, Mayor of Los Angeles, to R. E. Lucey, February 28, 1934, AASA; letter from James A. Farley, U.S. Postmaster-General, to R. E. Lucey, February 13, 1934, AASA; letter from W. F. Prisk, editor of *Long Beach Press-Telegram*, to R. E. Lucey, February 12, 1934, AASA.

52. Unidentified newspaper clippings (Long Beach, Cal.), April 27, 1934, and May 8, 1934, AASA.

Chapter 3

1. Bronder interviews with R. E. Lucey, July 6, 1976, and March 15, 1977.

2. *Amarillo Daily News*, May 15, 1934.

3. *Amarillo Daily News*, May 16, 1934.

4. "The Capital of the Plains," in *The Panhandle Anchor: An Installa-*

tion Publication (Amarillo: Privately published, 1934), pp. 42–43; "U.S. Bureau of Census," *Texas Almanac, 1976–77* (Dallas: A. H. Belo, 1976), pp. 178, 188.

5. *Panhandle Anchor*, p. 45; U.S. Department of Agriculture, *Report of the Chief of the Weather Bureau, 1934–1935*, p. 72.

6. Letter from R. E. Lucey to Cantwell, June 11, 1935, ADA.

7. Bronder interview with R. E. Lucey, March 8, 1977.

8. Archibald M. Bottoms, "A Tribute of the Diocese of Amarillo to the Catholic Church Extension Society of America on its Golden Jubilee, 1905–1955," *Amarillo Register*, August 12, 1955; *The Official Catholic Directory: Anno Domini 1928* (New York: P. J. Kenedy & Sons, 1928), pp. 218–19.

9. Bottoms, "Tribute"; M. F. Roche, *Recollections of Forty Years of the Diocese of Amarillo, 1927–1967* (Amarillo: Privately published, 1967), p. 3; Kuehler interview with Archibald M. Bottoms, n.d.

10. Bottoms, "Tribute."

11. *Official Catholic Directory: 1928*, pp. 218–19.

12. Kuehler interview with Msgr. Francis Smyer, n.d.

13. Bronder interview with R. E. Lucey, July 13, 1976; Bronder interview with Smyer, July 23, 1976; Bronder interview with Mrs. John Gulde, July 23, 1976; Bronder interview with Mrs. Carl Lutz, July 23, 1976; Kuehler interview with Bottoms, n.d.

14. Bronder interview with Lutz, July 23, 1976; Kuehler interview with Smyer, n.d.

15. Letter from R. E. Lucey to Rev. F. M. Kaminsky, March 20, 1934, ADA.

16. Letters from R. E. Lucey to Rev. Dr. Louis H. Motry, January 29, February 18, March 11, and August 2, 1935, ADA; letters from Motry to R. E. Lucey, February 12, March 7, June 28, and August 9, 1935, ADA.

17. Bronder interview with Gulde, July 23, 1976; Bronder interview with R. E. Lucey, March 15, 1977; memorandum from R. E. Lucey to Lay Board of Advisors, diocese of Amarillo, July 1, 1935. ADA; Bottoms, "Tribute"; Catholic Church Extension Society of America, records of stipends to the diocese of Amarillo, 1926–1941, CMLLUC.

18. Letter from R. E. Lucey to Rt. Rev. Eugene McGuiness, July 31, 1934, quoted in Sister Rosanna Lee, "The History of Catholic Education in the Diocese of Amarillo" (Master's thesis, Catholic University of America, 1952), pp. 42–43.

19. Lee, "History of Catholic Education," pp. 48–49, 52–53; R. E. Lucey, report to the American Board of Catholic Missions, 1939, ADA.

20. Letter from R. E. Lucey to Rev. Bernard Dolan, March 4, 1936, ADA; Bottoms, "Tribute."

21. Bronder interviews with R. E. Lucey, March 8 and March 15, 1977; R. E. Lucey, address to the Fourth Annual Banquet of the Catholic Welfare Bureau, Amarillo, March 12, 1939, ADA; Bronder interview with Hazel Kelly, July 23, 1976; Bronder interview with Lutz, July 23, 1976; Catholic Welfare Bureau, financial reports for 1935–1940, ADA.

22. David J. O'Brien, "The American Priest and Social Action," in *The Catholic Priest in the United States: Historical Investigations*, ed. John Tracy Ellis (Collegeville, Minn.: Saint John's University Press, 1971), p. 447.

23. Letter from R. E. Lucey to pastors of the diocese of Amarillo, February 15, 1936, ADA.

24. Questionnaire to all pastors—CCD progress report, April 18, 1936, ADA; CCD tally sheet, n.d., ADA.

25. CCD Study Club reports, November, 1936 through May, 1939, ADA; Bronder interview with Gulde, July 23, 1976; Bronder interview with Lutz, July 23, 1976.

26. Bronder interview with Smyer, July 23, 1976.

27. *Texas Panhandle Register*, Amarillo (cited hereafter as *TPR*), July 5, 1936.

28. Bronder interview with Smyer, July 23, 1976.

29. Cardinal Patrick Hayes, "The Leaven of Charity," *Catholic Charities Review* 17 (1933): 261; Archbishop John T. McNicholas, "Justice and the Present Crisis," *Catholic Mind* 29 (1931): 474.

30. Cardinal William O'Connell, "The Changed Condition of Labor," *Catholic Mind* 29 (1931): 3; *Brooklyn Tablet*, March 23, 1931; David J. O'Brien, *American Catholics and Social Reform: The New Deal Years* (New York: Oxford University Press, 1968), p. 103.

31. R. E. Lucey, "Economic Disorders and 'Quadragesimo Anno,'" *Homiletic and Pastoral Review* 35 (1935): 858–66; R. E. Lucey, "Apathy—Our Scourge," *Homiletic and Pastoral Review* 36 (1936): 468–77.

32. Letter from R. E. Lucey to Thomas J. Donahue, member of the building committee of Sacred Heart Church, Sweetwater, August 3, 1935, CATA.

33. Letter from R. E. Lucey to Rev. Austin Cubillo, C.M.F., pastor of Sacred Heart Church, Sweetwater, July 31, 1935, CATA.

34. Letter from R. E. Lucey to R. M. Simmons, member of the building committee of Sacred Heart Church, Sweetwater, August 9, 1935, CATA.

35. Letter from R. E. Lucey to John G. Becker, April 17, 1936, CATA.

36. R. E. Lucey, "The Need of Labor Organizations," *Catholic Messenger*, n.d.; "Labor in the Recession," *Commonweal* 28 (1938): 47.

37. *Brooklyn Tablet*, January 16, 1937, and February 27, 1937; Paul Blakely, "Labor Wages a Losing Battle," *America* 56 (1937): 417; *Social Justice*, October 5, 1936, and August 2–September 6, 1937; "Franklin D. Roosevelt and John L. Lewis," *Catholic World* 145 (1937): 385, 388.

38. O'Brien, *American Catholics and Social Reform*, pp. 111–12; Neil Betten, *Catholic Activism and the Industrial Worker* (Gainesville: University Presses of Florida, 1976), p. 80.

39. *Our Sunday Visitor*, January 10, 1937.

40. Hugh J. Nolan, ed., *Pastoral Letters of the American Hierarchy, 1792–1970* (Huntington, Ind.: Our Sunday Visitor, Inc., 1971), pp. 327–30.

41. Betten, *Catholic Activism*, pp. 75, 123, 131; O'Brien, *American Catholics and Social Reform*, pp. 112–13.

42. *TPR*, June 6, 1937; R. E. Lucey, "Are We Fair to the Church?" *Commonweal* 28 (1938): 491–92; R. E. Lucey, "Are We Fair to the Church?" *Commonweal* 28 (1938): 521–22; *TPR*, October 31, November 14, December 5, 1937, March 10, 1938; R. E. Lucey, moderator, "Principles of Legislation," *Summer School of Social Action for Priests* (Mundelein, Ill.: privately published, 1938), p. 330.

43. R. E. Lucey, address to the Fifteenth Annual Convention of the National Council of Catholic Women, Fort Wayne, Ind., November, 1935, ADA.

44. *Amarillo Daily News*, May 16, 1934; R. E. Lucey, address to International Association of Oil Field, Gas Well and Refinery Workers, Pampa, Tex., August 23, 1934, ADA; R. E. Lucey, address to the First Annual Catholic Action Congress, Oklahoma City, Okla., October 9, 1934, ADA; R. E. Lucey, address to the Fifteen Annual Convention of the National Council of Catholic Women. For the *Schechter* decision, see *United States Supreme Court Reports* 79 Lawyers' ed., U.S. 293–95 October term, 1934 (Lawyers' Cooperative Publishing Company, 1935), pp. 1570–93.

45. Quoted in John A. Garraty, *The American Nation: A History of the United States Since 1865* (New York: Harper and Row, 1966), p. 347.

46. *TPR*, August 2, 1936.

47. Report of address by R. E. Lucey to local study groups, *TPR*, March 7, 1937.

48. R. E. Lucey, address to the National Council of Catholic Women, Galveston, Tex., October 20, 1936, ADA.

49. Ibid.

50. Thomas E. Blantz, "Francis J. Haas: Priest in Public Service" (Ph.D. diss. Columbia University, 1968), pp. 233–34.

51. The Archives of the Archdiocese of San Antonio contain printed summaries of the programs for the Summer School of Social Action for Priests for 1937, 1938, and 1939.

52. *TPR*, August 8, 1937.

53. Charles Rankin, ed., *The Pope Speaks* (New York: Harcourt, Brace and Company, 1940), pp. 285–89, 293.

54. SAH transcripts, January 17, 1932, AASA.

55. *TPR*, August 23, 1936, February 14, May 2, May 23, 1937.

56. Nolan, *Pastoral Letters*, pp. 323–24; O'Brien, *American Catholics and Social Reform*, p. 86. See also Allen Guttman, *The Wound in the Heart: America and the Spanish Civil War* (New York: Free Press, 1962), chap. 3.

57. *TPR*, July 17, 1938.

58. *TPR*, September 13, 1936, January 10, 1937, January 21, 1938; Bronder interview with R. E. Lucey, March 29, 1977.

59. *TPR*, April 9, May 14, June 12, 1939; National Catholic Welfare Conference, News Release Service, July 24, 1939, Pittsburgh, Pa., AASA.

60. *TPR*, January 14, 1940; R. E. Lucey, address to the National Conference of Christians and Jews, Dallas, December 5, 1940, ADA.

61. Letter from Cicognani to R. E. Lucey, January 13, 1941, AASA.

62. R. E. Lucey, report to Cicognani, March 4, 1941, AASA.

63. Ibid.

64. Ibid.

Chapter 4

1. Telegram from Maury Maverick, Mayor of San Antonio, to R. E. Lucey, January 24, 1941, AASA; Maverick, address at civic reception, Municipal Hall, San Antonio, March 26, 1941, AASA; *San Antonio Express*, January 24 and January 25, 1941; "New Dealing Archbishop," *Time*, April 7, 1941, pp. 73–74; letter from Franklin D. Roosevelt to R. E. Lucey, March 18, 1941, FDRL.

2. *National Catholic Register*, March 23, 1941.

3. R. E. Lucey, address to the Holy Name Society, St. Paul, Minn., June, 1941, AASA.

4. Publicity brochure for the School of Social Justice, San Antonio, August 4–15, 1941, AASA; "Social Action in San Antonio," *Time*, August 25, 1941, pp. 60–61.

5. *San Antonio Express*, January 12, 1945.

6. R. E. Lucey, address to the State Convention of the American Federation of Labor, Houston, June 25, 1946, AASA; R. E. Lucey, address to the Eleventh Annual Convention of the Texas State Industrial Union Council, San Antonio, October 25–27, 1947, UTARL.

7. R. E. Lucey, "Work, Wages and Religion," *Texas State Federation of Labor Review* (1953): 55–60.

8. R. E. Lucey, address to the Twenty-Seventh National Conference of Catholic Charities, Houston, October 19, 1941, AASA; R. E. Lucey, address at a patriotic meeting, Memorial Stadium, Austin, December 21, 1941, AASA; R. E. Lucey, address at Incarnate Word College, San Antonio, June 19, 1944, AASA.

9. R. Lamanna and J. Coakley, "The Catholic Church and the Negro," in *Contemporary Catholicism in the United States*, ed. Philip Gleason (Notre Dame, Ind.: University of Notre Dame Press, 1969), pp. 153–60.

10. R. E. Lucey, statement to the Senate Committee on Education and Labor, Washington, D.C., September, 1944, AASA; Gunnar Myrdal, *An American Dilemma* (New York: Harper and Brothers, 1944); pastoral letter from R. E. Lucey, December 7, 1945, AASA.

11. R. E. Lucey, address to the Southwest Regional Conference of the National Council of Catholic Women, San Antonio, October 4, 1949, AASA; R. E. Lucey, sermon to the North Carolina Laymen's Association, St. Patrick Church, Charlotte, N.C., May 21, 1950, AASA.

12. Pastoral letter from R. E. Lucey to all pastors and superiors of private schools in the archdiocese of San Antonio, April 5, 1954, AASA.

On the *Brown* decision, see Richard Kugler, *Simple Justice* (New York: Alfred A. Knopf, 1975).

13. The *Express-News*, saluting Lucey on the fortieth anniversary of his ordination, said that his two-year-old integration order had "helped pave the way for smooth desegregation in our local public schools," in "a sharp and welcome contrast to current deplorable experiences elsewhere in the South." *San Antonio Express-News*, May 6, 1956.

14. R. E. Lucey, address to Little Flower Parish, San Antonio, March 24, 1957, AASA; *San Antonio Light*, March 25, 1957; *San Antonio News*, March 27, 1957; *San Antonio Light*, March 28, 1957.

15. Kuehler interview with Msgr. Paul Ehlinger, n.d.

16. Pastoral letter from R. E. Lucey, October 5, 1943, AASA.

17. *San Antonio Light*, August 3, 1943.

18. *San Antonio Light*, August 10, 1943.

19. R. E. Lucey, address to the Texas Association of Catholic Hospitals, San Antonio, March, 1945, AASA; pastoral letter from R. E. Lucey, July 13, 1945, AASA.

20. Kuehler interview with Ehlinger, n.d.

21. R. E. Lucey, address to the Southwest Regional Council of the National Association of Housing Officials, San Antonio, June 4, 1953, AASA.

22. Bronder interview with Callan Graham, April 4, 1976.

23. *Austin American-Statesman*, October 20, 1957; *San Antonio Light*, October 20, 1957.

24. *Official Catholic Directory: 1941*, p. 227.

25. Leo Grebler, Joan Moore, and Ralph Guzman, *The Mexican-American People: The Nation's Second Largest Minority* (New York: Free Press, 1970), pp. 449–50.

26. Ibid., p. 450.

27. Ibid., p. 451.

28. Ibid., p. 452.

29. R. E. Lucey, "History of the Bishops' Committee for the Spanish Speaking" (unpublished essay, September, 1972), pp. 1–8, AASA; Raymond McGowan, "The History and Necessity of the National Council for the Spanish Speaking" (unpublished essay, 1960), pp. 1–4, AASA.

30. Minutes of the Twenty-sixth Annual Meeting of the American

Hierarchy, Washington, D.C., November 15, 1944, AASA; minutes of the meeting of the archbishops and bishops of the four provinces of the Southwest for the general purpose of Mexican welfare, Oklahoma City, January 10–12, 1945, AASA; minutes of the meeting of the executive board of the Bishops' Committee for the Spanish Speaking (hereafter cited as BCSS), El Paso, Tex., February 21, 1945, AASA.

31. Bronder interview with Rev. John McCarthy, August 4, 1976; Kuehler interview with Ehlinger, n.d.; constitution of the Catholic Council for the Spanish Speaking, 1944, AASA.

32. Bronder interview with McCarthy, August 4, 1976; letters from Rev. Theodore Radtke to R. E. Lucey, March 8 and April 25, 1950, AASA; minutes of the meeting of BCSS, Catholic University, Washington, D.C., November 16, 1949, AASA; Radtke, report of the executive secretary of BCSS to the American hierarchy, Washington, D.C., November 15, 1950, AASA.

33. Agnes E. Meyer, "Forceful Archbishop Crusades for Mexicans of San Antonio," *Washington Post*, April 28, 1946.

34. *New York Times*, June 4, 1950.

35. Letter from R. E. Lucey to Radtke, July, 1950, AASA; Radtke, report of the executive secretary of BCSS to the American hierarchy, Washington, D.C., November 15, 1950, AASA.

36. Report of the President's Commission on Migratory Labor, "Migratory Labor and American Agriculture" (Washington, D.C.: U.S. Government Printing Office, 1951), pp. 56–64 (hereafter cited as Report of the President's Commission); Richard B. Craig, *The Bracero Program: Interest Groups and Foreign Policy* (Austin: University of Texas Press, 1971), pp. 36–64.

37. *New York Times*, March 25, March 26, March 27, March 28, 1951.

38. *New York Times*, April 5, 1959.

39. Report of the President's Commission, pp. 177–85.

40. Craig, *The Bracero Program*, pp. 72–77, 203.

41. "The Scandal of Migratory Labor," *America* 85 (1951): 213; telegram from R. E. Lucey to President Truman, July 3, 1951, AASA; R. E. Lucey, address at the Senate Hearing on Migratory Labor, Washington, D.C., February 5, 1952, AASA.

42. R. E. Lucey, address to the Biennial Convention of the National Farmers Union, Dallas, March 11, 1952, AASA; R. E. Lucey, address to the Fourth Annual Convention of the American G.I. Forum of Texas, San Antonio, July 5, 1952, AASA.

43. Rev. Matthew Kelly, statement to the Senate Subcommittee on Immigration and Naturalization, Washington, D.C., July 13, 1954, AASA; letter from R. E. Lucey to M. Kelly, July 20, 1954, AASA.

44. Letter from M. Kelly to R. E. Lucey, July 26, 1954, AASA.

45. Letter from R. E. Lucey to M. Kelly, July 28, 1954, AASA.

46. Letter from R. E. Lucey to M. Kelly, September 20, 1954, AASA.

47. Bronder interview with Rev. William O'Connor, O.M.I., August 14, 1976; memo from R. E. Lucey to O'Connor, April 2, 1956 (not sent), AASA.

48. Letters from Sen. Lyndon B. Johnson to R. E. Lucey, March 17, June 21, June 28, and July 7, 1954, LBJL; letters from R. E. Lucey to Lyndon Johnson, March 31, June 10, and June 28, 1954, AASA.

49. Letter from R. E. Lucey to James P. Mitchell, U.S. Secretary of Labor, February 5, 1957, AASA; Texas Legislature, Senate-House Concurrent Resolution No. 13, January 23, 1957, AASA.

50. Letter from R. E. Lucey to Msgr. George G. Higgins, February 11, 1957, AASA.

51. Memos from R. E. Lucey to M. Kelly, May 9, 1955, AASA; to O'Connor, August 26, 1955, and July 23, 1956, AASA; to Rev. John Wagner, October 2, 1958, and January 12, 1959, AASA.

52. Memo from R. E. Lucey to O'Connor, June 12, 1956, AASA.

53. Craig, *The Bracero Program*, pp. 150–97; R. E. Lucey, address to the Eleventh Conference of the National Council for the Spanish Speaking, Milwaukee, May 8–10, 1962, AASA; R. E. Lucey, report of the BCSS to the American hierarchy, Rome, November 1965, AASA.

54. Bronder interview with McCarthy, August 4, 1976.

55. Bronder interview with O'Connor, August 14, 1976.

56. Bronder interview with McCarthy, August 4, 1976; Bronder interview with O'Connor, August 14, 1976.

57. Bronder interview with O'Connor, August 14, 1976; Bronder interview with McCarthy, August 4, 1976.

58. Bronder interview with O'Connor, August 14, 1976.

59. Bronder interview with McCarthy, August 4, 1976.

60. Bronder interview with O'Connor, August 14, 1976; letter from Robert Sanchez, Latin American Affairs Advisor to the Texas State AFL-CIO, to Jerry Holleman, president of the Texas State AFL-CIO, April 24, 1958, AASA.

61. Bronder interview with R. E. Lucey, June 14, 1977.

62. Bronder interview with Wagner, April 27, 1976.

63. Bronder interview with Josephine McInnis, August 24, 1977; letter from R. E. Lucey to Mrs. John L. Sullivan, May 31, 1957, AASA.

64. Comment by Prof. Howard L. Harrod of Vanderbilt University on the author's paper "Chicano Champion: Archbishop Robert E. Lucey of San Antonio and the Spanish Speaking of the Southwest," presented at the Western History Association, Kansas City, Mo., October 16, 1980.

65. Letter from R. E. Lucey to Wagner, May 23, 1966, AASA; letter from R. E. Lucey to Msgr. William Quinn, May 24, 1966, AASA; letter from R. E. Lucey to Most Rev. Henry J. O'Brien, June 14, 1966, AASA.

Chapter 5

1. J. E. Kraus, "Confraternity of Christian Doctrine," in *New Catholic Encyclopedia*, 16 vols. (New York: McGraw-Hill, 1967), 4: 155. For a history of the Confraternity see Joseph B. Collins, ed., *The Confraternity Comes of Age: A Historical Symposium* (Paterson, N.J.: Confraternity Publications, 1956), and J. Shaw, *Edward Vincent O'Hara: American Prelate* (New York: Farrar, Straus and Cudahy, 1957).

2. Letter from Verona Spellmire to R. E. Lucey, February 16, 1965, AASA. See also the brochure of the Los Angeles Archdiocesan CCD Jubilee Congress, February 18–20, 1972, AALA; "Confraternity Notes," published by the Los Angeles Archdiocesan CCD, June, 1962, AALA; and Dennis Burke, "The History of the Confraternity of Christian Doctrine in the Diocese of Los Angeles, 1922–1936" (Master's thesis, Catholic University of America, 1965).

3. Minutes of the meeting of the Los Angeles Archdiocesan Confraternity of Christian Doctrine (hereafter cited as CCD), November 26, 1923, AALA. See also minutes for the meetings of April 16, June 17, September 5, and September 24, 1923, AALA, and the report of the Bureau of Catholic Charities, archdiocese of Los Angeles, 1922, AALA.

4. R. E. Lucey, address to the Cathedral Young People's Club, Amarillo, n.d., ADA.

5. Minutes of the meeting of the Study Club, Sacred Heart Cathedral, Amarillo, November 25, 1936, ADA.

6. Letter from Rev. W. F. Bosen, Sacred Heart Church, Littlefield, Tex., to Rev. Thomas Drury, November 28, 1936, ADA; Kuehler interview with Bottoms, n.d.

7. *TPR*, October 23, 1938.

8. Bronder interview with Rev. Joseph R. Till, March 22, 1976; Bronder interview with R. E. Lucey, October 26, 1976; pastoral letter from R. E. Lucey to the archdiocese of San Antonio, January 6, 1942, AASA.

9. R. E. Lucey, address to the First Regional Inter-American Congress of the CCD, San Antonio, October 23, 1947, AASA; Bronder interview with Till, March 22, 1976.

10. R. E. Lucey, address to the Diocesan Council of Catholic Women, Austin, October 9, 1949, AASA; R. E. Lucey, address to the Regional CCD Congress, Albuquerque, October 2, 1955, AASA; R. E. Lucey, address to the Regional CCD Congress, Oklahoma City, May 12, 1959, AASA.

11. Pastoral letter from R. E. Lucey to the archdiocese of San Antonio, March 25, 1944, AASA; memos from R. E. Lucey to Rev. Charles Drees, director of CCD, May 15 and November 10, 1953, AASA; Bronder interview with Till, March 22, 1976.

12. Letter from R. E. Lucey to pastors outside San Antonio, September 25, 1947, AASA; Bronder interview with R. E. Lucey, March 15, 1977; memo from R. E. Lucey to Drees, August 23, 1955, AASA.

13. *TPR*, August 30, 1936, and November 19, 1939.

14. Letter from R. E. Lucey to pastors, August 23, 1943, AASA.

15. Pastoral letter from R. E. Lucey to the archdiocese of San Antonio, July 3, 1953, AASA.

16. R. E. Lucey, unpublished essay on the history of the Latin American Relations Subcommittee of the National Catholic Welfare Conference–CCD, 1945–1956, AASA.

17. Excerpt from the minutes of the CCD Inter-American Congress, Buffalo, N.Y., September 26–30, 1956, AASA.

18. Letter from R. E. Lucey to Rev. Frederick A. McGuire, executive secretary of the Mission Secretariat of the National Center of CCD, October 17, 1956, AASA.

19. Letter from R. E. Lucey to Most Rev. Raymond A. Lane, M.M., September 9, 1955, AASA.

20. Bronder interview with Till, March 22, 1976; Bronder interview with Rev. James McNiff, April 13, 1976; minutes of the CCD committee at the annual meeting of the American hierarchy, Washington, D.C., November 15, 1956, AASA.

21. Bronder interview with McNiff, April 13, 1976; Kuehler interview with Most Rev. Jose Gabriel Calderon, March 15, 1973; Kuehler interview with Rev. John Gorham, March 16, 1973.

22. McNiff worked alone on Operation Latin America from 1957 to 1961. At that time another Maryknoll priest, John Gorham, was added to the staff. Lucey also sent one of his own priests, Ramon Garcia, to help with the work in the early 1960s. These three constituted the Archbishop's Latin American team.

23. Letter from R. E. Lucey to Most Rev. Domenico Tardini, Secretary of State of Vatican City, January 3, 1957, AASA; letter from R. E. Lucey to Lane, February 4, 1957, AASA.

24. Letter from Msgr. Julian Mendoza Guerrero, secretary general of CELAM, to R. E. Lucey, April 9, 1957, AASA; letter from R. E. Lucey to Mendoza, April 22, 1957, AASA; letter from Mendoza to R. E. Lucey, May 2, 1957, AASA.

25. Bronder interview with McNiff, April 13, 1976.

26. Letter from R. E. Lucey to M. Marks, executive secretary of the NCWC-CCD, May 9, 1957, AASA; R. E. Lucey, unpublished essay on the history of the Latin American Relations Subcommittee, AASA; letter from R. E. Lucey to Marks, January 11, 1957, AASA; memo from R. E. Lucey to Till, August 18, 1959, AASA; letter from R. E. Lucey to Most Rev. Antonio Samoré, January 11, 1960, AASA.

27. Report on the conclusions of the third meeting of CELAM, Rome, November, 1958, AASA; letter from McNiff to R. E. Lucey, May 25, 1959, AASA; pastoral letter from Cardinal Luque, Archbishop of Bogota, April 27, 1959, AASA.

28. Bronder interview with McNiff, April 13, 1976; letter from Msgr. Paul Tanner to R. E. Lucey, August 10, 1960, AASA; letter from R. E. Lucey to McNiff, October 10, 1960, AASA; letter from R. E. Lucey to McNiff, October 18, 1960, AASA.

29. Letters from R. E. Lucey to McNiff, December 27 and December 28, 1960, AASA.

30. Letter from McNiff to R. E. Lucey, January 29, 1961, AASA.

31. Letter from Gorham to Rev. John W. Comber, M.M., Superior General of the Maryknoll order, September, 1962, AMM; letter from Gorham to R. E. Lucey, October 2, 1962, AASA.

32. Letter from R. E. Lucey to McNiff, August 6, 1962, AASA.

33. Letter from R. E. Lucey to Rev. Ramon Garcia, October 25, 1962, AASA.

34. Letters from R. E. Lucey to McNiff, January 7 and January 23, 1963, AASA; letter from McNiff to R. E. Lucey, January 17, 1963, AASA.

35. See J. Hofinger and T. Sheridan, eds., *The Medellin Papers* (Manila: East Asian Pastoral Institute, 1969).

36. Letter from R. E. Lucey to Gorham, March 13, 1967, AASA; memo from Gorham to Most Rev. John McCormack, M.M., July 28, 1968, AMM; from a Report on Catechetics in Latin America: Program under the Direction of R. E. Lucey, AMM.

37. Letter from R. E. Lucey to Garcia, February 15, 1965, AASA; letters from R. E. Lucey to Gorham, March 31 and May 24, 1965, AASA.

38. R. E. Lucey, report to the meeting of the American hierarchy, Washington, D.C., November, 1967, AASA.

39. Bronder interview with Rev. Virgil Elizondo, March 23, 1976; Kuehler interview with Calderon, March 15, 1973.

Chapter 6

1. *Pacem in Terris* (New York: American Press, 1963), p. 24. For an account of the civil rights movement in the 1960s, see Martin Luther King, Jr., *Why We Can't Wait* (New York: Harper and Row, 1963), and Benjamin Muse, *The American Negro Revolution: From Nonviolence to Black Power, 1963–1967* (Bloomington: Indiana University Press, 1968).

2. Letter from R. E. Lucey to Rev. Sherrill Smith, December 13, 1957, AASA.

3. Bronder interview with Rev. Sherrill Smith, November 4, 1977.

4. R. E. Lucey, address to the Texas Christian University Seminar on Interracial Relations, Fort Worth, June 14, 1961, AASA; letter from Smith to R. E. Lucey, April 19, 1963, AASA.

5. Hugh J. Nolan, ed., *Pastoral Letters of the American Hierarchy, 1792–1970* (Huntington, Ind.: Our Sunday Visitor, Inc., 1971), pp. 577–79.

6. R. E. Lucey, homily at the investiture of monsignori, San Antonio, April 16, 1964, AASA; pastoral letter from R. E. Lucey, May 22, 1964, AASA.

7. News release from National Catholic Welfare Conference News Service, May 21, 1964, AASA.

8. Letter from R. E. Lucey to Smith, May 27, 1964, AASA.

9. *Alamo Messenger*, March 19, 1965.

10. *San Antonio Express*, March 19, 1965; *San Antonio Light*, March 18, 1965.

11. *Texas Catholic Herald*, March 25, 1965.

12. For a sampling of opinions see the *New World* (archdiocese of Chicago), March 26, 1965; the *Pilot* (archdiocese of Boston), March 27, 1965; the *Criterion* (diocese of Indianapolis), March 26, 1965; the *Catholic Chronicle* (diocese of Toledo), March 26, 1965.

13. Letter from R. E. Lucey to Smith, March 29, 1965, AASA.

14. Pastoral letter from R. E. Lucey, August 11, 1965.

15. Letter from R. E. Lucey to Quinn, September 8, 1965, AASA.

16. Ibid.

17. Letter from Lyndon Johnson to R. E. Lucey, September 10, 1965, LBJL; *San Antonio Express-News*, August 26, 1967; memo from R. E. Lucey to himself, January 15, 1968, AASA; Bronder interview with Rev. John Yanta, October 28, 1977.

18. *San Antonio Light*, April 8, 1966; *San Antonio Express-News*, April 9, 1966.

19. Letter from Pope Paul VI to R. E. Lucey, March 3, 1966, AASA; telegram from Lyndon Johnson to R. E. Lucey, May 10, 1966. AASA; R. Sargent Shriver, address at the triple jubilee celebration of R. E. Lucey, San Antonio, March 14, 1966, AASA.

20. See John Tracy Ellis, "American Catholics and the Intellectual Life," *Thought* 30 (1955): 351–88, and Thomas F. O'Dea, *American Catholic Dilemma: An Inquiry into the Intellectual Life* (New York: Sheed and Ward, 1958).

21. Joann Wolski Conn, "From Certitude to Understanding: Historical Consciousness in the American Catholic Theological Community in the 1960's," (Ph.D. diss. Columbia University, 1974), pp. 26–70; Sydney Ahlstrom, *A Religious History of the American People* (New Haven: Yale University Press, 1972), pp. 1009–15.

22. For a detailed account of all the sessions of the Second Vatican Council, see the four-volume work of Xavier Rynne, *Letters from Vatican City: Vatican Council II, Background and Debates* (New York: Farrar, Straus and Company, 1963); *The Second Session* (London: Faber and Faber, 1963); *The Third Session* (New York: Farrar, Straus and Giroux, 1965); *The Fourth Session* (London: Faber and Faber, 1965).

23. Robert B. Kaiser, *Pope, Council and World: The Story of Vatican II* (New York: Macmillan, 1963), p. 12.

24. Walter M. Abbott, ed., *The Documents of Vatican II* (New York: Association Press, 1966).

25. "Address of the Pope," public session, December 7, 1965, in Rynne, *Fourth Session*, p. 324.

26. *San Antonio Light*, December 7, 1963; R. E. Lucey, address to the Southwest Liturgical Conference, San Antonio, January 27, 1964, AASA; R. E. Lucey, address to the Antonians, March 12, 1964, AASA.

27. Msgr. Roy Rihn, homily at the jubilee mass for the class of 1941, San Antonio, June 1, 1966, AASA.

28. Ibid.

29. Bronder interview with Msgr. Roy Rihn, November 7, 1977; pastoral letter from R. E. Lucey, July 8, 1966, AASA.

30. Jan Hart Cohen, "To See Christ in Our Brothers: The Role of the Texas Roman Catholic Church in the Rio Grande Valley Farm Workers' Movement in 1966–1967" (Master's thesis, University of Texas at Arlington, 1974), pp. 24–28. On June 8 the membership of the IWA voted to become Local 2 of Chavez's National Farm Workers Association.

31. Ibid., p. 23; *Corpus Christi Caller*, July 5 and July 6, 1966.

32. Cohen, "To See Christ in Our Brothers," pp. 28–29.

33. Ibid., pp. 29–31.

34. Bronder interview with R. E. Lucey, July 19, 1977; letter from Most Rev. Egidio Vagnozzi to R. E. Lucey, April 16, 1966, AASA.

35. Quoted in Cohen, "To See Christ in our Brothers," p. 32.

36. Memo from Rev. William Killian to R. E. Lucey, June 12, 1966, AASA; *Houston Post*, June 12, 1966; *Alamo Messenger*, June 17, 1966.

37. *Valley Evening Monitor*, June 20, 1966.

38. Ibid.

39. R. E. Lucey, statement to the San Antonio news media, June 20, 1966, AASA; letter from R. E. Lucey to Robert Sanchez, June 2, 1966, AASA.

40. Quoted in Cohen, "To See Christ in Our Brothers," pp. 43–45.

41. R. E. Lucey, address at the installation of Bishop Humberto Medeiros, Brownsville, Tex., June 29, 1966, AASA.

42. Cohen, "To See Christ in Our Brothers," pp. 44–45; Bronder interview with Most Rev. Humberto Medeiros, April 14, 1976.

43. Ibid., pp. 46–47.

44. R. E. Lucey, homily at the mass for the Valley marchers, San Antonio, August 27, 1966, AASA.

45. "The Confrontation," *Texas Observer*, September 16, 1966, pp. 10–11; *Dallas Morning News*, September 6, 1966; "The March: A Triumph, A Task," *Texas Observer*, September 16, 1966, p. 3.

46. Letter from R. E. Lucey to Higgins, September 19, 1966, AASA.

47. Letter from R. E. Lucey to Smith, February 23, 1959, AASA; letter from W. E. Thomas to R. E. Lucey, July 22, 1964, AASA; letter from R. E. Lucey to Thomas, July 27, 1964, AASA; R. E. Lucey, address to the Antonians, San Antonio, March 10, 1966, AASA.

48. Letter from Jack E. Coughlin to R. E. Lucey, April 22, 1966, AASA; letter from R. E. Lucey to Smith, April 25, 1966, AASA.

49. Letter from A. J. Range to Smith, April 26, 1966, AASA.

50. See *San Antonio Light* and *San Antonio Express* for strike coverage, August, 1966.

51. Memo from R. E. Lucey to himself, September 2, 1966, AASA.

52. Memo from R. E. Lucey to Smith, October 10, 1966, AASA.

53. Ibid.

54. Letter from Smith to R. E. Lucey, November 9, 1966, AASA.

55. Ibid.

56. Ibid.

57. Ibid.

58. Telegram from Cesar Chavez to R. E. Lucey, November 9, 1966, AASA.

59. Memo from Rev. Charles Grahmann to R. E. Lucey, November 10, 1966, AASA; letter from Smith and Killian to R. E. Lucey, November 10, 1966, AASA.

60. Memo from R. E. Lucey to Smith and Killian, November 14, 1966, AASA.

61. Bronder interview with Walter Corrigan, June 15, 1978.

62. *Alamo Messenger*, December 22, 1966; letter from R. E. Lucey to Smith, January 4, 1967, AASA.

63. Letter from R. E. Lucey to Smith, January 13, 1967, AASA; letter from R. E. Lucey to Edward Sullivan, January 9, 1967, AASA.

64. Memo from Msgr. J. Leroy Manning to Whom It May Concern, January 13, 1967, AASA.

65. *Alamo Messenger*, October 6, 1966; Bronder interview with Rev. Charles Herzig, October 31, 1977; University of Texas at Arlington Oral History Project (cited hereafter as UTAOH Project), UTARL, interview with William Killian, March 3, 1972.

66. Cohen, "To See Christ in Our Brothers," p. 86.

67. Letter from Most Rev. Humberto Medeiros to R. E. Lucey, January 2, 1967, AASA; letter from R. E. Lucey to Roy Evans, January 30, 1967, AASA.

68. The three priests arrested with Smith and Killian were Marvin Doerfler, Donald Hefferman, and William Hayes. The other five people arrested were Isabel Diaz, Leonor Gorga, Gregoria Solis, Benito Rodriquez, and Antonio Orendain.

69. *San Antonio News*, February 2, 1967; letter from R. E. Lucey to Smith, February 2, 1967, AASA.

70. Bronder interview with R. E. Lucey, July 19, 1977.

71. Letter from R. E. Lucey to Medeiros, February 2, 1967, AASA.

72. *San Antonio Express*, February 2, 1967; *San Antonio Express-News*, February 5, 1967; telegram from Evans to R. E. Lucey, February 3, 1967, AASA; telegram from Hank Brown to R. E. Lucey, February 7, 1967, AASA.

73. *San Antonio Express*, February 6, 1967.

74. Kuehler interview with R. E. Lucey, October 26, 1972.

75. *San Antonio Express-News*, February 4, 1967; Bronder interview with Rev. Joseph Deane, June 13, 1978.

76. *San Antonio Express-News*, February 12, 1967.

77. Memo from R. E. Lucey to himself, February 14, 1967, AASA.

78. Letter from Msgr. Erwin Juraschek to Sherrill Smith, March 8, 1967, AASA; *San Antonio News*, March 14, 1967.

79. Letter from William Elizondo to R. E. Lucey, March 21, 1967, AASA.

80. Letter from Grahmann to Elizondo, March 28, 1967, AASA.

81. UTAOH Project, interview with Sherrill Smith, March 2, 1972.

Chapter 7

1. R. E. Lucey, inaugural invocation, January 20, 1965, AASA.

2. R. E. Lucey, homily at mass for the Latin American ambassadors, San Antonio, April 2, 1967, AASA.

3. *New York Times*, April 3, 1967; *Los Angeles Times*, April 3, 1967; Washington, D.C., *Evening Star*, April 3, 1967.

4. Saint Mary's University *Rattler*, April 14, 1967.

5. *National Catholic Reporter*, April 12, 1967.

6. Letter from R. E. Lucey to Johnson, August 22, 1967, AASA; letter from R. E. Lucey to Ralph Yarborough, August 25, 1967, AASA.

7. *San Antonio News*, September 7, 1967; R. E. Lucey, statement to the San Antonio news media, September 8, 1967, AASA; *San Antonio Express-News*, September 9, 1967; letter from R. E. Lucey to Johnson, September 13, 1967, AASA.

8. Letter from R. E. Lucey to Most Rev. Francis Spellman, September 11, 1967, AASA; letter from R. E. Lucey to Msgr. Franco Brambilla, chargé d'affaires to Apostolic Delegation, September 22, 1967, AASA.

9. *San Antonio Express*, April 30, 1967.

10. UTAOH Project, interview with Smith, March 2, 1972; Bronder interview with Deane, June 13, 1978.

11. *San Antonio Express*, April 30, 1967.

12. *San Antonio News*, May 2, 1967; *San Antonio Express*, May 2, 1967; *San Antonio Sun*, May 4, 1967.

13. Memo from Henry Munoz, Jr., to Brown, May 4, 1967, AASA; *San Antonio Express*, May 5, 1967.

14. Unsigned letter to the editor, *San Antonio Express*, May 10, 1967; memo from R. E. Lucey to himself, May 15, 1967, AASA.

15. Letter from R. E. Lucey to Rev. John Orr, June 8, 1967; letter from R. E. Lucey to Rev. Maurice Dillane, June 8, 1967; letter from R. E. Lucey to Rev. Donald Heffernan, June 8, 1967; letter from R. E. Lucey to Lawrence Murtagh, June 13, 1967; letter from Manning to Deane, September 6, 1967; memo from R. E. Lucey to himself, May 22, 1967; letter from R. E. Lucey to Rev. Robert Walden, June 12, 1967 (all in AASA); *Houston Chronicle*, December 17, 1968.

16. Minutes of the meeting of the Priests' Senate, June 29, 1967, AASA; *San Antonio Express-News*, July 9, 1967.

17. Letters from R. E. Lucey to Walden, December 9 and December 19, 1966, AASA.

18. Letter from R. E. Lucey to Walden, July 17, 1967, AASA.

19. Letter from Rev. Clarence Leopold to the San Antonio archdiocesan clergy, October 27, 1967, AASA.

20. Letter from R. E. Lucey to Leopold, October 30, 1967, AASA.

21. Ibid.

22. Letter from Leopold to R. E. Lucey, November 17, 1967, AASA.

23. *National Catholic Reporter*, November 29, 1967.

24. Letter from Rev. John L. McKenzie to the editor, *National Catholic Reporter*, December 12, 1967.

25. Ibid.

26. *Alamo Messenger*, December 22, 1967.

27. Minutes of the meeting of the Priests' Senate, November 29, 1967, AASA; letter from R. E. Lucey to Manning, February 19, 1968; pastoral letter from R. E. Lucey, March 5, 1968, AASA.

28. Minutes of the meeting of the Priests' Senate, February 20, 1968, AASA.

29. Letter from the Priests' Association of the Archdiocese of San Antonio Steering Committee to R. E. Lucey, March 3, 1968, AASA; *San Antonio News*, March 8, 1968.

30. Letter from Manning to Rev. Marion Swize, March 8, 1968, AASA.

31. Letter from Swize to R. E. Lucey, March 16, 1968, AASA.

32. Letter from Leopold to R. E. Lucey, March 26, 1968, AASA; letter from R. E. Lucey to Swize, March 20, 1968, AASA.

33. Letter from Leopold to R. E. Lucey, March 21, 1968, AASA.

34. Letter from the Priests' Association Steering Committee to R. E. Lucey, April 6, 1968, AASA.

35. Memo from R. E. Lucey to himself, April 15, 1968, AASA.

36. *San Antonio Express-News*, April 28, 1968.

37. Letter from Rev. Joseph Till to R. E. Lucey, May 21, 1968, AASA; *San Antonio Express*, May 22, 1968.

38. Letter from R. E. Lucey to Till, June 14, 1968, AASA.

39. *San Antonio News*, June 13, 1968.

40. Letter from R. E. Lucey to Rev. James Brandes, June 18, 1968, AASA.

41. Pastoral letter from R. E. Lucey, August 6, 1968, AASA.

42. Letter from James Brandes to the editor, *San Antonio Express-News*, August 14, 1968.

43. Letter from R. E. Lucey to Till, September 4, 1968, AASA.

44. Memo from Manning to R. E. Lucey, September 5, 1968, AASA.

45. Letter from Till to R. E. Lucey, September 8, 1968, AASA.

46. Letter from R. E. Lucey to Leopold, September 11, 1968, AASA; letter from R. E. Lucey to Till, September 10, 1968, AASA.

47. Letter from Till to R. E. Lucey, September 18, 1968, AASA.

48. Bronder interview with Rihn, November 7, 1977.

49. Bronder interview with Smith, November 4, 1977; Bronder interview with Rihn, November 7, 1977.

50. Letter from fifty-one priests to Pope Paul VI et al., September 16, 1968, AASA.

51. Ibid.

52. Ibid.

53. Bronder interview with Herzig, October 31, 1977.

54. Letter from R. E. Lucey to Most Rev. Luigi Raimondi, September 20, 1968, AASA.

55. Letter from R. E. Lucey to Raimondi, September 26, 1968, AASA.

56. Letter from Raimondi to Rihn, October 10, 1968, AASA.

57. Letter from R. E. Lucey to Raimondi, October 14, 1968, AASA.

58. Letter from R. E. Lucey to Rev. Carlos Quintana, October 17, 1968, AASA; letter from R. E. Lucey to Rihn, October 17, 1968, AASA.

59. Letter from Rihn to R. E. Lucey, October 20, 1968, AASA.

60. Fact Sheet, published by Assumption Seminary Awareness Committee, October 21, 1968 (cited hereafter as Fact Sheet), AASA; Bronder interview with Rihn, November 7, 1977.

61. Telegram from Rev. Louis Michalski to Raimondi, October 17, 1968, AASA.

62. Letter from Raimondi to R. E. Lucey, October 21, 1968, AASA.

63. Letter from R. E. Lucey to Rev. Eustace Struckoff, October 22, 1968, AASA.

64. Fact Sheet, October 22, 1968, AASA; Bronder interview with Eustace Struckoff, May 26, 1978.

65. Fact Sheet, October 22, 1968, AASA.

66. Statement of fifty-one priests of the archdiocese of San Antonio, Texas, concerning the resignation of Archbishop Robert E. Lucey, October 24, 1968, AASA; *San Antonio Express-News*, October 25, 1968; *New York Times*, October 25, 1968; *National Catholic Reporter*, October 30, 1968.

67. Letter from 127 Assumption Seminary students to Pope Paul VI et al., October 25, 1968, AASA; Fact Sheet, October 23, 1968, AASA.

68. Letter from Raimondi to R. E. Lucey, October 30, 1968, AASA.

69. Letter from R. E. Lucey to Rihn, October 30, 1968; letter from R. E. Lucey to Walden, October 30, 1968; letter from R. E. Lucey to Michalski, October 30, 1968; letter from R. E. Lucey to Raymond Henke, October 30, 1968 (all in AASA); *San Antonio Express-News*, October 31, 1968; letter from seventeen priests of the archdiocese of San Antonio to Pope Paul VI et al., October 30, 1968, AASA; *San Antonio Express*, October 31, 1968; *San Antonio Light*, October 31, 1968.

70. Memo from Killian to R. E. Lucey, October 30, 1968, AASA.

71. Ibid.

72. R. E. Lucey, remarks to pastors at chancery meeting, October 31, 1968, AASA.

73. Memo from Killian to R. E. Lucey, October 31, 1968, AASA.

74. Ibid.

75. Memo from R. E. Lucey to Killian, November 4, 1968, AASA.

76. Letter from R. E. Lucey to Raimondi, October 31, 1968, AASA.

77. Pastoral letter from R. E. Lucey, November 3, 1968, AASA; *San Antonio Express*, November 4, 1968; *San Antonio Light*, November 4, 1968.

78. Letter from Rihn to R. E. Lucey, November 4, 1968; letter from Walden to R. E. Lucey, November 4, 1968; letter from Henke to R. E. Lucey, November 4, 1968; letter from Michalski to R. E. Lucey, November 4, 1968 (all in AASA); request for the resignation of R. E. Lucey as Archbishop of the archdiocese of San Antonio, petition delivered to chan-

cery office, November 7, 1968, AASA; "The Priests' Rebellion," *Newsweek*, November 11, 1968, p. 71; *Washington Post*, November 13, 1968; *New York Times*, November 17, 1968; *San Antonio Light*, November 12, 1968; *San Antonio Express*, November 13, 1968.

79. Letter from R. E. Lucey to Raimondi, November 18, 1968, AASA.

80. Letter from R. E. Lucey to Drury, December 3, 1968, AASA.

81. Letter from Most Rev. William Connare to the archdiocesan clergy, December 2, 1968, AASA.

82. Letter from Raimondi to R. E. Lucey, November 29, 1968, AASA.

83. Bronder interview with Most Rev. William Connare, April 30, 1976.

84. Letter from R. E. Lucey to Raimondi, December 4, 1968, AASA.

85. Letter from R. E. Lucey to Cicognani, December 4, 1968, AASA.

86. Letter from Cicognani to R. E. Lucey, December 21, 1968; letter from Raimondi to R. E. Lucey, December 7, 1968; letter from R. E. Lucey to Raimondi, December 10, 1968 (all in AASA).

87. Bronder interview with Rev. J. L. Manning, October 26, 1977.

88. Letter from R. E. Lucey to Cicognani, December 13, 1968, AASA.

89. Letter from Connare to the archdiocesan clergy, December 7, 1968, AASA; *Alamo Messenger*, December 13, 1968; letter from R. E. Lucey to the Archdiocesan Fact Finding Committee, December 10, 1968, AASA.

90. Letter from Raimondi to R. E. Lucey, December 12, 1968, AASA.

91. Letter from Msgr. Joseph Nowak to R. E. Lucey, December 29, 1968, AASA; letter from R. E. Lucey to Connare, January 13, 1968, AASA.

92. Priests' Association *Newsletter* 2, no. 1, February 7, 1969; 2, no. 2, March 25, 1969, AASA.

93. Letter from Pope Paul VI to R. E. Lucey, May 23, 1969, AASA; R. E. Lucey, resignation statement to the San Antonio news media, June 4, 1969, AASA.

94. *San Antonio Express*, July 2, 1969; R. E. Lucey, remarks at testimonial dinner, San Antonio, July 1, 1969, AASA.

95. Letter from Pope Paul VI to R. E. Lucey, September 6, 1969, AASA; letter from Connare, June 4, 1969, AASA.

96. Bronder interviews with R. E. Lucey, June 28, July 5, and July 19, 1977.

Epilogue

1. Bronder interview with R. E. Lucey, July 13, 1976. See also "Satellites" file, Robert E. Lucey Papers, AASA.

2. Bronder interview with R. E. Lucey, June 14, 1977.

3. Bronder interviews with Rihn, November 7, 1977; Smith, November 4, 1977; Till, March 22, 1976; Kuehler interview with Killian, n.d.

Bibliography

Archives and Manuscript Collections

The principal source materials used in this study were the papers of Archbishop Robert E. Lucey. When I arrived in San Antonio in the spring of 1976, I found the Archbishop's papers stuffed in two large filing cabinets in the storage cellar of the San Antonio chancery office. The papers were in no discernible order. During my two-year stay in the city, I was able to more than double the archival holdings of the Lucey papers, principally by persuading the Archbishop to deposit the large volume of letters, memos, sermons, and addresses that he had taken to his residence on retirement. After spending nearly six months putting the papers into workable order, I began my research.

Archives of the Archdiocese of Los Angeles, Los Angeles, California

The Archives of the Archdiocese of Los Angeles were especially helpful in filling out the Archbishop's early years. They contain information on Saint Vincent College, the Bureau of Catholic Charities, the Confraternity of Christian Doctrine in Los Angeles, and Lucey's correspondence with various Los Angeles priests. Across the street from the archive building is the headquarters of the *Tidings*, the official archdiocesan newspaper, where one can find back copies of the paper. The archives are in excellent condition.

Archives of the Archdiocese of San Antonio, San Antonio, Texas

The San Antonio Archives presently contain most of the papers of Archbishop Lucey. Included in the collection are letters and correspondence relating to the Confraternity of Christian Doctrine, the Bishops' Committee for the Spanish Speaking, the Catholic Welfare Bureau, Catholic Action, organized labor in Texas, the Archbishop's pastoral letters from 1941 through 1969, voluminous addresses and sermons, family correspondence, several diaries, the transcripts of "Saint Anthony's Hour," twelve large scrapbooks of newspaper clippings and personal letters, correspondence relative to the Priests' Senate and the Priests' Association as well as a large collection of miscellaneous correspondence dating from the Archbishop's years in Los Angeles. In addition, the San Antonio Archives contain an extensive collection of interviews with the Archbishop, priests, and lay people who became part of this story. Located upstairs in the chancery office are the "live" files that contain the personal dossiers of every priest currently in the archdiocese and correspondence on numerous archdiocesan programs. Downstairs are the "dead" files, those relating to deceased clergy of the archdiocese, and extensive records on every parish in the archdiocese. The Lucey papers in this archive are quite substantial and in excellent condition for future research.

Archives of the Diocese of Amarillo, Amarillo, Texas

The most valuable holding in the Amarillo archives is the complete record of the *Texas Panhandle Register*, containing Bishop Lucey's editorial column as well as a full account of Catholic life in the diocese under his episcopacy. The archives also contain a sizable collection of Lucey letters to the American Board of Catholic Missions, the Extension Society of America, and the Catholic Association for International Peace. There are also diocesan financial records and correspondence between Lucey and Raymond McGowan. In addition there are records of the activities of the Confraternity of Christian Doctrine and the Catholic Welfare Bureau.

Archives of the Maryknoll Missionaries, Maryknoll, New York

The personal correspondence files of James McNiff and John Gorham, two members of Lucey's Latin America Confraternity team, shed some light on this complex operation and on Lucey's manner of dealing with the Latin American hierarchy.

Archives of the Missionary Society of Saint Paul the Apostle, New York, New York

The archives of the Paulist Fathers contain several folders of correspondence between Lucey and the Paulists staffing the Newman Center at the University of Texas at Austin. The correspondence details the Archbishop's discontent with several Paulists over the implementation of various decrees of the Second Vatican Council and his subsequent withdrawal of support from them.

Baylor University Library, Waco, Texas

Baylor University's Program for Oral History contains two lengthy interviews with the Archbishop, which were of only general interest.

Catholic Archives of Texas, Austin, Texas

These archives are the principal repository for the diocese of Austin but are thin on material relating to Archbishop Lucey's career.

Cudahy Memorial Library, Loyola University of Chicago, Chicago, Illinois

The library contains the records of the Catholic Church Extension Society of America, which provided information dealing with the Society's financial contributions to the diocese of Amarillo in the 1930s.

Catholic University of America Library, Washington, D.C.

At the time of my research, the papers and records of the National Catholic Welfare Conference at the Catholic University of America Library were not in workable condition and thus were useless for this study.

Franklin D. Roosevelt Library, Hyde Park, New York

The Roosevelt Library contains several letters between Lucey and the President but little of significance for this study.

Harry S. Truman Library, Independence, Missouri

The Truman Library contains some correspondence between Lucey and the President, but on the whole, this was not an important source of information.

Lyndon B. Johnson Library, Austin, Texas

The Johnson Library contained several folders of correspondence between Lucey and Johnson during the latter's career as a Congressman, Senator, and President. Most of the material was declassified, although there were three letters that I was not permitted to read. The Lucey-Johnson correspondence contained some interesting reading, especially the letters between the Apostolic Delegation and the White House regarding Vietnam and the Johnson Administration's assessment of the pecking order of the American hierarchy. The numerous letters and memos exchanged by Lucey and Jack Valenti reveal a warm friendship between the two.

Low Memorial Library, Columbia University, New York, New York

The oral history collection at Columbia contains an interview with Mr. H. L. Mitchell, the man responsible for having President Truman select Archbishop Lucey for membership on the President's Commission on Migratory Labor.

Marquette University Memorial Library, Milwaukee, Wisconsin

The Marquette University Memorial Library holds the correspondence of the Catholic Association for International Peace, of which Lucey was once a member and vice-president.

University of Notre Dame Library, South Bend, Indiana

On retiring from the archdiocese in 1969, Lucey was irritated that none of the three Catholic colleges in San Antonio asked him for his papers. Father Thomas Blantz, archivist at Notre Dame, did ask and received several boxes of original Lucey letters, which are now located in the university's fine collection. The Lucey collection here consists mainly of papers dealing with the Archbishop's Confraternity work in the United States and Latin America, the Bishops' Committee for the Spanish Speaking, personal correspondence, travel schedules, birthday and seasonal greeting cards, and the like.

University of Texas at Arlington Library, Arlington, Texas

The University of Texas at Arlington archives were useful principally for the material they contained regarding Lucey's labor activities in Texas and his association with the Rio Grande Valley farm workers' movement. Jan Hart Cohen interviewed key people involved in the farm workers' strike and march, and her master's thesis on the Roman Catholic Church's participation in the movement was especially helpful to me.

University of Texas at Austin Library, Austin, Texas

The principal collection at the University of Texas at Austin relating to the Archbishop is the Maury Maverick papers, which made for interesting reading but added little to my understanding of Lucey's friendship with the former Mayor of San Antonio. The Oral History Program of the University of Texas at Austin contains one interview with Archbishop Lucey. Unfortunately the interviewer allowed the Archbishop to stray repeatedly from the questions, and thus the interview was of little value.

Personal Interviews

From the spring of 1976 until two weeks before his death, I interviewed Archbishop Lucey on Tuesday afternoons for approximately forty-five minutes per interview. In addition to Archbishop Lucey, the following people kindly took time to talk with me: Cardinal Humberto Medeiros; Archbishop Joseph McGucken; Bishop William G. Connare; Fathers Joseph Deane, John Dunne, Virgil Elizondo, Charles Grahmann, Charles Herzig, John McCarthy, James McNiff, J. Leroy Manning, Augustine O'Dea, Bernard Popp, Roy Rihn, Sherrill Smith, Francis Smyer, Eustace Struckoff, Lawrence Stuebben, Joseph Till, Joseph Truxaw, John Wagner, Alexander Wangler, and John Yanta; Rabbi David Jacobsen; Sisters Dolores Girault and Angela Clare Lucey; and Walter Corrigan, Joseph Edelein, Callan Graham, Mrs. John Gulde, Hazel Kelly, Mrs. Carl Lutz, Mrs. Josephine McInnis, Mrs. Luci Johnson Nugent, Robert Walden, and Senator Ralph Yarborough. I am also grateful to the following for having answered my interview requests by mail: Fathers Matthew Kelly and William O'Connor, Mrs. Mary E. Carson, William Grady, Mrs. Lady Bird Johnson, Edmund T. Lucey, Jr., Mrs. Mary E. Lucey. All of my interviews remain in my possession. Some have been transcribed, others remain on tape, and still others are in the form of hand-written notes.

In addition to the interviews conducted for oral history projects by various universities as noted above, Marilyn Kuehler conducted several dozen interviews in preparation for a biography of Archbishop Lucey that, unfortunately, was never completed. The following is a select list of the Kuehler interviews that I consulted: Archbishop Robert E. Lucey; Cardinal Dario Miranda; Bishop Jose Gabriel Calderon; Fathers Clifford Blackburn, James Boyle, Paul Ehlinger, Ramon Garcia, John Gorham, Erwin Juraschek, William Killian, James Lockwood, Roy Rihn, Sherrill Smith, and John Wagner; and Marguerite and Esperanza Batz, Archibald Bottoms, Julia May, Genevieve and Florence Kelly, and Edward O'Flaherty. All of the Kuehler interviews have been transcribed and are located in the Archives of the Archdiocese of San Antonio.

Reports

National Catholic Welfare Conference Report. "Organized Social Justice: An Economic Program for the United States Applying Pius XI's Great Encyclical on Social Life." New York: Paulist Press, 1935.

Report of the President's Commission on Migratory Labor. "Migratory Labor and American Agriculture." Washington, D.C.: U.S. Government Printing Office, 1951.

Report of the San Antonio Archdiocesan Fact Finding Committee. 494 pages of testimony. Unpublished, 1968, AASA.

U.S. Department of Agriculture. Agricultural Economic Report number 77. "Termination of the Bracero Program: Some Effects on Farm Labor and Migrant Housing Needs." Washington, D.C.: U.S. Government Printing Office, 1965.

U.S. Department of Agriculture. Annual Meteorological Summaries. "Report of the Chief of the Weather Bureau, 1934–1935." Washington, D.C.: U.S. Government Printing Office, 1936.

U.S. Department of Labor. *Farm Labor Fact Book*. Washington, D.C.: U.S. Government Printing Office, 1959.

United States Supreme Court Reports. 67 Lawyers' ed. U.S. 260–62. October term, 1922. Rochester, N.Y.: Lawyers' Cooperative Publishing Company, 1924.

———. 79 Lawyers' ed. U.S. 293–95. October term, 1934. Rochester, N.Y.: Lawyers' Cooperative Publishing Company, 1935.

Newspapers

Alamo Messenger
Amarillo Daily News
Amarillo Globe
Amarillo Sunday News and Globe
Austin American-Statesman
Brooklyn Tablet
Boston Pilot
Brownsville Herald
Catholic Messenger (Davenport, Iowa)
Corpus Christi Caller
Dallas Morning News
Dallas Times Herald
Denver Register
Evening Star (Washington, D.C.)
Fort Worth Star Telegram
Houston Chronicle
Houston Post
Long Beach Press-Telegram

Long Beach Sun
Los Angeles Examiner
Los Angeles Times
National Catholic News Service
National Catholic Reporter
New York Times
L'Osservatore Romano
Our Sunday Visitor
Pampa Advocate
Pampa Daily
Rattler
San Antonio Express
San Antonio Express-News
San Antonio Light
San Antonio News
Sun (*San Antonio Express-News* Sunday supplement)
Texas Panhandle Register
Tidings
Valley Evening Monitor
Valley Morning Star
Washington Post

Magazines

America
Ave Maria
Catholic Charities Review
Catholic Mind
Catholic World
Commonweal
Harper's
Homiletic and Pastoral Review
Month
Nation
Newsweek
Official Catholic Directory
Progressive
Social Justice
Texas AFL-CIO News
Texas Almanac, 1976–1977
Texas Observer
Texas State Federation of Labor Review
Time

Books

Abbott, Walter M., ed. *The Documents of Vatican II.* New York: America Press, 1966.

Abell, Aaron I. *American Catholicism and Social Action: A Search for Social Justice, 1865–1950.* Garden City, N.Y.: Doubleday, 1960.

Ahlstrom, Sidney E. *A Religious History of the American People.* New Haven: Yale University Press, 1972.

Barry, Colman J., ed. *Readings in Church History.* 3 vols. Westminster, Md.: Newman Press, 1965.

Betten, Neil. *Catholic Activism and the Industrial Worker.* Gainesville: University Presses of Florida, 1976.

Bokenkotter, Thomas. *A Concise History of the Catholic Church.* Garden City, N.Y.: Doubleday, 1977.

Bremner, Robert H. *From the Depths: The Discovery of Poverty in the United States.* New York: New York University Press, 1956.

Broderick, Francis L. *Right Reverend New Dealer: John A. Ryan.* New York: Macmillan, 1963.

Brogan, D.W. *The American Character.* New York: Alfred A. Knopf, 1944.

Brusher, Joseph S. *Consecrated Thunderbolt: Father Yorke of San Francisco.* Hawthorne, N.J.: Joseph F. Wagner, 1973.

Chabot, Frederick C. *With the Makers of San Antonio: Genealogies of Early San Antonio Families.* San Antonio: Privately published, 1937.

Collins, Joseph B., ed. *The Confraternity Comes of Age: A Historical Symposium.* Paterson, N.J.: Confraternity Publications, 1956.

Corner, William, ed. *San Antonio de Bexar: A Guide and History.* San Antonio: Bainbridge and Corner, 1890.

Corwin, Arthur F., ed. *Immigrants—and Immigrants: Perspectives on Mexican Labor Migration to the United States.* Westport, Conn.: Greenwood Press, 1978.

Craig, Richard B. *The Bracero Program: Interest Groups and Foreign Policy.* Austin: University of Texas Press, 1971.

Cross, Robert D. *The Emergence of Liberal Catholicism in America.* Cambridge: Harvard University Press, 1958.

DeVito, Michael J. *The New York Review, 1905–1908.* New York: United States Catholic Historical Society, 1977.

Ellis, John Tracy. *American Catholicism*. Chicago: University of Chicago Press, 1969.

————, *Essays in Seminary Education*. Notre Dame, Ind.: Fides Press, 1967.

————, ed. *The Catholic Priest in the United States: Historical Investigations*. Collegeville, Minn.: Saint John's University Press, 1971.

Flynn, George Q. *Roosevelt and Romanism: Catholics and American Diplomacy, 1937–1945*. Westport, Conn.: Greenwood Press, 1976.

Fogelson, Robert M. *The Fragmented Metropolis: Los Angeles, 1850–1930*. Cambridge: Harvard University Press, 1967.

Galarza, Ernesto; Gallegos, Herman; and Samora, Julian. *Mexican-Americans in the Southwest*. Santa Barbara, Cal.: McNally and Loftin, 1969.

Gannon, Robert I. *The Cardinal Spellman Story*. Garden City, N.Y.: Doubleday, 1962.

Garraty, John A. *The American Nation: A History of the United States Since 1865*. New York: Harper and Row, 1966.

Gavin, Donald. *The National Conference of Catholic Charities*. Milwaukee: Bruce Press, 1962.

Gleason, Philip, ed. *Contemporary Catholicism in the United States*. Notre Dame, Ind.: University of Notre Dame Press, 1969.

Grebler, Leo; Moore, Joan; and Guzman, Ralph C. *The Mexican-American People: The Nation's Second Largest Minority*. New York: Free Press, 1970.

Guttman, Allen. *The Wound in the Heart: America and the Spanish Civil War*. New York: Free Press, 1962.

Hays, Samuel. *The Response to Industrialism, 1885–1914*. Chicago: University of Chicago Press, 1957.

Hofinger, J.; and Sheridan, T., eds. *The Medellin Papers*. Manila: East Asian Pastoral Institute, 1969.

Hofstadter, Richard. *The Age of Reform*. New York: Harper and Row, 1955.

Kaiser, Robert B. *Pope, Council and World: The Story of Vatican II*. New York: Farrar, Straus and Company, 1963.

King, Martin Luther, Jr. *Why We Can't Wait*. New York: Harper and Row, 1963.

Kugler, Richard. *Simple Justice*. New York: Alfred A. Knopf, 1975.

Lemius, J. B. *Catechism on Modernism: Founded on the Encyclical "Pascendi Dominici Gregis" of His Holiness, Pius X.* New York: Society for the Propagation of the Faith, 1908.

Leuchtenburg, William. *The Perils of Prosperity, 1914–1932.* Chicago: University of Chicago Press, 1958.

Liu, William T., and Pallone, Nathaniel J., eds. *Catholics/U.S.A.: Perspectives on Social Change.* New York: John Wiley and Sons, 1970.

McAvoy, Thomas T. *A History of the Catholic Church in the United States.* Notre Dame, Ind.: University of Notre Dame Press, 1969.

McGowan, Raymond A. *Toward Social Justice: A Discussion and Application of Pius XI's "Reconstructing the Social Order."* New York: Paulist Press, 1935.

McKenzie, John L. *Authority in the Church.* New York: Sheed and Ward, 1966.

McNamara, Robert F. *The American College in Rome, 1855–1955.* Rochester, N.Y.: Christopher Press, 1956.

Moore, Edmund. *A Catholic Runs for President: The Campaign of 1928.* New York: Ronald Press, 1956.

Mowry, George E. *The California Progressives.* Berkeley: University of California Press, 1951.

Muse, Benjamin. *The American Negro Revolution: From Nonviolence to Black Power, 1963–1967.* Bloomington: Indiana University Press, 1968.

Myrdal, Gunner. *An American Dilemma.* New York: Harper and Brothers, 1944.

New Catholic Encyclopedia. 16 vols. New York: McGraw-Hill, 1967.

Nolan, Hugh J., ed. *Pastoral Letters of the American Hierarchy, 1792–1970.* Huntington, Ind.: Our Sunday Visitor, Inc., 1971.

O'Brien, David J. *American Catholics and Social Reform: The New Deal Years.* New York: Oxford University Press, 1968.

O'Dea, Thomas F. *American Catholic Dilemma: An Inquiry into the Intellectual Life.* New York: Sheed and Ward, 1958.

Pacem in Terris. New York: American Press, 1963.

Panhandle Anchor: An Installation Publication. Amarillo: Privately published, 1934.

Parison, P. F., and Smith, C. J., comp. *History of the Catholic Church in the Diocese of San Antonio, Texas.* San Antonio: Carrico and Bowen, 1897.

Putz, Louis J., ed. *The Catholic Church, U.S.A.* Chicago: Fides Publishers Association, 1956.

Ramsdell, Charles. *San Antonio: A Historical and Pictorial Guide.* San Antonio: Naylor, 1959.

Rankin, Charles, ed. *The Pope Speaks.* New York: Harcourt, Brace and Company, 1940.

Ratte, John. *Three Modernists: Alfred Loisy, George Tyrell, William L. Sullivan.* New York: Sheed and Ward, 1967.

Reisler, Mark. *By the Sweat of Their Brow: Mexican Immigration Labor in the United States, 1900–1940.* Westport, Conn.: Greenwood Press, 1976.

Roche, M. F. *Recollections of Forty Years of the Diocese of Amarillo, 1927–1967.* Amarillo: Privately published, 1967.

Ryan, John A. *A Living Wage.* New York: Macmillan, 1906.

Rynne, Xavier. *Letters from Vatican City: Vatican Council II, Background and Debates.* New York: Farrar, Straus and Company, 1963.

———. *The Second Session: The Debates and Decrees of Vatican Council II, September 29 to December 4, 1963.* London: Faber and Faber, 1963.

———. *The Third Session: The Debates and Decrees of Vatican Council II, September 14 to November 21, 1964.* New York: Farrar, Straus and Giroux, 1965.

———. *The Fourth Session: The Debates and Decrees of Vatican Council II, September 14 to December 8, 1965.* London: Faber and Faber, 1965.

Shaw, J. *Edward Vincent O'Hara: American Prelate.* New York: Farrar, Straus and Cudahy, 1957.

Strumberg, Robert, comp. *History of San Antonio and the Early Days of Texas.* San Antonio: Standard Printing Company, 1920.

Summer School of Social Action for Priests. Mundelein, Ill.: Privately published, 1938.

Treacy, Gerald C., ed. *Five Great Encyclicals.* New York: Paulist Press, 1939.

Truxaw, Joseph. *Diary of a Seminarian, 1907–1917.* Los Angeles: Privately published, n.d.

Wertenbaker, Green Payton. *San Antonio: City in the Sun.* New York: McGraw-Hill, 1946.

Wiebe, Robert. *The Search for Order, 1877–1920.* New York: Hill and Wang, 1967.

Yzermans, Vincent A., ed. *American Participation in the Second Vatican Council.* New York: Sheed and Ward, 1967.

Articles

Blakely, Paul. "Labor Wages a Losing Battle." *America* 56 (1937): 417–18.

Donovan, John D. "The American Catholic Hierarchy: A Social Profile." *American Catholic Sociological Review* 19 (1958): 98–112.

Ellis, John Tracy. "American Catholics and the Intellectual Life." *Thought* (1955): 351–88.

"Franklin D. Roosevelt and John L. Lewis." *Catholic World* 145 (1937): 385–89.

Hales, E. E. Y. "The Americanist Controversy." *Month* 31 (1964): 36–43.

Hayes, Patrick Cardinal. "The Leaven of Charity." *Catholic Charities Review* 17 (October 1933): 259–63.

"Labor in the Recession." *Commonweal* 28 (1938): 47.

McAvoy, Thomas T. "The Catholic Church in the United States between Two Wars." *Review of Politics* 4 (1942): 409–31.

McNicholas, Archbishop John T. "Justice and the Present Crisis." *Catholic Mind* 29 (1931): 473–81.

O'Connell, William Cardinal. "The Changed Condition of Labor." *Catholic Mind* 29 (1931): 1–4.

Parsons, Wilfred. "The Social Thought of the American Hierarchy: Our Bishops Speak." *Social Order* 2 (1952): 259–78.

Ryan, John A. "The Study of Social Problems in the Seminary." *American Ecclesiastical Review* 39 (1908): 113–21.

Schneider, Louis, and Zurcher, Louis. "Toward Understanding the Catholic Crisis: Observations on Dissident Priests in Texas." *Scientific Study of Religion* 9 (1970): 197–207.

Weber, Francis J. "What Ever Happened to Saint Vincent's College," *Pacific Historian* 14 (1970): 76–90.

Dissertations and Theses

Blantz, Thomas E. "Francis J. Haas: Priest in Public Service." Ph.D. dissertation, Columbia University, 1968.

Burke, Dennis. "The History of the Confraternity of Christian Doctrine in the Diocese of Los Angeles, 1922–1936." Master's thesis, Catholic University of America, 1965.

Cohen, Jan Hart. "To See Christ in Our Brothers: The Role of the Texas Roman Catholic Church in the Rio Grande Valley Farm Workers' Movement, 1966–1967." Master's thesis, University of Texas at Arlington, 1974.

Conn, Joann Wolski. "From Certitude to Understanding: Historical Consciousness in the American Catholic Theological Community in the 1960's." Ph.D. dissertation, Columbia University, 1974.

Foppe, Regina E. "The Response of the Roman Catholic Church to the Mexican-Americans in West Texas, 1938 into Post–Vatican II." Master's thesis, Texas Tech University, 1976.

Harter, John M. "The Creation and Foundation of the Roman Catholic Diocese of Amarillo, 1917–1934." Master's thesis, West Texas State University, 1975.

Lee, Rosanna. "The History of Catholic Education in the Diocese of Amarillo." Master's thesis, Catholic University of America, 1952.

Rooney, Nellie. "A History of the Catholic Church in the Panhandle-Plains Area of Texas from 1875–1916." Master's thesis, Catholic University of America, 1954.

Smith, Rosemary E. "The Work of the Bishops' Committee for the Spanish Speaking on Behalf of the Migrant Worker." Master's thesis, Catholic University of America, 1950.

Index

Acerbo Nimis, 87
Adkins v. *Children's Hospital*, 28
AFL, 57, 67
AFL-CIO, 133
Alamo Messenger: Selma March, 103; support of farm workers' movement, 112; declining subscriptions, 124; report of Lucey letter to Senate, 137; withdrawal of support for Smith, 153
Alazan-Apache Courts, 72
Alter, Archbishop Karl J., 56
Amarillo, Texas, 42–43; diocese, 43, 44–45, 63–64
Amarillo Globe, 42
Amat, Bishop Thaddeus, 11
America, 55–56, 79
American Association of Social Workers, 27
American Board of Catholic Missions, 43–44, 47–48
American Federation of Labor, 57, 67
American Federation of Labor-Congress of Industrial Organizations, 133
Andrade, Erasmus, 124, 127
Association of Catholic Trade Unionists, 59
Assumption Seminary, 145, 146, 147, 151, 153, 154

Barnes, Rev. C. Rankin, 39
Benedict XV, Pope, 60
Bishops' Committee for the Spanish Speaking, 74–76, 83, 110
B'nai B'rith, 73
Braceros, 77, 82–83
Brandes, Rev. James, 138, 142
Brooklyn Tablet, 55
Brophy, John, 56, 59
Brown, Hank, 126
Brown v. *Board of Education*, 69
Bureau of Catholic Charities, Los Angeles, 21–22, 24, 25–26

California Department of Industrial Relations, 30
California State Department of Social Welfare, 27
Callahan, Rev. William, S.J., 163
Cantwell, Bishop John J., 21, 34, 38, 39, 43, 88
Casso, Rev. Henry, 106, 110, 123–24, 164
Catholic Action, 49
Catholic Church, and nativism, 32
Catholic Conference on Industrial Problems, 28
Catholic Theological Society of America, 136
Catholic University of America, Washington, D.C., 46

Catholic Welfare Bureau, Amarillo, 48–49
Catholic Welfare Bureau, San Antonio, 70–71
Catholic World, 56
CELAM. *See* Latin American Bishops' Council
Chavez, Cesar, 83, 109, 114, 122
Children's Protective Association, Los Angeles, 39
Christian Brothers, 48
Cicognani, Cardinal Amleto Giovanni, 158–60
CIO, 55–57, 67
Civil Rights Act (1964), 154
Civil rights movement, 100
Civil Rights Sunday, 102
Conaty, Bishop Thomas, 15
Confraternity of Christian Doctrine: history of, 87–88; in Los Angeles, 88; in Amarillo, 49–50; in San Antonio, 89–91, 94–95; Operation Latin America, 92–99; Inter-American Relations Committee, 92, 93
Congress of Industrial Organizations, 55–57, 67
Connally, John, 114
Connare, Bishop William G., 156–57, 158, 160, 161
Coughlin, Rev. Charles, 56, 58
Court-packing plan, 58
Cronin, Rev. John, 59
Cursillo, 93, 95, 97
Cyer, George, 27

Day, Dorothy, 85–86
de Lubac, Henri. 107
Depression, 33, 37–38, 43–44. *See also* Lucey, Robert E., and New Deal
Dietz, Rev. Peter, 59
Divini Redemptoris, 61
Donahue, George, 59
Dougherty, Cardinal Dennis, 61

Drinan, Rev. Robert, 164
Drossaerts, Archbishop Arthur J., 41, 65, 70
Drury, Bishop Thomas, 113, 156

Ehlinger, Rev. Paul, 70
Evans, Roy, 126
Evening Star (Washington, D.C.), 131
Extension Society, 43–44, 47

Fair Employment Practices Committee, 68
Farley, James, 39–40
Fitzsimon, Bishop Lawrence, 80
Franco, General Francisco, 61–62
Furey, Archbishop Francis J., 163

Gannon, Michael, 16–18
Gerkin, Bishop Rudolph, 43–46, 47, 48
Gutierrez, Gustavo, 98

Haas, Rev. Francis, 59
Hague, Frank, 56
Hales, E. E. Y., 17
Hayes, Cardinal Patrick, 53
"Hemisfair 68," 119–20, 130
Henke, Rev. Raymond, 152, 156
Herzig, Rev. Charles, 124, 146
Higgins, Msgr. George G., 81, 117
Hill, Gladwyn, 77–78
Hitler, Adolph, 62, 63
Ho Chi Minh, 130
Hoover, Herbert, 36
Houston Post, 112
Hughes, Archbishop John, 18
Humanae Vitae, 142
Humphrey, Hubert, 161

Incarnate Word Guest House, 157
International Ladies Garment Workers Union, 117
International Union of Electrical, Radio and Machine Workers, AFL–CIO, 119, 121

John XXIII, Pope, 100, 107
John Paul II, Pope, 164
Johnson, Lyndon Baines, 73, 81, 104, 105, 106, 119, 130–31, 161
Jordan, Barbara, 114

Kelly, Rev. Matthew, 80
Kendrick, Archbishop Francis Patrick, 18
Kennedy, Robert F., 114
Killian, Rev. William: as editor of *Alamo Messenger*, 106; and IWA strike, 110, 111, 112; and Cesar Chavez, 122; return from Via Coeli, 128; strategy toward dissident priests, 152–55; origins of fact-finding board, 154; death, 164
Ku Klux Klan, 32
Küng, Hans, 164

LaCasita Farms, 109–10, 114, 125
LaFollette-Costigan bill, 36
Laning, Msgr. Daniel, 112, 114
LaSage Shoe Store, 11, 12
Latin American Bishops' Council (CELAM), 92–99
Leo XIII, Pope, 12, 22–23, 27, 28, 30, 33
Leopold, Rev. Clarence, 136, 143
Letter from "51," 145–46
Lewis, John L., 55, 57, 67
Long Beach Building Trades Council, 39
Long Beach Press-Telegram, 40
Los Angeles, 6, 8–9, 12, 13, 14, 24
Los Angeles Community Chest, 29
Los Angeles County Welfare Federation of Community Chests, 39
Los Angeles Municipal Housing Commission, 27
Los Angeles Times, 39, 130
Lucey, Catherine, 9
Lucey, Dennis, 8, 9
Lucey, Edmund, 9, 10

Lucey, John, 6–9
Lucey, Leroy, 9
Lucey, Margaret, 9
Lucey, Mark John (Jack), 8, 11, 12, 14, 21
Lucey, Mary Ellen, 8, 10
Lucey, Mary (Nettle), 6, 8, 10
Lucey, Robert E.: on death of father, 6–7; boyhood of, 9–11; at St. Vincent College, 11–12; at St. Patrick's Seminary, 12–15; at North American College, 15, 18–19; ordination of, 19; early pastoral assignments of, 21; appointment of, to Bureau of Catholic Charities, 21; transfer of, to St. Anthony Parish, 34; appointed Bishop of Amarillo, 39; elevated to Archdiocese of San Antonio, 63; Triple Jubilee of, 105; and Vatican II, 108; resignation of, 159; retirement years of, 163–64; death of, 163
and Bishops' Committee for the Spanish Speaking: origins of, 74–75; early work of, 75–76; as farm worker organization, 76–77, 80, 81–82, 110, 123–24; criticism of, 80; control over by Lucey, 81; accomplishments of, 82–83
and conflict with clergy: Via Coeli incident, 127–28; disciplinary transfers, 134; controversy with Priests' Senate, 134–38, 139; conflict with Priests' Association, 140–45; demand for resignation of, 145–46; Assumption Seminary investigation, 147–49; publication of "51" letter, 151; fires seminary personnel, 152; deals with dissidents, 153–55; impasse with priests, 160–61, 164
and Confraternity of Christian

Doctrine: in Los Angeles, 87–88; in Amarillo, 49–50, 88–89; in San Antonio, 89–92; in Latin America, 92–99

and international relations: endorses collective security, 60–61, 62–63; and Spanish Civil War, 61–62; and Vietnam War, 130, 131–32, 133

and labor: interprets *Rerum Novarum*, 27–28; and living wage, 27–31; responds to *Adkins* decision, 28; interprets *Quadragesimo Anno*, 33–34, 36; attacks open shop, 39; as Bishop of Amarillo, 53–54; defends Lewis, 57; criticizes AFL, 57; attacks Catholic critics of labor, 57; summer schools for priests, 59–60; as Archbishop of San Antonio, 66–68, 101; Project Equality, 104; supports Smith, 117–18; reprimands Smith, 119, 120, 123

and migrant farm workers: work on President's Commission, 76–77, 78–79, 83; opposes exploitation of, 79–81; program of material aid to, 81–82; supports Rio Grande Valley strike, 110, 112–13, 114; remarks at Medeiros installation, 113–14; evaluates significance of strike, 117; withdraws support of Smith and Killian, 122–23, 125; responds to picketing, 127

and New Deal: supports Roosevelt, 57; and Christian social order, 57–58; criticizes Coughlin, 58; supports court-packing plan, 58–59; attacks Supreme Court, 58–59

and poverty: philosophy of charity work, 25; experience in Los Angeles, 25–27; Catholic Welfare Bureau, Amarillo, 48–49; Catholic Welfare Bureau, San Antonio, 70–72; SANYO, 104–5; relationship with Johnson, 105, 106

and race: appeals for equality, 68–70; desegregates archdiocesan schools, 69–70; endorses civil rights movement, 101–4; and Toolen, 103; and Project Equality, 104

McAuliffe, Rev. Michael, 9, 11
McCarthy, Rev. John, 84
McGowan, Rev. Raymond, 15, 74
McIntyre, Cardinal Francis, 80
McKenzie, Rev. John F., S.J., 135, 136–37
McNicholas, Archbishop John T., 53
McNiff, Rev. James, M.M., 93, 94, 95, 96
Magnin, Rabbi Edgar, 39
Majestic Theater, 101
Manning, Msgr. Leroy, 142, 143, 153, 154
March on Austin, 114
Martin, Msgr. William, 154
Marx, Bishop Adolph, 110
Maverick, Maury, 65
Medeiros, Bishop Humberto, 111, 113, 114, 122
Mendoza, Msgr. Julian, 94, 96
Mexican Americans, 65, 73–74
Michalski, Rev. Louis, 149, 150–53, 152, 156, 164
Migrant farm workers, 76–77, 78–79
Miranda, Archbishop Dario, 96
Mitchell, James P., 81
Modernism, 16–18
Mooney, Archbishop Edward, 57, 58

Morrow, Dr. J. T., 70
Mundelein, Cardinal George, 57, 58, 65, 67
Murray, Philip, 55, 59
Murtagh, Rev. Lawrence, 102
Myrdal, Gunnar, 69

National Association for the Advancement of Colored People, 70
National Catholic Reporter, 131, 136, 137
National Catholic Welfare Council (Conference), 43–44, 67, 81, 95
National Conference of Christians and Jews, 63
National Farm Workers Association, 109, 114
National Industrial Recovery Act, 58
National Union for Social Justice, 58
National Youth Corps, 105
Nelson, Eugene, 109
New Deal, 34, 36, 40, 41, 53, 58, 65, 67, 89
Newman Center, 21
Newsweek, 156
New York Review, 17–18
New York Times, 130, 156
Noll, Bishop John, 56
North American College, Rome, 15, 18–19
Nowak, Msgr. Joseph, 138, 150–51

O'Connell, Cardinal William, 53
O'Connor, Rev. William, 82, 83–84
Office of Economic Opportunity, 105
Operation "Foodstuff," 110
Operation Latin America, 92–99
Organized labor, 55, 56–57. *See also* Unions
Our Sunday Visitor, 56

Pacem Dei Munus, 60
Pacem in Terris, 100
Parents Club of Assumption Seminary, 151–52
Paul VI, Pope: on Lucey's Triple Jubilee, 105, 111; and Vietnam War, 130, 131, 133; *Humanae Vitae*, 142; letters to, from dissident priests, 145, 152; accepts Lucey's resignation, 161; testimonial letter to Lucey, 161
Pearl Brewing Company, 118
Pioneer Flour Mill Company, 123
Pius IV, Pope, 87
Pius IX, Pope, 19
Pius X, Pope, 16–18
Pius XI, Pope, 22, 33, 43, 53, 58, 61, 87
Pius XII, Pope, 65, 107
Pontifical Commission for Latin America, 95
Price, Mrs. Katherine E., 48
Price Memorial College, 48
Priests' Association of Archdiocese of San Antonio, 138, 140, 144–45, 146, 151, 156, 160
Priests' Senate, San Antonio, 108, 134, 139
Progressivism, 7
Prohibition, 32
Project Equality, 104, 118, 123
Public Law 78, 79, 83

Quadragesimo Anno, 31, 33, 34, 66; Lucey's interpretation, 35–36; and National Industrial Recovery Act, 36; and Christian social order, 53, 57–58; and CIO, 55

Radtke, Rev. Theodore, 77
Rahner, Karl, 106
Raimondi, Luigi, Apostolic Delegate, 111, 145, 146, 147, 149, 151, 152, 156, 157–58, 159, 161–62

Ralph, James, Jr., 27
Rattler (Saint Mary's University), 131
Reeb, James, 102
Rerum Novarum, 12, 14, 22–23, 27, 28, 30, 31, 33
Richardson, Friend, 27
Rihn, Msgr. Roy, 108–9, 138, 145, 146, 147, 148–49, 150–51, 152, 156, 163
Rio Grande Valley, 78, 104
Rio Grande Valley farm workers' strike, 109, 110, 114–17, 124–25
Roosevelt, Eleanor, 72
Roosevelt, Franklin D., 33, 57–58, 62, 65, 66, 68
Ryan, Rev. John A., 14, 28, 33, 34; influence on Lucey, 15; social reform by Catholics, 23–24; and Summer School of Social Action, 59, 60

Sacred Heart Cathedral, Amarillo, 88–89, 91
Sacred Heart Church, Los Angeles, 9
Sacred Heart Church, Sweetwater, 54
Saint Anthony Church, Long Beach, 34
"Saint Anthony's Hour," 34–38, 60
Saint George College, 43, 48
Saint Patrick Church, Brasher Falls, 8
Saint Patrick's Seminary, Menlo Park, 12–15
Saint Vincent College, 11, 12
Samoré, Archbishop Antonio, 96
San Antonio, 66–68, 69–70
San Antonio archdiocese, 46, 73
San Antonio Catholic Interracial Council, 69
San Antonio Community Chest, 71
San Antonio Convention Center, 155–56

San Antonio Council of Churches, 70
San Antonio Express, 65, 66–67, 127, 132–33
San Antonio Express-News, 134, 140, 142, 156
San Antonio Home Builders Association, 72
San Antonio Light, 156
San Antonio Neighborhood Youth Organization (SANYO), 104–5, 106
San Antonio News, 133, 142
San Antonio Sun, 133
San Fernando Cathedral, 66, 130
Santa Fe Railroad Company, 10–11
Santa Rosa Hospital, 71, 118
SANYO, 104–5, 106
Schrembs, Bishop Joseph, 51
Search, Rev. Paul, 138
Second Vatican Council, 4, 18, 97, 99, 121, 133, 136, 144, 157; antecedants of, 106–7; and John XXIII, 107; documents of, 107–8; and authority in Church, 108; and Paul VI, 108; Lucey's enthusiasm for, 108
Segundo, Juan Luis, 98
Selma, Alabama, 103, 104
Shaw, Frank, 40
Sheen, Bishop Fulton J., 132
Sheil, Bishop Bernard, 57
Shriver, Sargent, 105–6
Smith, Alfred E., 32
Smith, Rev. Sherrill, 106, 124, 126, 127, 140; appointment to Social Action Department, 100; desegregation in San Antonio, 100–101; Selma march, 102–3; appointment to Project Equality, 104; and farm workers' strike, 110, 111, 112, 122, 125; labor activities of, 115–19, 123; reprimand from Lucey, 120; reply to Lucey, 120–22; transfer of, 123;

banishment to Via Coeli, 125; statement after return from Via Coeli, 128; dismissal from Social Action Department, 128–29; formation of Priests' Association, 138; co-author of "51" letter, 145; loss of support from *Alamo Messenger*, 153; reconciliation with Lucey, 163
Social Justice, 56
Southern Pacific Railroad Company, 6, 8–9
Spanish Civil War, 61–62
Spellman, Cardinal Francis, 132
Spellmire, Verona, 88
Starr County, Texas, 110
Steves, Marshall, 119, 120, 123
Struckoff, Rev. Eustace, O.F.M., 150, 151
Sullivan, Edward, 123
Summer School of Social Justice for Priests, 59–60, 66
Swize, Rev. Marion, 139, 140, 141, 164

Tardini, Cardinal Domenico, 94
Texas Panhandle Register, 50, 62, 63, 89, 91
Texas State Federation of Labor *Review*, 67
Tidings, 29, 30, 31, 39

Till, Rev. Joseph, 95, 138, 140–44, 146, 164
Time magazine, 65, 66
Toolen, Archbishop Thomas J., 103, 104, 126
Tower, John, 102
Tranchese, Rev. Carmine, S.J., 72
Truman, Harry S., 76, 78, 79

Unions, 66–68. *See also* Organized Labor

Valley Evening Monitor, 112
Valley Farm Workers' Assistance Committee, 127
Vaughan, George, 117
Via Coeli, 125, 153
Vietnam War, 130, 131–32
von Braun, Werner, 163

Wagner, Rev. John, 86, 106
Wagner, Robert, 66
Walden, Rev. Robert, 134–35, 138, 150–51, 152, 156, 164
Walsh, Archbishop Thomas J., 56
Walsh, Bishop Emmet, 61
Washington Post, 76, 156
Wetbacks, 77–78

Yanta, Rev. John, 104, 106
Yarborough, Ralph, 102, 131
Yorke, Rev. Peter C., 14, 24